MW01579446

From THE ALICE
to THE ARCTIC

Other books by Jeff Carter:

People of the Inland (Rigby)
Life and Land of Central Australia (Angus & Robertson)
Outback in Focus (Rigby)
In the Tracks of the Cattle (Angus & Robertson)
Stout Hearts and Leathery Hands (Rigby)
In the Steps of the Explorers (Angus & Robertson)
Four-Wheel Drive Swagman (Rigby)
Bush Battlers (Rigby)
Ungezahmetes Land (Englebert, W. Germany)
The New Frontier (Angus & Robertson)
Wild Country (Rigby)
Surf Beaches of Australia's East Coast (Angus & Robertson)
Guide to Central Australia (Sun Books)
All Things Wild (Rigby)
Wild Animal Farm (Rigby)
Jeff Carter's Great Book of the Australian Outdoors (Rigby)
The Australian Explorer's Handbook (Hodder & Stoughton)
The Complete Guide to Central Australia (Hodder & Stoughton)

From THE ALICE to THE ARCTIC

40 Years of Motoring with Jeff Carter

HODDER & STOUGHTON
SYDNEY AUCKLAND LONDON TORONTO

"Take what you want—and pay for it."
(Old Middle Eastern proverb.)

First published in 1989
by Hodder & Stoughton (Australia) Pty Limited,
10–16 South Street, Rydalmere, NSW, 2116.

© Jeff Carter, 1989.

This book is copyright. Apart from any fair dealing for
the purposes of private study, research, criticism or
review as permitted under the Copyright Act, no part may
be reproduced by any process without written permission.
Enquiries should be addressed to the publisher.

National Library of Australia Cataloguing-in-Publication entry

Carter, Jeff, 1928– .
    From the Alice to the Arctic.

    ISBN 0 340 51857 X.

    1. Carter, Jeff, 1928– .
    —Journeys. 2. Voyages and
    Travels. 3. Automobiles—
    Touring. I. Title.

910.4

Typeset by G.T. Setters Pty Limited, Kenthurst
Printed in Hong Kong by Colorcraft Ltd.

Contents

Foreword

Most of us take life seriously. I do. But when something funny happens or the chance comes for enjoyment, I get a good grip on the situation with both hands and make the most of it—because such opportunities are too precious to waste. Anyone of intelligence, experience or imagination knows that perturbation is waiting around the corner to wipe the smile from our faces—Murphy's immutable Law.

This book is largely about the more amusing episodes of my motoring career (the ones fit to print); there is no point labouring the hard times, which most readers could match. You can search between the lines for the shadows cast by these peaks, if you like. But this is intended as an entertainment, so grasp it with both hands and enjoy it. If one day we meet, don't say you envy me, because like you, I've had my ups and downs. These are just the good bits!

The following chapters cover most of my adult life (I like to think there's more to come), from the mid 1940s to the late 1980s. Many of the stories originally appeared in Australian, British, American or German motoring magazines. I have recast them somewhat, taking out topical and technical material. But I have left the style of writing alone, because I think it's interesting to note the changes that took place over the years (for better or worse) and the way 'slants' varied to suit different magazine audiences and editors. As with the motor car, nothing stays the same.

So that you may better understand the chronology of these rather intermittent recollections, the following summary of my motoring and journalistic career (a loose term) may be useful. From 1946 to 1953 I was a freelance fiction writer, hitch-hiker and motorbike pillion rider, plying between Melbourne in Victoria and Rockhampton in Queensland, fetching up as editor of *Outdoors & Fishing* magazine while living first in a tent and then in a shack on the banks of Sydney's Woronora River.

Before I was twenty, I was the father of Karen and Thor, whose Scandinavian mother was the somewhat amazing motorcyclist mentioned in several chapters.

In 1954 I broke rank completely, changed from motorbikes to motor cars (Land Rovers) and became a full-time non-fiction freelance writer and photographer, in partnership with another immigrant, this time an

American pulp novelist. True to form, I was again quickly the father of two: Goth and Vandal. In the ensuing years I wrote and illustrated countless magazine articles, plus sixteen adventure-travel books. Mare Carter, as she became known, moved from pulp fiction to radio and magazine writing. Together we produced the *Wild Country* television documentary series and established Wild Country Park on our forty-five hectare property at Foxground, a unique wildlife refuge in the rainforest with its own museum and cinema.

During this period we owned a number of off-road vehicles, culminating in a Range Rover. These were strictly workhorses for our constant safaris through outback Australia. We had different individual preferences for personal transport. Mare always yearned for a beach buggy, but owned a 1928 Essex, a Honda Accord and three Subaru four-wheel drive station wagons.

I have owned eight Porsches, including three outstanding vehicles: the 2.8-litre Kremer Porsche, 'Little Red', the 2.7 Carrera I raced for some years and my current 3.4-litre 911 Carrera Club Sport. Lack of imagination, if you like, but there really is something about Porsches. Once hooked, you stay hooked, particularly if you are attracted to them for the right reasons: performance, reliability, durability—and resale value! Unfortunately, in my opinion, a lot of people have Porsches for the wrong reasons.

The classic 911 Porsche which has endured almost unchanged for twenty-five years was not designed as a vehicle for *poseurs*. It is a driver's car, meaning it is for people who enjoy high-speed motoring as a recreation, or sport. Even the new-style, comparatively grandiose 928 Porsches remain essentially drivers' cars.

In all my years of association with the marque, I have received no favours or considerations from the manufacturers or Australian importers. So I can offer the honest opinion, based on personal experience and a study of the comments of other motoring writers, that the 911 Porsche, in its field, is the best car in the world.

Off-road, the Range Rover continues to retain a similar position. Once you have experienced the best, nothing else will do. If I have had one lucky streak in my life, it has been to consistently enjoy 'the best' (to me) vehicles, places, companions, particularly women, adventures and encounters. Some of which you can now read about. But first my thanks to those exceptional friends who helped preserve my sense of humour over the years: Frances, Jules, Ayleen, Athol, Mare (most of all), Otto, Les, Anne, Paul, Christine, Roger, Bronwyn, Monika, Hermann, John, Madge, Lolita, Jennifer and Jacqueline. Also my children, now adults: Karen, Thor, Goth and Vandal, plus their offspring, those tiny tots who know me as 'Abuelo'.

1 Sons of the father

'That boy is limping. Why is that boy limping?' My question, from the head of our Great Table, was addressed to various lowered heads, bobbing over soup bowls.

Thor, the eldest of my three sons, had just come in to join our evening meal. Clearly, he was lame on the nearside. The only reply to my question was a nervous rattle of soup spoons. Eventually, my mate, Mare, cleared her voice and said gently 'He hurt his foot'.

'*How* did he hurt his foot?' I wanted to know. My suspicion was that he had crashed or upended his Renault R10 for the umpteenth time.

Thor Carter in his Renault R10 competing in a local car gymkhana.

Only a fortnight earlier he had rolled it through a netting fence into Conroy's sheep paddock, severely twisting his wrist—to his own discomfort and my annoyance. A farm boy with a sprained wrist is just about useless around the place (and we had wasted half a day mustering Conroy's sheep, drunk with freedom, from all over Foxground).

'He fell in the creek,' mumbled Goth, my number two son, speaking into his soup bowl. Vandal, youngest of the trio, suddenly jumped up and began a noisy round of the table in his clumping motocross boots, saying cheerfully 'Anyone for seconds?' This transparent diversion failed to distract me.

'What were you doing in the creek?' I asked Thor directly.

'I jumped in, off the bridge,' he replied sheepishly.

'What the devil for? It's a five-metre drop,' I exclaimed.

'I was in a hurry. I had battery acid on my leg and it was burning.'

'How the dickens did you get battery acid on your leg?' I demanded.

'From the Land Rover,' Thor responded, studying his soup bowl as if he expected to find a gold nugget there.

'I'm hanged if I see how you managed to get acid from the battery on to your leg,' I said. 'Tell me.'

Everyone at the table fell silent. Not a soup spoon clinked.

'It was upside down,' Thor said at last.

'The battery?' I said incredulously.

'No. The Land Rover. . .'

I was not really surprised. Our family lore is rich in such motoring tales. My male offspring began doing hair-raising things in vehicles from their early teens. Lately they have mostly grown conservative. Only the patriarch and the youngest heir continue the family tradition. I have only myself to blame. All three boys, Thor, Goth and Vandal, virtually grew up in the back seats of Land Rovers and Porsches. This no doubt coloured their views on motoring. They came to believe that a vehicle can go anywhere and at any speed, provided you are in the right one. And that they had charmed lives—because we never crashed. What they failed to appreciate was the eminent suitability of our vehicles for the work they did. Land or Range Rovers for cross-country adventures and Porsches for high-speed tours. Both types of vehicles are designed from the ground up for their special tasks—and are not interchangeable. Further, ours were always in near-new condition.

It took all the junior Carter menfolk a lot of painful trial and error to learn that old wrecks welded and bolted back together in our hayshed did not emerge as hybrid Land Rover/Porsches.

In fact, the first vehicle created by the boys showed little resemblance to either marque. The brainchild of Goth, my second eldest, it was a three-wheeled wind-driven travelling machine. The sail was square, after the style of a Chinese junk. There were no brakes. To stop, you hauled down the sail. This took a while, but there was no problem in open paddocks, where long grass and soft ground exerted a braking effect.

In defiance of orders issued from my end of the Great Table, Goth road-tested his sail-car on the locally famous 'concrete strip' section of the Foxground Road. This is a quarter-mile length of cement road through what was once a swamp. It has been used, since the arrival of the Carter family in Foxground in the early 1960s, for acceleration testing of everything from FJ Holdens to Kremer Porsches. Aided by a stiff breeze and the smooth road surface, Goth achieved a hitherto unattainable speed—unfortunately at the same time as our neighbour George Cullen chose to drive his herd of milking cows across the road.

Frantically trying to down sail, Goth crashed headlong into the astonished animals and had his masterpiece trampled to pieces in the resultant stampede. He escaped with only minor abrasions—until I got my hands on him that night.

Goth's next effort was a motorised pushbike which also came to grief on the concrete strip in Foxground Road, this time with more serious results. Apparently the vehicle somersaulted when the driving mechanism fouled the wheel spokes, causing Goth to take a header on to the concrete.

By chance, I arrived on the scene in a Land Rover only minutes after the accident and can report that it is not pleasant to find one of your sons lying unconscious in the middle of the road. Nor is the subsequent anguished loitering around various hospital corridors. But it all ended well and proved to be the only really serious mishap to befall a Carter boy during his motoring apprenticeship. Which is another way of saying they were very lucky boys.

All learned to drive at the wheel of various Land Rovers, first in our paddocks and then along the lonely bush tracks above our farm. I took care not to show any of them how to get the vehicles out of low range during the early stages. This meant that my students did most of their learning at walking pace or a slow trot—and when they went solo, I could still run after them and save the situation if anything went wrong! But in retrospect, I think those ponderous early lessons may have been the reason they all later turned into hotfoots. The slowness of the Land Rovers made them hungry for speed.

Thor, my eldest son, was first to own his own wheels. Only weeks into his first job, he somehow bought a controlling interest in a 125cc Honda road bike. This was followed about a year later by a 175cc Honda trail bike and then a CB250 Honda road model. On this he subsequently disappeared for a full day, leaving home at dawn and not returning until

Thor and Van Carter outside the farmhouse, Foxground.

Thor aboard his first motorbike, ready to emulate his 'Four Wheel Drive Swagman' father.

almost 11 p.m. When I wanted to know where he had been, he said 'to Melbourne'. I took this to be some form of callow evasion, aimed at disguising the fact that he had entered the girl-chasing stage. But I discovered much later that he *did* go to Melbourne, to visit elder sister Karen, then a student at Monash University. The outward bound journey took seven and a half hours (from Foxground), the return eight hours neat, with a lunch break of about an hour in the middle! The Honda, not new in the first place, was never much good after that. Thor traded it on a 250cc Alpine Bultaco trail bike and passed his 175cc Honda over to Vandal.

For the best part of a year, the peace of backblocks Foxground was shattered daily as Thor and Vandal chased each other around our high paddocks and up and down ridges as far afield as Saddleback Mountain above Kiama. Much of their riding was along narrow, rough trails through the rainforest, where wet and slippery conditions made falling off easier than staying on. This practice made them pretty good riders, to say the least—and I frequently watched open-mouthed as they sped over country that would have terrified a mountain goat. I didn't know it then, but a lot of their riding was done at night, although only Thor's Bultaco was fitted with a headlight. Vandal had to follow close behind his brother's silhouette, memorising the track a long way ahead and more or less riding blind. Not easy when the leading rider has only one speed: flat out!

One memorable night, Thor crashed while racing downhill across paddocks below Saddleback Mountain. This left Vandal rocketing full tilt into the black night over wet grass until his descent was halted by a clump of lantana bush.

Around that time I was practising in my 356C Porsche to become a dark-horse rally driver. I had developed a short obstacle course in our lower creek paddocks where I could practise such things as handbrake turns, slowing without brakes, controlling (?) slides, remaining cool (?) after a spin, clutchless gear changes and so on. I never mastered any of these techniques, but had a lot of fun trying. My efforts provided amusement for the family and did the rock-like C Porsche no harm at all. Inspired by my example, the boys decided to install their own motocross practice track.

A bulldozer working on a neighbouring farm was hired for three hours to carve out a hair-raising figure-of-eight trail along the edge of the jungle in our highest paddocks. Half a mile long, the track cost the three Carter brothers and two other youthful shareholders with trail bikes a total of thirty dollars. A large and a small jump and two creek crossings were part of the course.

Without a bike of his own, Goth found rides few and far between, but was content to act as timekeeper (he was still under medical advice to avoid sustaining further head injuries). Thor, Vandal and their two neighbourhood mates used the track almost daily for half a year, then the two visitors slowly lost interest and dropped out. Thor and Vandal persisted, avowed but friendly rivals. Watching them develop their two quite different riding styles, I was aware they were both on the threshold of becoming very competitive motocrossers. Thor was the more spectacular, faster rider while he was upright, but fell off so often, he rarely equalled the lap times of his steadier younger brother. Vandal seldom crashed or did anything flamboyant but was deceptively quick. His times crept steadily downward.

Thor was working at the time and when the chance came to acquire a second-hand Husqvana CR400 motocross competition bike, he mustered nearly all of the eight hundred dollars necessary to buy it— for Vandal! Thus our youngest, then aged fifteen, was mounted on just about the most powerful, accelerative motocross bike in the country—a sort of two-wheel version of Mr Shelby's Cobra. And didn't he go! Strangely, while pursuing his brother around their private practice track, Thor's times also improved dramatically. But now he was falling off at higher speeds and his Bultaco suffered.

A few more months of practice and the pair of them joined a local motocross club and unleashed themselves on the competitive circuit. In his first race on the Bultaco, Thor took the lead in spectacular fashion, but maintained his position intermittently, falling off six times in five laps! He regained the lead several times in sensational style, demonstrating

Thor on Van's Husqvarna.

to a delighted crowd that he was unbeatable when upright—but finished the race well down in the field. In a later event, he fell while leading in the final lap, was ridden over by two following bikes, then got up and finished in second place. From memory, this was the only placing he ever achieved during his brief motocross career.

Vandal, on his mighty Husky in the Open Division against much stiffer competition, made a less flamboyant debut. But within half a dozen meetings on various tracks he was consistently finishing close on the heels of the leading NSW riders of the time, 'Woody' Woodham and 'Ampol' McDonald (who both went on to compete successfully

Van, just into his third teen year, leading star NSW motocrosser 'Woody' Woodham.

overseas). Thor, like a young Jack Brabham, continued to amuse the spectators with his displays of inspired riding and sensational falls. He led many races but never placed. Eventually the Bultaco was unable to continue and Thor contented himself with driving Vandal (too young for a car licence) and his Husky to the various race meetings.

Unfortunately, or fortunately, I have never been able to decide, after six months the great CR400 Husky needed complete rebuilding, a project far beyond Vandal's pocket. The brothers Carter retired from competitive motocross and their respective mothers (I had been already twice 'married') breathed a collective sigh of relief.

Around this period, Thor and Goth had been bitten by the motor car bug. Thor bought a Standard Super 10, which cost far less than Vandal's Husky. (A licence-holder for several years, Thor had previously driven only the family Land Rovers.) Not to be outdone, Goth purchased a fleet of two Morris Oxfords from a neighbouring farmer. One, more or less a going concern apart from a host of major and minor defects, cost five dollars. The other vehicle, bought as a source of spares, changed hands for one dollar and had to be towed on to our property by Land Rover. Neither vehicle was registered, of course, nor had any prospect of ever achieving roadworthiness. Not that it mattered, because Goth had no licence.

Thor's Standard 10 had seen many better days, but had the redeeming feature of six month's rego. Given Thor's uncompromising driving style, I doubted the vehicle would go the distance. But I reckoned without Thor's mechanical aptitude and determination. As fast as the Standard 10 fell to bits, he rebuilt it, not always according to the maker's specifications, but with admirable ingenuity.

At the time I was driving a Porsche 912 shod with fat, Belgian-made Goodyear Grand Prix tyres. My car handled very well and this caused Thor to assume that all he needed was some wide rubber and he could give me a run for my money. Somehow he managed to get a couple of wide rims wearing Goodyear G800 tyres on to the back of his Standard 10. With no more funds available, this left him with two worn-out cross-plies on the front—and the world's ultimate under-steering car. This didn't stop him trying to improve on the local record for fastest time through the notorious Kiama Bends (a tortuous sector of the Princes Highway just south of that seaside town).

All he achieved was a spate of local stories about journeys through barbed wire fences and road workmen running for safety into the bush whenever they saw a Standard 10 approaching (the road was being upgraded at the time).

In due course, this rough treatment reduced the Standard 10 to 'paddock-car' status. When he stopped laughing, the garageman where

Thor took his car for its pink 'roadworthy' slip merely pushed it into his backyard with the other wrecks and sold Thor a Renault R10. I judged this car to be terminally ill in several departments, but Thor cheerfully worked on it nightly and at weekends for several months. The result: not a car one would lust after, but a moderately reliable, tough, noisy little goer.

I imagine Thor saw it as a Porsche 912. He certainly drove it that way. At the gravel intersection of Foxground and Free Selectors' Road, he used to practise handbrake turns outside Bill Mitchell's cowyard. I heard about this from Bill, who rang up hopping mad one evening because Thor had crashed through the fence and frightened his cows off into the night when he was in the middle of milking them. According to Thor, it was all due to circumstances beyond his control. At the critical point of his turn, the spare-wheel bib under the Renault's chin had come adrift, dropping the spare down so that it ploughed like a bulldozer blade. This caused the car to kangaroo-hop out of control through the fence, into the middle of Bill's cowyard. The startled animals rushed out through the break and disappeared in four different directions down the crossroads.

Meanwhile, Goth was having car and cattle problems too. His hybrid Morris Oxford had absolutely no brakes. To stop, you got into as low a gear as possible and switched off the ignition and/or steered for rising ground. While climbing Foxground Hill into our property, the vehicle stalled. Luckily Goth was able to grab reverse gear, which at least slowed his rearward progress down the steep slope.

Once through our front gate, he had the choice of aiming for the narrow bridge over the creek or trying to swing in through our neighbour's gate, over a cattle grid. As mentioned earlier, it's a five-metre drop into the creek if you miss the bridge, so Goth proceeded backward into the property of Colin Cook, next door. Miraculously, he got through the gate and grid, but then careered down a bumpy, grassy slope, still backward, into the post-and-rail fence of Colin Cook's bull yard.

The car broke two of the rails and came to a halt, wedged under the top rail, halfway through the fence. The broken rails, still secure in their upright posts, effectively wedged the car doors shut. Not that Goth wanted to get out. Mr Cook's notoriously ornery Brahmin bull happened to be in the yard, with a cow left there for servicing. The bull regarded the Morris Oxford as some form of rival and spent the next couple of hours intermittently horning the vehicle and snorting through the windows at Goth. We eventually rescued him when my mate noted a vacant seat at the Great Table during our evening meal.

Goth's next effort was an illegal two-kilometre jaunt along the tar-surfaced public section of Foxground Road. After successfully climbing the hill up to the Princes Highway, he turned his unregistered Morris Oxford and began a much faster return journey. Alas, he was confronted by a large truck coming the other way along the narrow strip of bitumen.

He panicked and swerved off the road, down through a barbed wire fence into one of Jimmy Waite's paddocks. The car stalled, refused to start again and had to be left overnight. Next morning Goth and Vandal returned with one of our Land Rovers to tow the Morris Oxford home. Jimmy Waite was just finishing repairing his fence, muttering darkly. After apologising for the damage, the boys sheepishly towed the car out through the paddock gate and up the track toward the road, Goth riding in the Morris to steer. As they climbed the steep last pinch on to the road, the towrope broke and Goth once more careered down the slope through the fence, this time backward. Result: a free lesson in fence mending for them both, under the baleful eye of a not-amused Jimmy Waite.

Vandal's first car had once been an FJ Holden. I think he found it abandoned and rusting behind someone's hayshed and when he unexpectedly got it going, the owner insisted he drive it off the property. The body style was table-top truck, a model never produced at Fisherman's Bend. No brakes, no oil pressure, no lights, no doors, no windows. The motor was good, the clutch strong but intermittent. The gearbox was a sort of lucky dip (if you found a cog going in your direction, no questions were asked).

A rule had been passed down from my end of the Great Table that henceforth no unregistered vehicles were to be taken upon the public roads. Vandal nevertheless had plenty of fun and excitement with his FJ Holden. The bonnet was removed and towed over the grassy paddocks as a sort of sled. This proved a popular sport until a particularly exuberant slalom took Goth into Foxground Creek where he nearly drowned.

After that, the FJ continued as a tow vehicle, this time for huge home-made kites fashioned from polythene fertiliser bags stretched over plastic pipes. These were capable of lifting a teenage farmboy to a height of ten metres when towed into a strong head wind—a record height achieved in farmer Doug Blow's empty corn field. The flyer was a neighbour-hood boy, Ray Parker, who would have gone higher if Vandal had not driven the FJ Holden under the telephone wires leading to the Blow farmhouse. The towline did not break the wires, but lifted them from their insulators, whereupon the weight of the wires plucked Master Parker from the sky. (Ray continued upward in later years, to become NSW manager of a chain of supermarkets.)

No, the Blow family was not impressed. Yes, the Carter boys were not popular with our neighbours during this period. And need I say that of course I was generally unaware of these escapades at the time and was not permitted to learn the Terrible Truth until age had softened me.

Thor at this stage had become interested in trials driving and spent his spare time practising on the back roads of Kangaroo Valley, Foxground, Kiama and Albion Park. His navigator was an ex-schoolmate, Steve Owers, who became one of Australia's top rally passengers, accompanying such eminent drivers as Barry Ferguson. Steve is known for his iron nerve, which he no doubt developed while accompanying Thor in the Renault R10 and later vehicles.

Once, in heavy rain near Albion Park, Thor conducted his car off the road, through a ditch and *over* a barbed wire fence, parking it on its head in a field. While Thor and Steve hung upside down in their seat belts, they noticed an interesting thing: the windscreen had popped neatly out, leaving the wipers sadly flailing back and forth across nothing! Thor, a thoughtful lad, held his hand against the roof while he released his belt, but Steve impetuously thumped the release button and landed hard on his head, sustaining a cricked neck. The car was soon righted with the aid of a couple of farm workers and the intact windscreen retrieved. The motor started readily and they arrived home only an hour late.

Occasionally the Renault R10 served a useful purpose. Stripped inside for rally driving, it had a lot of room for firewood. This was a help when the Land Rover was otherwise engaged and caused Thor to develop an uncanny skill at driving vehicles backward at speed. This came about when he was toiling fully-laden up the hill through our farm. After missing a gear change, the R10 started to roll back and the brakes proved to be out for the day. 'That's when I first learned to drive fast backward,' Thor told me years later.

Vandal mastered the same art when his first road-registered car, a Holden HK, stuck in reverse. Unaware of the simple under-the-bonnet cure, he drove twelve kilometres backward along the Princes Highway to a garage in Gerringong! On another occasion, while towing a trailer-load of gravel home from Gerringong with the HK, the clutch master cylinder collapsed as he tried to change up from first to second. In the resultant struggle with the steering-column shift, the lever came off in his hand, so he drove home the twelve kilometres in first without stopping.

Goth had his own trouble with trailers. Fetching a small load of fence posts down from the high country above our farm, he got into strife on a hairpin bend overlooking a steep ravine. Lack of brakes again. He finished up jack-knifed on the corner, with the Morris Oxford half off the road and unable to push the loaded trailer back out of the way.

Thinking to shift the trailer clear, he unhitched it—and watched his beloved car plunge into the jungle-filled ravine, where it remains to this day. Fortunately he saved my load of fence posts.

Battered and worn out by countless trial runs and gymkhana meetings, Thor's Renault R10 also retired from active motoring at around this period, without ever having engaged in organised rally competition. It was replaced by a 1960 model Renault Dauphine that seemed to have little to recommend it, other than it was going. My 912 was then mounted on Michelin XAS tyres and I had achieved some local notoriety as a daredevil wet-weather pedaller. The combination of car and tyres was the secret—there was no great skill required. Such is the faith of the young, Thor purchased two Michelin XAS tyres for the back wheels of his Dauphine and confidently awaited rain. None fell for more than a month, which was almost a Foxground record. Disgusted, Thor went off to Sydney on his motorbike for a few days. Vandal, too, had expressed an interest in trying Michelin XAS tyres in the wet on his own car (he was now an eighteen-year-old licensed driver).

Rain began to fall but there was no sign of Thor. Vandal busied himself in our hayshed, working on his newly acquired second-hand Torana, parked next to Thor's Dauphine. Late that afternoon he drove off into the rain and did not return until nightfall. Around midnight, I was awakened by the sound of Thor's returning motorbike. Rain drummed

Thor competing in the Renault Dauphine at a local car gymkhana.

the roof as I dozed off. At dawn I stirred again at the sound of the Dauphine driving off. It was still pelting down. Off to test the Michelin XAS tyres, I mused.

At breakfast, I remarked to Vandal that Thor had returned late and gone off first thing to test his tyres. (Vandal is a heavy sleeper and never hears anything in the night short of a shotgun blast at close range.) 'Did he, by Jingo!' Vandal shouted. He jumped up and galloped out of the room.

'That boy should be made to stay put and eat his meals properly,' I said to Mare across the Great Table. 'He looks downright pale, probably malnutrition.' For once she agreed with me and sped outside to remonstrate with her youngest. Seconds later I heard Vandal's Torana start up and roar away. Then my mate returned to our interrupted breakfast. This time she looked pale.

'What's up?' I wanted to know.

'Vandal says he borrowed Thor's Michelin XAS tyres to try in the rain yesterday and didn't swap them back. Thor's gone off on his old rims and smooth tyres!'

About half-way through the Kiama Bends there is a very scenic point where you can look down over a lush green slope to the blue of the Tasman Sea. Far below, almost a kilometre from the road, is the railway line. When trains pass, they appear as small toys, silhouetted against the white waves breaking on the rocks. It is a favourite view for photographers with a head for heights.

This is where Thor discovered he was on smooth tyres. He took out a barbed wire fence and proceeded in a series of spins down the wet grassy slope toward the railway line and the sea. Without suffering a scratch to himself and only superficial damage to the startled Dauphine. We learned all this from Vandal, who arrived home after an hour to borrow the Land Rover. This was needed to tow Thor back up to the highway, where his smooth rear tyres might find some traction on the bitumen. I expected mayhem, but they both arrived home laughing and full of high spirits. Later the same day they went off in the Dauphine, wearing its Michelin XAS tyres at the rear. These were not a great success, I gathered, because the Dauphine returned home more battle-scarred than ever. (Thor's test driving method never varied—he pressed on until something broke, blew up or he left the road. Miraculously he was never seriously hurt, except when falling off horses and skis.)

All three boys, in fact, came closer to injury at the hands of their sire than they did in their vehicles. All had lucky escapes after performing some mischief with my Land Rover or 'Big Red' the Range Rover. The rules were: no driving my Porsches and if they wanted to drive any one of my other vehicles, they paid for all damages. By and large they were lucky. The long-wheelbase Land Rover station wagon inverted by Thor suffered no visible damage at all, although some of the doors were harder to open and close than previously. An old-style Land Rover that took out a gate post with its front corner needed only a replacement bolt-on front fender. This was before Leylands became trendy and began putting the headlights and blinkers in the front guards. The most serious damage was sustained when someone left a tame wombat inside the Range Rover while they had a meal at the Busy Bee Cafe near Dapto, south of Wollongong. The bored animal, named 'William the Terrible', spent an hour biting and clawing large clumps out of the rear seat. The damage cost around two hundred dollars to set right.

Vandal, destined to become the fastest driver of us all, crashed only once during his driving apprenticeship. In the Kiama Bends, of course— and all his own work. Later he had two near misses in an early Holden Torana. On his way to work as a male nurse on nightshift at Port Kembla District Hospital, he turned on the heater and got his feet sprayed with scalding water and the windscreen obscured by clouds of steam. In the same car, the front-rising bonnet flew up at high speed, totally obscuring his vision.

Constantly hard-driven, the poor Torana eventually tossed it in completely and was just able to be driven to the tip. There Vandal met an old schoolmate about to dump a Holden HK station wagon that had two months' rego and not much else. After a push start (the battery was flat), Vandal drove home in that. He spent the ensuing months keeping out of the way of the local policeman, who could have papered the entire windscreen with defect notices, again reducing Vandal's visibility to nil.

During this period, Vandal was also trying to keep out of the way of his future father-in-law. This proved difficult, because every time he visited his young lady at home and was sent packing, he had to ask her dad to help push-start the HK!

Thor, meanwhile, had been reduced to driving an ancient Singer 'sports car' in what I can only describe as laughable condition. This he tipped on its side repeatedly, without injury, until a heavyweight male passenger, too big for the seat-belt, fell on him during an 'incident', breaking several of his ribs. Soon after that, Thor used an axe to chop the R10, the Dauphine and the Singer into transportable-sized pieces, carted them to the tip and married a girl from Tasmania with an almost new Mini Cooper Clubman.

Goth, never a great car enthusiast and somewhat unlucky with wheels, was for a time the best mounted of the Carter boys. Living in Sydney while trying to break into show business, he went into a butcher's shop to buy some chops and came out with a Valiant station wagon in excellent condition! The butcher had just won a new car in a lottery and offered

Goth the Valiant for a song if he would drive it away that day. Luckily, this was just the amount Goth could muster.

A month later, he returned home to Foxground one weekend to show us his new vehicle. On the Sunday, while on his way to visit friends in the nearby town of Berry, he was confronted by an out-of-control car on the wrong side of the Princes Highway. This he dodged by (you guessed it) driving off the road through a barbed wire fence into a ditch. Result: no injuries, but one written-off excellent Valiant station wagon. Uninsured.

Around that time, Mare and I escaped to Europe and swanned around for 30 000 kilometres and almost two years in a white three-litre Porsche Carrera. When we returned, the boys and their various girlfriends and wives organised a welcome-home party. It was a fancy-dress turnout. Vandal and another local lad came as ladies. Not in your city 'drag' style, but as proper last-generation farm ladies, wearing long floral print dresses, straw hats with flowers in them and enamel brooches pinned over enormous, shapeless bosoms. Vandal is over six feet and built to match, but his friend is a giant. The two presented a formidable duet.

On the night of the party it rained cats and dogs, which is normal for Foxground. Just after the first guests arrived, someone phoned from a neighbouring farm to say there was a tree down across the road about a kilometre from our place. Vandal and his friend, Phillip Wells, offered to attend to this. They drove off into the rainy night in a Land Rover, taking with them a chainsaw and an axe. Imagine the spectacle that confronted arriving guests. The switchback road to our farm burrows through a dark tunnel of overhanging rainforest trees. You plunge alarmingly down a steep hill into this tunnel. On rainy, wind-torn nights, car headlights cast dancing leaf shadows on the tree trunks, creating an eerie spectacle. All around is ominous, brooding blackness. Splashing rain gleams in the moving light and drifting mist plays tricks with the eyes.

Suddenly a procession of guests' cars jams up on the road, headlights playing downhill on the leafy obstruction ahead. But what is this? Two giant ladies wielding a roaring chainsaw and gleaming axe attacking the fallen tree. Large branches are sawn and hacked from the trunk and hurled aside like matchwood. Then the thick trunk is expertly reduced to several post-sized logs which are rolled and hoisted aside by the muscular Amazons. The weird scene has overtones of a late-night horror show.

The guests crouch open-mouthed in the dryness and safety of their motor cars, immobilised with astonishment. Eventually the monstrous ladies toss the final log aside and beckon the cavalcade of cars through. Everyone drives straight on, windows wound up tightly against the rain. No one stops to thank the ladies.

Today, late in the 1980s, Vandal's family car (he is now father of two) is an old Holden Commodore station wagon. He races a twenty-year-old Holden XU1 Torana and for a hobby buys early 1970s Porsches in Germany for rebuilding to Australian specifications. Thor's wife still drives her Mini Clubman and Thor rides a pushbike to work (in Hobart, where he is in charge of the photographic department of CSIRO's Division of Oceanography). Goth, professional entertainer, educator and photographer, goes his various ways in an ancient Holden Commodore sedan that has seen better days. Previously, he had an old V8 Holden station wagon, but some likely lads from Sydney's western suburbs stole it, stripped it and burnt it in a side street of Ambervale. Mare Carter travels in the latest Subaru four-wheel drive Sportswagon, her third of that marque. I drive a Porsche 911 Carrera Club Sport, number eight in my line of purchases from Stuttgart. Between the current Carter-family car-scene and the early events described in this chapter, we've experienced a variety of adventures, some of which follow.

2 Looking backward

I didn't know it then, but during the early 1960s I reached the zenith of my photographic career. *Life* magazine bought some of my pictures. So did *Esquire, Paris-Match, Stern* and *Epoca*. The highest-paying magazine in the world, the *National Geographic*, gave me a series of assignments. They also gave me an expense account.

The rule-of-thumb on expenses was that they could equal the page rate. A ten-page feature was worth $10 000! I couldn't believe it. I hired twin-engined Aero-Commanders from Avis to fly over Lake Eyre, and helicopters to spy on oil drillers in the Simpson Desert. When I flew in by private charter to Alice Springs, a fully provisioned Land Rover, laden with Scotch and caviar, waited to take me on safari. None of this fazed the *National Geographic*, who paid up without a murmur.

The situation went to my head. On my third assignment I bought a four-cylinder 356C model Porsche and entered it in my expense account book under 'travel costs'. Someone in Washington DC rang me up about this. Eventually I was informed in writing that the *National Geographic* did not care to buy me a Porsche, which they referred to as a 'hard item'. They didn't give me much work after that. In time I was reduced to writing books and making television films for a living.

My 356C Porsche cost $4500 and was the last example of that model sold in Australia. It came to me from Alec Mildren, who was in the process of switching agencies from Porsche to Alfa-Romeo. He wanted it out of his window. The correct list price was $5000. This was early 1965 when the first six-cylinder 911 Porsches were arriving, superseding the 356 range.

I really liked that first Porsche. It was 'Bali' blue in colour, with a partly tinted windscreen and discreet, rich chrome work, including a bullet-shaped external rear-vision mirror. It had a rocklike solidity—the doors thudded shut like bank vaults and you could literally walk all over

Jeff Carter's first 1965 model Porsche, the last 356C-type sold new in Australia by agent Alex Mildren for $5000, just before the introduction of the 911 series.

Thor with Dad's brand-new 356C Porsche at a south-coast beach not far from the farm at Foxground.

Down on the farm at Foxground with the author's first Porsche, the 356C.

it (in silk socks, of course) without making dents. Its official model name was 356C. Engine capacity 1500 cc, producing 88 bhp.

By the standards of the day, it was quick off the mark (0 to 60 mph in 13.5 seconds). And it went around corners like no other car. Provided you knew what you were doing. Ralph Nader would have wanted the car banned from all public roads.

The early Porsches were known as oversteering cars. This meant they went around corners sideways—or backwards. If you really blew it, they spun like catherine wheels.

None of this happened at ordinary cruising speeds, but no enthusiast drives Porsches at the normal rate. I certainly didn't. Consequently I saw rather more of where I had been than where I was going in my C model. (For the interested student, I suggest that once the car is going backwards or spinning, pull on the handbrake and maintain a firm pressure on the brake pedal—and do not forget to declutch!)

Eventually, with the aid of a book by Baron von someone-or-other, I learned how to negotiate corners at quite high speeds. The Baron was then the doyen of Porsche rally drivers and an exponent of the art of *wischening*, a German skiing term, meaning 'to slip sideways'.

Once you accept that it is not necessarily disastrous to move sideways in a motor car, the art of *wischening* is readily mastered. Provided your car oversteers. The early Porsches oversteered like billyo, particularly when shod with their standard issue cross-ply 'sport' tyres.

To *wischen*, all you had to do was select a gear that left you with plenty of reserve acceleration and then go into the chosen corner much too fast. Quite small but rapid sawing motions of the steering wheel and firm acceleration controlled the resultant slide. After practising on lonely roads, I eventually learned to *wischen* and stay on my side of the driving line.

The worst thing you could do while *wischening* was to ease off on the loud pedal. Any hesitation with the right foot caused the vehicle to swap ends or spin, even if you backed off only by the thickness of your socks.

Though I mastered the art of *wischening* to my own satisfaction, nobody else was impressed. Passengers wanted to get out. Oncoming traffic took violent evasive action. My children paled and fell silent. Mare, their mother and my longtime fellow-traveller, bought herself a 1928 Essex.

Another problem with *wischening* was tyre wear. All four of my tyres were smooth at 10 000 kilometres.

'Is there any way of going quickly around corners with less drama and expense?' I asked the new Sydney Porsche agent, Richard Cocks (who had taken over from Alec Mildren).

'Yes,' said Richard brightly. 'We shall fit a set of the new radial tyres. Also a compensating spring between the rear wheels, to maintain the

Jeff as auto-engineer, attempting to remedy a gear-shift problem in his 912 Porsche. This photograph did not please the makers or their Australian agents, who threatened legal action.

negative camber, which we'll increase slightly. And the suspension will be lowered one inch.'

The car looked as if it had two broken rear axles, but the suspension modification and the radial tyres provided an astonishing improvement. High speed cornering no longer required *wischening*. People began to ride with me again. Of course, there was a modest amount of tyre slip at times, but not enough to make passengers want to get out.

The tyres lasted 15 000 kilometres, a marked improvement on the cross-plies. The lowered suspension caused occasional underbody scraping on bush roads, which meant the heater gates were usually jammed shut or open. A small price to pay for the phenomenal handling.

As I recall, the C Porsche's top speed was 104 mph on the clock— preferably down a slight incline. On longish country cruises it could travel 30 miles on a gallon of petrol. The overall average was about 25 mph, getting down to 22 mph when I was brave.

The only breakage in two years and 27 000 miles was the clutch diaphragm spring. When the car was out of warranty, of course. But after some terse correspondence with the Australian importers and the Porsche factory in Stuttgart, Germany, I was refunded half the price of the spring.

Apart from a set of brake pads, my first Porsche cost nothing further in the way of repairs and replacements. It had the normal services, plus two sets of radials. Nothing went wrong during the two years, except water dripped on my feet the first time it rained. Mr Mildren grudgingly fixed that, gratis.

Although they had been on the market seventeen years, Porsches in 1966 were rare beasts. Only forty-eight came yearly to Australia. Most of their wealthy owners cherished and mollycoddled them, rarely venturing forth on the highways and byways. Or so it seemed, because I seldom glimpsed another Porsche to flash my lights at. (According to the German Porsche house magazine *Christophorus*, you were supposed to greet fellow Porsche owners thus.)

I never flashed my lights much. The only other Porsches I saw were at Richard Cocks's Porsche Service Centre, or parked outside expensive restaurants in Double Bay. The Porsche mystique was pretty strong even in those early days. They were famous for the quality of their construction, their durability, the innovative brilliance of their basic design, their extraordinary speed and handling qualities, their reliability, ease of maintenance and their excellent resale value. In this last field, no other exotic car could match them.

Porsche's racing victories were piling up around the world and so was their reputation as the ultimate road car. Legend had it that once you owned a Porsche, no other vehicle would do. When Porsche owners reluctantly parted with their car, they invariably went out and bought another Porsche. Doyen of motoring writers, Ken Purdy, described the Porsche as 'the best car in the world'.

My first two years as a Porsche owner convinced me that most of their reputation was justified. Overall, I found the C model magnificent. It always started. It never stopped. No squeaks or rattles developed. No speck of rust appeared, despite two years totally out of doors. (I've never been able to afford a garage for any of my cars.) The 356C never went off song (except when I fed it muddy petrol pumped from an old drum); performance hardly varied in two years. Tuning and tinkering were totally uncalled for. Although it was in the exotic company of Ferrari and Maserati, the C was less trouble and cheaper to maintain than a mass-produced family sedan.

My Bali-blue model did have some minor faults, though, in addition to leaking rain water on my feet during its first few weeks. The fresh-air ventilation system was hopeless. The only way to get cool air into the car was to open a window. (They have not improved much to this day.) The heater had two positions: blast furnace and off. The scorching blast of air could be directed at your feet or at the windscreen—you couldn't have a little of both. The foot-activated windscreen washer was a joke.

The two back seats were strictly for children, small children. The boot under the front bonnet was supplied already full by the manufacturer—with a spare wheel and the petrol tank. Careful packing allowed you to stow perhaps four cut lunches and a few neatly folded handkerchiefs. The car was in truth designed for two people—with the 'child' rear seats folded down, luggage space was adequate.

My second set of radials were smooth after 12 000 kilometres. While pricing new rubber at Richard Cocks's emporium, I looked with envy at some of the new model six-cylinder 911 Porsches in for maintenance. They looked roomier and sharply contemporary in contrast with my slightly old-fashioned, rounded C model. But their price was astronomical, even allowing for their better looks, greater speed and power.

'You should have one of these,' Richard said tentatively.

'Can't afford one,' I snapped irritably. 'Besides, no one in their right mind would spend over $9000 on a motor car.'

'The 911's do cost rather a lot,' Richard agreed. 'But for country work, one of these should suit you. It has six inches ground clearance, fully laden. Your present car has only four and a half inches.' He indicated one of the new Porsches, light green in colour.

'Only $7500, to you.'

'Why?' I asked, full of suspicion.

'This is a 912 model, identical with the 911 in appearance, and it has the proven four-cylinder motor, instead of the...ah...newer six-cylinder model, which has yet to stand the test of time. It has been on the market only two years.'

'Hmm,' I said, getting into the 912. It fitted very well.

'Six inches more leg room for the rear passengers,' Richard said, poking his head inside the car. 'Improved heater and fresh-air system, plus *electric* windscreen washers,' he added smoothly.

'Any room in the boot?' I enquired sarcastically.

Richard walked to the front of the car, smirking. He threw open the boot lid with a flourish, revealing space for scores of cut lunches and countless folded handkerchiefs. ·

I gaped enviously. Richard, sensing his advantage, followed up quickly. 'If you buy this vehicle, you won't have to buy new tyres for your old C model. See, it already has new tyres!'

That was the clincher. I went home in my green 912 Porsche shod with fat Belgian-made Goodyear Grand Prix low-profile cross-plies. All brand new. The deal? $4000 for the 356C, which had cost me $4500 two years ago. Price of the 1967 model 912, with no extras, was $7500.

As a matter of fact, there were a lot of extras, compared with the C model. The 912 had an extra gear for starters, making five in all. And extra large doors, allowing easier access to the enlarged rear passenger area. The electric washers combined with the three-speed wipers meant you no longer had to stop and get out of the car to clear the windscreen.

The higher ground clearance handled the roughest bush roads and made scudding around our farm paddocks a rather tame exercise. (We had our own gymkhana course, including a permanent skidpan area down near the creek.)

Thor with 1928 Essex, Jeff with 912 Porsche, and Mare with Land Rover.

On the road, the 912 handled infinitely better than the C model. It never wanted to go sideways and was basically neutral. You could lift your foot off in corners and all the car did was slow down! Hurled into corners under acceleration, the 912 would squeal its front tyres and if you persisted, it would gently begin to slide out at the back. The only way you could get it *wischening* was to jump on the accelerator in first or second gear in very tight hairpins.

If you were too brave on wet bitumen, the car's mild understeer characteristic allowed it to run inexorably wide—no matter what you did with the steering wheel, until you eased off. Once front traction was restored, it resumed going where you steered it. The 912 was somewhat quicker than the C type: 0 to 60 mph in 11.5 seconds. Top speed was 112 mph indicated on the flat, occasionally 120 downhill. Through the famous 'Kiama Bends' near our farm at Foxground, it was faster than the C model, with no hint of drama. Even at quite high speeds, you were never *busy*, as you were required to be in the 356 cars. Few of my passengers wanted to get out.

Another advantage of the 912, so far as I was concerned, was the engine compartment. The Porsche people had designed this for their six-cylinder motor, but our motor was only four cylinders. This left enough room

to stow at first three and later four Paddy Pallin sleeping bags! Very handy for a family that liked to go camping in style.

The bags rode behind the rear engine mounts on a flat metal plate above the exhaust muffler. The plate got hot, so we placed a row of canned foods on it, before stowing the bags. When we stopped, there was always a piping hot meal ready to eat. 'We' comprised my long-haired mate, Mare, and my two youngest sons, Goth and Vandal, then aged eleven and fourteen years. On camping trips, we found the 912 easily carried us, our tent, inflatable beds, food, clothing, cooking stove, utensils, drinking water, etc., plus four sleeping bags. The space for the additional bag came about as follows. After a few months, the 912 developed a habit of jumping out of gear when it hit certain types of bumps on bitumen or dirt roads. It turned out a lot of the 912s were doing the same. Various engine mount modifications, provided gratis, only made things worse. One notable effort by Porsche Service Centre had the car jumping out of gear fifty-six times in twenty-seven miles on a corrugated road. The House of Hamilton in Melbourne was equally nonplussed by the problem.

After a year, a solution of sorts was found. I could never find out exactly what was done, from Messrs Hamilton or Cocks. Richard mumbled something about installing 'hard mounts, as used in the rally cars'. What I think they did was remove all the rubber bushes from the mounts and bolt the engine-gearbox direct on to the car body, metal to metal. At least, it felt like that. Anyway, the change made room for a fourth sleeping bag in the engine compartment! The vibration was irritating, especially on idle. While waiting at traffic lights, I could see three of everything.

The big fat Belgian Grand Prix cross-plies lasted 30 000 kilometres, although I was travelling quicker than in my Bali-blue C Porsche. Richard Cocks fitted the 912 with a set of what were then the radical Michelin XAS radials. They looked a mite skimpy in comparison with the previous tyres, but their performance was vastly superior, particularly in the wet. At first they wallowed and squealed, but a twenty per cent increase in pressure all round quelled the din and restored the 912's cornering tidiness. Another gain was the longevity of the XASs. They lasted 44 000 kilometres!

Winter was nigh, there was frost in the valley. The first grey thrushes of the season appeared in our garden. The phone rang. It was Richard, calling regardless of expense from Sydney.

'It's here,' he announced.

'Winter? Yes, I know,' I responded.

'No, no. The 911E. The new fuel-injected model. I'll bring one down next weekend so you can get the feel of it.'

I knew what he was talking about, but feigned ignorance in front of my family, who were wont to grow apprehensive when a new model Porsche came on the market. This particular one was supposed to be the ultimate product from Stuttgart, featuring not only the new-fangled fuel-injection system (doing away with carburettors), but a unique Porsche 'automatic' gearbox, operated by the traditional lever through the 'H' pattern, but lacking a clutch pedal!

Fuel injection was then in its infancy, several manufacturers using different types—but of course Porsche had delayed introducing it until they had decided on the system best suited to their vehicles: the Bosch mechanical manifold injection system, first used on their Daytona race cars in 1966. It was now early 1969, but Porsche had taken that long to decide that the electronic Bosch fuel injection system already being used in Volkswagen cars was unsuitable for their higher-revving sporting vehicles.

The just-arrived 911E was reputed to have fifty more horses under its bonnet than my 912 model, plus bigger, better brakes and other improvements. So I was secretly agog to encounter the new wonder vehicle, though I maintained my normal outer calm.

Next Saturday morning, a startling, resonant drone echoed up the valley to our homestead. There was a stampede of youthful feet downstairs and outside. Number two son, Goth, a budding aircraft buff, thought

With Richard Cocks and the 911E Porsche at Foxground.

it was an overseas jet off-course. Number three, Vandal, hoped it was the council grader. Number one, Thor (an engineering student) said it was 'a fuel-injected six-cylinder air-cooled motor of about two litres approaching at speed'.

It was. Bright orange, too. As it came up the hill, our cattle stampeded into the gully. 'What do you think of it? Isn't she a beauty?' said Richard, beaming.

'Strewth!' I said. 'It'd be a fair cow in wet weather. What's that big hole in the top?'

'That's the sunshine roof,' said Richard coolly. 'It closes in bad weather at the touch of a button. There are also power windows, radio, aerial, electrically heated rear window, with wiper, foglights and of course Sportomatic transmission.'

'How much is all this?' I said.

'In round figures, say $13 000,' Richard said.

'Strewth!' I said again. Mare came out of the kitchen.

'It seems a lot,' she put in. 'Just to get new tyres. And it doesn't look any bigger than the other one.' She went back inside to her scones and the Saturday roast.

'This is my demonstration car,' Richard put in quickly. 'It has every conceivable extra. Yours won't cost so much. $11 000 in fact.'

'That's a big saving,' I said. 'Show me how it all works.'

He did, and it was quite an experience, even for a seasoned Porsche voyager. I had never realised before that what my 912 lacked was another fifty horsepower!

Due to the incredible roadholding and the quietness of the engine, there was little illusion of speed. You could argue that the combination of power, effortless handling and shush made 911E driving almost matter of fact. Sitting beside Richard and staring out at the flashing scenery as we stormed up Woodhill Mountain at 90 mph, there was never the slightest thought that we might run out of bitumen on the corners. Or that we couldn't go even faster if we wished. Or that we couldn't stop if we encountered Ron Ingold's cows on the road around the next bend. Coming home it was my turn. Getting used to the lack of a clutch pedal was easy. Gear changes were made in the same manner and for the same reasons as in a normal car, except that you didn't have to complicate proceedings with your left foot. You could even double shuffle on down-changes, pausing with the lever in neutral while treading on the loud pedal. But for standard gear changes, you just lifted your foot momentarily from the accelerator, then pushed the gear lever into the required slot.

The 911E's automatic gearbox provided the normal engine braking effect of down-changes, unlike some automatic transmissions. Richard told me Porsche called it the 'Sportomatic' system.

Back at the farm, I asked Richard to tell me precisely how much I might have to pay for a 911E with Sportomatic transmission, but *no* extras. He did some scribbling on his jotter. 'On the road, you won't get much change out of $11 000,' he replied. We had just entered the kitchen and there was a hushed silence among my assembled family. Rain had begun to pour down outside, as it often does at Foxground, making an ominous drumming sound on the corrugated iron roof. A fire blazed cheerfully in the big black fuel stove, but a coolness seemed to pervade the room.

Eventually Mare spoke up: 'Is there anything *wrong* with the car he has?' she asked Richard.

'Well, no,' he responded. 'It's in tip-top condition. Very well maintained...by us. Ah...' he paused. 'It could do with new tyres, that's about all.'

'How much are they?' Mare pursued.

'About $175 for another set of Michelin XAS's... Plus balancing,' Richard just got in as Mare cried: *'Done!'*

After a few glasses of warming red wine, Richard and the 911E drove off into the dusk and rain, after booking me up for a set of new tyres, instead of a new car. A saving of some $10 875, Mare pointed out.

About a year later, I visited Richard's Sydney workshop to have my 912 Porsche serviced (necessary only at 10 000 kilometre intervals, plus oil changes at 5000 kilometres).

'Your tyres are smooth,' he said. 'I'll order a new car.'

'Hold on, not so fast,' I responded. 'What sort of car?'

'A 911E, of course, similar to the one I showed you,' Richard said oilily.

'Where's the advantage?' I wanted to know. 'It still looks the same as my 912 and...'

'Try not to interrupt,' Richard interjected. 'You already know the 911E is faster and handles much better than yours. Due to the extra fifty horsepower and more sophisticated suspension.'

'I reckon my hundred and eight horses are enough,' I got in.

'Do you *mind*?' Richard said, holding up a quieting hand. 'There are a few other advantages I didn't get a chance to explain last time— such as the hydropneumatic suspension at the front, larger tyres and quartz headlights...and of course the big, two-litre, six-cylinder fuel-injected motor.'

'Yes, what exactly is the advantage of fuel injection?' I asked.

'Well, ah...no carburettors. Much less complicated. No fiddling with jet adjustments and float levels.' He flipped his order book open. 'I'll put you down for an orange 911E. I have one arriving next month.'

'I don't know about orange,' I said. 'And what's all this cost?'

'Still only $11 000,' Richard said casually.

'How much for my 912?' I countered.

'Let's say $7250.' Richard was writing busily in his book.

The offer seemed too good to be true—only $250 less than I paid for the car more than two years ago! 'That seems reasonable,' I said. 'But it means I have to find almost $4000.'

Richard stopped writing and looked at me with surprise. Richard was the sort of person who finds it hard to imagine how anyone could be caught short of a measly $4000. 'No problem. You can lease the car,' he said absently, continuing to write.

'What's leasing?' I wanted to know.

'Just like hire-purchase, but you pay the deposit at the end of the contract period, instead of the beginning. Interest rates and conditions are much the same. You just sign these documents, I write you a cheque for your car, less the first monthly lease payment, and you drive home in your 911E.' He pushed the papers towards me. I went home in my orange 911E, with Richard's cheque for $7000 in my pocket.

The car turned out to be a phenomenal improvement on the 912, in almost every way. What I had been lacking, obviously, was an additional fifty horses. There had been times in the 912 when young men in hotted-up Holdens and Fords had been able to hold me off on the straights—then make me follow at their chosen speed through the ensuing bends. In the 911E, I seemed unchallengeable.

So far as I can recall, my orange car outgunned everything I encountered on the highway—and was of course uncatchable on winding roads. I began to drive faster than I had ever driven, but with rather less drama.

My improved performance was duly noted by the south-coast police patrolling twixt Nowra and Wollongong. I learned after the fact that on a number of occasions I had been unsuccessfully chased by police in Cooper S patrol cars. These affronts to officialdom were eventually put right by assorted motorbike patrolmen, who seemed to have a ticket with my name on it every time I drove past.

The demerit points system had been recently introduced and I was soon in correspondence with the motor registry people, who wanted me to show cause why my licence should not be suspended. At the time I felt this was adding insult to injury—the fines being sizeable and frequent. Eventually, my encounters with the law made me wonder if I could much longer afford to drive the 911E. Another problem concerned my passengers, who frequently pleaded to get out. Not due to any

wischening manoeuvres, just the speed. Their heads would swivel back and forth like spectators at a ping-pong match as they stared white-eyed first at the road ahead, then the speedo, then back to the prospect before us. No doubt at every approaching corner it seemed that only luck could save us. Useless to explain this was a 911E Porsche and all was well.

Successfully negotiating the corner didn't convince them of anything except that we had been very lucky. I could have put up with this, but nervous passengers have a habit of clutching at things as they fall about during cornering. In the 911E this always seemed to be the gear lever. Which in the Sportomatic transmission is a sort of instantaneous electric clutch. Touch it and you're out of gear.

As we all know, it is not a good idea to de-clutch at the apex of a full-power corner. This destroys the driver's illusion that he is Jack Brabham and confirms the passenger's worst fears—that the car is out of control. Which it is.

After several monumental dramas not entirely of my own doing, I found myself travelling mostly alone, except for the frequent police escort. In fairness, I must say Porsche's Sportomatic transmission was an excellent concept. Provided passengers left it alone.

However, by 1970, due to a continuing sense of isolation and a consuming, lemming-like urge to go into television documentary film making, I parted company with my orange 911E. The pain of our separation was assuaged by my coming into possession of one of the first Range Rovers landed in Australia. This was a press evaluation vehicle which became known in the trade as 'Big Red', being that colour, registered number DIN 616. We spent two years together, poking into

Thor (at left) and Jeff (centre) filming for the Wild Country *TV series at Anna Creek station, South Australia.*

the remotest corners of the continent during my film-making expeditions, which resulted in the television series *Wild Country*. This showed first on the Australian Channel 7 network and later worldwide, in some twenty countries.

3 Over my shoulder

1963. It happened like this. We had been settled on our farm and wildlife refuge at Foxground a couple of years and I was firmly resolved to keep out of the hurly-burly of photo-journalism. Then the Australian chief of the prestigious international photo-agency, Black Star, rang and offered me the job of covering Donald Campbell's Bluebird land speed record attempt on Lake Eyre. I said no thanks, I would rather stay home with my cows, kangaroos and wombats. The Black Star boss said 'We will pay you two hundred dollars weekly, plus all expenses.' I said no again. 'Your pictures will be in *Life*, *Stern*, *Epoca* . . . all the famous magazines— maybe even *Paris-Match* if he kills himself.' I continued to be negative. 'We will pay you four hundred dollars a week and all expenses,' the great man said. This offer could not be refused. The average weekly wage then was around thirty dollars.

We arranged to meet a few days later at dawn at Mascot airport, where Mr Black Star would have a private charter plane waiting. He would come with me to Lake Eyre. At the appointed hour he arrived—with a four-man film crew, plus a mountain of movie equipment. The pilot shook his head and told us in a strong German accent that his aeroplane could not safely carry such a load. Mr Black Star had not got where he was by accident. A man of instant decisions, he said 'Okay, two of us will drive to Lake Eyre.' He meant me and him. The car was an Armstrong-Siddeley.

Mr Black Star drove this gentleman's hack to Goulburn, where he confessed he was accustomed to being chauffeur-driven. This had been terrifyingly obvious for two hours.

After that, I drove and Mr Black Star alternately dozed and delivered long monologues about the trials and tribulations of his chosen way of life. Late that night he shouted me to my first-ever stay in a motel, at

Mildura, where he somehow charmed the sleepy manager's wife into cooking us up a midnight feed of grilled Murray cod.

We got to Marree halfway through the following night, with a chronically ill, battered Armstrong-Siddeley. In the town we were met by one of the film crew, asleep over the wheel of a four-wheel drive International Scout. Mr Black Star had thoughtfully phoned ahead to Muloorina station on Lake Eyre and asked for a guide to be waiting. This turned out to be Les ('Rhubarb') Wasley, veteran newsreel camera-man and today one of the doyens of ABC television photographers. I fancied a glow in the eastern sky when we finally put our heads down to rest in our barrack-style accommodation at Muloorina sheep station. But Mr Black Star tugged me awake for a dawn breakfast in the mess hut and hurried me and my cameras across the dusty road to a rough airstrip where a Cessna plane waited, its motor running. 'Get photos of the homestead, the countryside, the lake, the track, Bluebird, Campbell, everything. . .' Mr Black Star instructed. He shoved me into the Cessna and no doubt went back to bed. One of the two men in the twin pilot seats in front of me was the German accented gentleman I had met at Mascot two days earlier. The door had been removed from the plane, to facilitate photography, so conversation was impossible above the noise of the engine.

The pilot gave me a wave and then we were tearing down the strip while I struggled to fasten my seat belt. Probably ex-Luftwaffe, I mused, as we banked sharply after take-off and I stared down through the unobstructed doorway at gibbers and saltbush. Soon we were over Lake Eyre, which glared like ice under the hard autumn sun. Trucks were moving slowly across the blinding salt, dragging scraping implements to smooth one of several tracks that were prepared for Bluebird. They were following the path of a grader, lost in the white blankness that rolled off to every horizon. Some four-wheel drive vehicles and sedan cars were scurrying near a large army tent set up in what was unquestionably the middle of nowhere. A blue line, painted on the salt, arrowed off into the great blinding yonder.

I photographed all this as well as I could, thumping the pilot several times and pointing, trying to get him to circle and give me a better angle of view. But he seemed preoccupied with his companion, into whose ear he shouted almost continuously. I could not make out what he was saying and didn't care much, being intent on my photography. Then, far ahead, I glimpsed three stationary cars and a huddle of human figures. The Cessna throttled back and began to lose altitude. Good, I thought. We're going to land and maybe one of the men down there is Donald Campbell.

I took a couple of photos and then for want of something better to

do, concentrated my attention on the two gentlemen seated ahead of me. The Luftwaffe pilot was certainly obsessed with his companion, an elderly, bull-necked man with greying hair and leather-brown skin. I leaned closer to listen and heard German accented shouts such as 'A liddle more throddle, a liddle more... nein, nein, zat's too much! Achtung! Nose up, steady...'

He was giving the elderly gentleman a flying lesson! Worse, a *landing* lesson. I buckled myself down tightly, which took me out of earshot, closed my eyes and hoped. We made a sort of controlled crash landing and after a bit of swerving came to a halt. 'Congratulations, Herr Price. You haf made your first solo landing!' said the pilot.

Thus, in a jangled state of nerves, I met the legendary King of Muloorina, Elliott Price, the man who carved a million-dollar sheep empire out of the desert. Aged sixty-six, he was master of two and a half thousand square kilometres of sand and saltbush, including much of Lake Eyre, venue for the Bluebird land speed record attempt. Flying held a fascination for the leathery, iron-willed desert patriarch. A few years earlier he had knocked up an American kit autogyro and merrily roamed the skies above Lake Eyre until grounded by the Department of Civil Aviation, who ordered the Marree police to dismantle the contraption.

The gaggle of parked cars on the rock-hard surface of the lake contained Donald Campbell, journalist (later novelist) Evan Green and assorted experts. They were scouting a site for a new Bluebird track, because the others were too soft or wet or bumpy. Donald reluctantly took a brief, limp grip of my outstretched hand when we were introduced and allowed me to occupy the remaining spare seat in the back of his Valiant.

Evan drove, Campbell beside him. The man next to me had a stop-watch and notepad. We kept starting and stopping with a series of skids and the atmosphere was so charged with boffin waffle I didn't dare ask why. We would reach a certain speed and Evan would announce this and then say 'Neutral...coasting... (pause) speed exactly umpteen miles an hour.' At which point the man beside me would shout 'Now!' and press his stop-watch as Evan slammed on the brakes. When we stopped, the length of the skid was measured, also the depth of the furrows we had made. There followed much learned discussions and kicking of the salt surface. The man with the notebook made calculations and reported the results to other boffins. Then we got back in the car and did it all again, and again...

Later on, the job got more interesting when Donald Campbell began test driving Bluebird. Also when I met Tonia Campbell, who was as vivacious as her husband was taciturn. A Belgian-born nightclub singer, she was tomboyishly attractive and, in sharp contrast with Donald, co-operative with the press. Very co-operative. On one memorable sunny day, she took an outdoor bubble bath in the trough of an artesian bore a few kilometres from Muloorina homestead, to the delight of some visiting newspaper photographers. Unfortunately Tonia was not such a gift to newspaper writers or radio interviewers, because much of what she said was unprintable, though often funny.

Bluebird's test runs were infrequent, uncertain affairs. Base camp at Muloorina homestead was about fifty kilometres from the prepared track on Lake Eyre. The most favoured time for test runs was soon after sunrise, which meant those without aeroplanes had to leave Muloorina in darkness to be sure of being set up beside the track with photographic gear when Bluebird screamed down the salt. If it ran. With the other two full-time photographers (both movie men), I frequently spent whole days standing beside my tripod out on the glaring salt, waiting in vain for Bluebird— or news that the test run had been called off, again. A two-way radio would have been handy, but the army signal corps had a monopoly on these. So we waited until hunger, heat, wind, cold, boredom or angry frustration forced us to pack up and drive back to the starting line for news. Several times when we did this, Bluebird whizzed un-announced down the track and we missed our pictures! On other occasions we arrived back at the starting line where Bluebird was garaged to find the camp deserted, everyone having gone back to Muloorina hours ago. The drive had been called off, but no one ever bothered to drive out to our lonely station and tell us.

More by good luck than good management, we occasionally contrived to be ready with our cameras beside the track when Donald drove by. On the early runs we were allowed to set up our gear about two hundred metres from the blue line that Donald straddled as he tore across the lake. This was hardly close enough for good photos, even with our biggest telephoto lenses. We campaigned to get closer, but the army retaliated by insisting we *retreated* to the service track, which paralleled the blue line at a distance of five hundred metres, an impossible distance for photography.

After that we played cat-and-mouse games with the army patrols that whizzed up and down the service track before each run. It was all very unsatisfactory and finally we approached Donald Campbell and wheedled from him the only smidgin of co-operation he ever granted us. For just one practice run, one way only, we could set up our cameras fifty metres from the blue line. He would not be travelling at full speed, perhaps 300mph, but we were on no account to make any movement that might distract him. Apparently at that speed, the sight of photographers fleeing their post in terror could cause a flicker of the great man's wrist that would have us all killed.

We thought this was a reasonable enough favour to be granted. After all, we were there for the sole purpose of increasing Donald's fame (and fortune) by recording his exploits. My agency, Black Star, had no doubt paid for the privilege of exclusive world magazine photography rights. Les 'Rhubarb' Wasley was part of a documentary team working for Ajax Films and Keith 'KB' Loon (who liked that brand of beer) was filming in 35mm colour for the Ovaltine people, who had paid a large sum to produce a cinema-release commercial starring Donald and Bluebird. So if we wanted to risk our necks, why shouldn't we?

Naturally, as this was to be our only chance of getting shots of Bluebird at speed heading almost directly at our cameras, we cribbed closer to the line than agreed—to within twenty-five metres in fact. (Yes, photographers *are* irresponsible lunatics.) When Bluebird eventually appeared, screaming almost directly toward us, we were dismayed to observe through our viewfinders that the shrieking monster was not straddling the line as usual, but was a couple of metres our side of it!

All intelligent people, we realised the futility of running from a car moving at perhaps 300mph and kept our fingers on the shutter buttons. A split second after Donald thundered past, we were whirling and falling about like autumn leaves in a gale, cameras and tripods toppling in all directions. But we had our pictures.

When we recalled the incident that evening, Donald explained that he had followed a new path to save wear and tear on the track proper. It was one of the rare occasions he offered us a grin—at our discomfiture.

No doubt under great stress himself, Campbell seemed to take pleasure in making things difficult for other people. The Ovaltine commercial called for a dawn scene of Donald sitting in Bluebird before going out to break the world land speed record and downing a mug of Ovaltine. He and Bluebird were to be silhouetted against the huge orange orb of the rising desert sun. Donald refused to do the scene in the morning, because he disliked getting up early unless he was really doing a run in Bluebird. So it was agreed to shoot the scene against the setting sun, which looks much the same as sunrise to most cinema-goers.

It was a full-scale Cinemascope production, requiring truckloads of hired generators and klieg lights from Adelaide and a crew of a dozen technicians to be organised on to Lake Eyre. Preparations took a week. The director and crew were very uptight as zero hour approached because they knew they had barely two minutes to get their shot against the great blazing disc of desert sun before it slipped below the horizon. The scene required about forty seconds and there would be no chance of a re-shoot if anything was muffed.

Donald was to be seated in the cockpit of Bluebird. Leo Villa, his chief mechanic, would hand him a large coloured mug with the word 'Ovaltine' embossed on it. Donald would pretend to drink (I think there was some rum in the mug), smile at the camera as he handed Leo the empty mug, then slowly lower Bluebird's cockpit canopy. Alas for the film director, his crew and the Ovaltine company. Instead of smiling into the camera when he finished his drink, Donald pulled a wry face, ruining the shot and wasting a day's work by the film crew—at a cost of several thousand dollars. Very funny.

Despite all these expensive, time-wasting shenanigans, after six weeks my two movie friends and I felt we had photographed every conceivable angle of the Bluebird enterprise. All that was needed was the actual record-breaking run and the resultant handshakes.

By then it was established that Donald wouldn't run on a Friday, which he thought unlucky. A pattern had emerged whereby Donald, Tonia and entourage flew off to the fleshpots of Adelaide each Friday and returned late Sunday but more likely mid Monday. This meant we could enjoy four-day weekends.

Well, Donald and company could, but for those of us stranded at Muloorina, the delights of counting sheep was a poor substitute for recreation. At breakfast one Friday morning our Luftwaffe pilot whispered to 'Rhubarb' Wasley and myself that he was slipping home to Sydney for the weekend in the twin-engined Aero-Commander plane that was being hired or loaned to the Bluebird project (no one was sure). Campbell and party had dodged off to Adelaide in assorted aeroplanes belonging to wealthy admirers and the Aero-Commander would not be required until Monday to ferry them back to Muloorina. So off the three of us went, to enjoy a weekend of compassionate leave at home.

I made it to Foxground around eight o'clock that night, where Mare had prepared a champagne dinner by candlelight. Alas, this was interrupted by a midnight phone call from the distraught Luftwaffe pilot. He had to leave Mascot at dawn for Adelaide, whence he had been summoned by his masters. Campbell, it seemed, had decided to make his first attempt at the record on Monday and wanted to take the official timekeepers to Muloorina on Saturday afternoon.

By leaving home more or less immediately, I made it to Mascot just in time to clamber aboard the already moving Aero-Commander at dawn. 'Rhubarb' was not his bright usual self. Nor was I—and the Luftwaffe man had reverted sulkily to his native tongue. We flew in glum silence all the way to Adelaide, brooding over our lost weekend.

On arrival, Mr Campbell was not amused to find two free-booters in his aeroplane. He had with him the chief timekeepers, Tonia and assorted others. When heads were counted, there were two too many for the Aero-Commander. Ours: Carter and Wasley. Donald was very dark about this. At the last minute one of his wealthy Adelaide mates offered him the loan of a Piper Comanche aircraft. Donald and I would fly in this to Muloorina. Unfortunately, the Piper was garaged at a minor air-strip some kilometres from Adelaide.

We drove there in a borrowed car and eventually took off early in the afternoon, Donald muttering about how he hated single-engined aircraft because they were 'deucedly damned, dangerous things' if they chose to stop. He tugged, pushed and swore at the controls in the manner of a man unfamiliar with them. This caused me to fall into a deep, introspective silence. The situation was not improved some hours later when Donald announced tersely 'It's going to be pretty damned dark when we land at Muloorina.' The sun was sinking dramatically toward the western horizon, but I had no eyes for its grandeur. 'You should be able to see a town on your side,' Donald said. I looked hard, but there was no town. 'Can you see a railway line?' There was no railway line. Clearly, we were lost, above an uninviting desert landscape across which shadows were now creeping ominously. At last the railway line appeared, and beside it the Marree Road. 'I think we might land at Marree,' Donald stated. 'It could be too bloody dark by the time we get to Muloorina.' It was the longest speech he ever made to me and I agreed with every word he said. Some cars on the road below us already had their lights on.

But Donald calmly overflew Marree and proceeded into the gathering dusk toward Lake Eyre, requesting via radio that a few cars be parked along the Muloorina airstrip with their lights on. 'Just in case. . .' Soon after, Campbell all smiles and Carter all shakes, we climbed safely out of the Piper after a rather bumpy landing. Maybe I had been punished for stuffing the great man about—I will never know.

He did not make his run on Monday, as announced, but several days later, when the timekeeping crew were threatening to take their Longines clocks home.

The run failed to shake John Cobb's record of 394mph, established seventeen years earlier. The timekeepers went home, but returned a week or so later, when Donald announced he would have another try. After various delays, he did this, again when the timekeepers were on the point of mutiny. The run was slower than his first attempts. The timekeepers went home. The press went home. The world lost interest in the Bluebird land speed record attempt.

Typically, I suppose, Donald Campbell and a somewhat reduced entourage returned quietly to Lake Eyre a month later and set a new world speed record for a wheel-driven car of 403mph (Craig Breedlove had already recorded 407mph in a free-wheeling jet-powered vehicle). The Bluebird project, which had dragged on at several venues around the world for ten years, had finally improved on John Cobb's seventeen-year-old record by nine miles per hour.

The reputed cost of the venture was ten million dollars. In retrospect, I think Donald Campbell's greatest achievement must have been in the field of fundraising. Somehow, over a period of ten years, he managed to attract a never-ending stream of commercial sponsors, from lemonade makers to car distributors. When you think of it, a million dollars a year for ten years has to be some sort of world record.

Long before the Muloorina marathon I had some more amusing outback adventures with another famous man, Eric Worrell. Well, he was on his way to becoming famous—as a reptile expert (it was in the early 1950s). Later he was awarded an MBE and then, the final accolade, was the subject of television's greatest crowd-pleaser *This is Your Life*. Eric was also an up-and-coming author.

For his snake-hunting safaris, Eric had somehow cajoled his bank manager into buying him a Holden utility (the first commercially produced such vehicle in the world, the ute being an Australian invention). Eric wanted publicity for his small reptile park (then near Woy Woy), and I wanted exciting stories and photos to sell to magazines, so we fell in together. I was envious of his wheels and planned to buy my own vehicle with the proceeds of my story and photo sales.

With an eye toward the day when I would be at the helm of my own car, I used to study Eric's driving technique and ask questions as we went along. Gear changing fascinated me and I watched intently each time he declutched, moved the gear lever, lifted off the clutch and simultaneously pressed back on the accelerator. It sounds pretty dopey now, but I fell into the habit of mimicking Eric's feet movements, pressing and releasing imaginary pedals. On some trips I think I saw more of Eric's feet than I did of the countryside. The inevitable happened, when he finally let me have a drive. I made immaculate gear changes, but kept looking at my feet instead of the road—which we left, several times! Eric finally suggested that perhaps it would be better if I continued my studies at 'a proper driving school'. (I did this in 1954, after finding a bank manager willing to buy me a vehicle.)

On one of our early trips, Eric was lumping a canvas bag full of tiger snakes across a paddock near Tocumwal on the Murray River when a squatter galloped up on his thoroughbred. Apparently he thought we had something of his in the bag and demanded noisily to see inside it. When Eric suggested he had only a few snakes, collected for scientific purposes, the squatter roared 'Balderdash!' and threatened to bring up some troopers if the bag wasn't opened forthwith. So Eric undid the neck of the bag and the squatter peered down from his saddle into it. The horse had a quicker eye and reared up violently, pawing the sky like Roy Roger's famous mount, Trigger. The squatter, thinking his horse was going to topple over backward, slipped his feet from the stirrups. But the terrified animal bounded forward and took off in a frenzied gallop, the squatter clinging on precariously with his knees. They may be travelling still.

On a later snake-gathering safari, we toured the Murray River from old Tallangatta (later submerged by Lake Hume) to Swan Hill. After several days, Eric had the floor of his new Holden panel van covered with flat wooden crates containing three hundred tiger snakes. At this stage, we decided to return to Sydney via Bourke, which is rather the long way round, if you look at a map. I don't know why, except that it seemed like a good idea at the time.

It was not a good idea. Rain plagued us and somewhere between Roto and Gilgunnia we got slightly lost and bogged down for a few days. Tucker was scarce, but luckily I had brought along a huge jar full of shelled hard-boiled eggs, preserved in mayonnaise.

This was a Scandinavian recipe, prepared for us by my partner of the time (mother of Karen and Thor Carter), a wildly individual Norwegian motorbike rider. The idea was that mayonnaise preserved the eggs (from my small poultry farm). Normally we slept in swags on the ground, but due to the constant rain and muddy conditions, we bedded down each night in the van, on top of the crates of tiger snakes. Now, snakes have some rather disgusting habits and tend to get very smelly when kept in confined quarters—to the extent that our sleeping conditions could at best have been described as appalling. The constant slithering and hiss of the reptiles, only inches from our heads, didn't help. We tended to sit up late in the cabin of the van until we were really tired, yarning in the feeble overhead light and swallowing down our hard-boiled eggs in mayonnaise, which we both pronounced delicious. Until one morning, in better light, we discovered the contents of the jar was crawling with maggots and had obviously been thus for several days!

Eventually we made it to Cobar, after finding nothing at Gilgunnia, the place we had been making for, except the ruin of a pub or homestead. We stormed into the cafe and were treated like lepers by the waitress. No matter, we thought, it takes all types—and pressed on to Bourke. There, in another cafe, we were similarly treated, the waitress standing away from the table as we ordered, then literally throwing our plates down as she served us, before scurrying off in wide-eyed disgust. We couldn't make it out.

Later, in a pub, we were put right. We stank to high heaven of decomposing snake effluent. Having lived and slept with the reptiles for ten days, we had grown accustomed to the stench!

Garage mechanics kept cross-threading the filler plug in the differential of my first vehicle, a 1954 Peugot 203 light lorry. This allowed the worm drive to pump the oil on to the road as you went along, whereupon the mechanism became red hot and destroyed itself. Twice. I could not afford this sort of thing and switched to Holden panel vans. In these I travelled around 80 000 *miles* each year, when I would trade up to the new model. In three years I used as many Holdens, travelled a quarter of a million miles and never broke down.

This record is better than it sounds, because travelling the roads of outback NSW in the late 1950s was tough on vehicles. Generally speaking, bitumen was unknown anywhere west of what is now the Newell Highway. Even the Hume Highway had its horror stretches, particularly between Tarcutta and Albury. In one memorably wet year, scores of trucks, tourist buses and private cars bogged down near Little Billabong and had to be supplied with aerial drops of food. Getting to places like Bourke, Wilcannia or Hay could be a nightmare if it rained. Even the major 'highways' across the red and blacksoil plains were impassable after a day of heavy showers.

These major roads were little more than graded tracks spearing across the western plains. After a heavy shower, they offered as much traction

Jeff Carter's first vehicle, a 1954 Peugeot light lorry, encamped near Buchan in north-east Victoria.

as ice. If you stopped, it was hard to get moving again. So you pressed on, as smoothly and swiftly as possible, in a series of just-controlled slides, first toward one side of the road and then the other. Where the road was elevated above flood plains, it was like driving along a dyke wall: on either side, water or deep mud waited to claim you. Because of the corrugations, you needed to travel at between sixty and one hundred kilometres per hour, which required tremendous concentration and a degree of skill.

Sustained rain soaked deep into the road surface, which adhered to the tyres in ever-thickening layers and slowly filled the wheel arches until they were packed solid. Eventually the wheels jammed against the packed mud and clay. There was no answer to this problem, but you could delay the inevitable by travelling in a low gear with your foot heavy on the accelerator. The spinning drive wheels would then pick up less mud and cut down through it to the dry road surface underneath. If there *was* dry road surface, the wheels would grip for a few metres. Then, as you gained momentum, they would ride up on to the mud again, spin wildly and bore down to dry ground, grip again briefly, and so on . . . It was tough on the car, nerve-racking for the driver, particularly as the vehicle tended to fishtail every time it lost traction. But on occasions I proceeded in this manner for hour upon hour, at an average speed of 25 km/h. If there was no hard or dry surface under the mud, you bogged instantly.

After a few years at this sort of thing, I became wise in the ways of the west and learned to use lesser-known roads and tracks, rather than the alleged 'highways' in wet weather. These often took a more tortuous but more commonsense path than the major routes, following along the crests of sand dunes instead of spearing direct across claypans that would become impassable after a heavy dew. Another advantage of the back track was that you rarely found it churned up by semi-trailers, which left wheel tracks too deep for a conventional small vehicle to follow. Of course, there was nothing magical about minor roads and station tracks—after a day or so of heavy rain they become impassable, too. When this happened, I used to make camp and practise taking photos in the rain.

Beyond the Darling, particularly in the north-west 'corner' country, I found that sand bogging in dry weather was a common hazard for the Holden driver. The run from Wanaaring to Tibooburra could be very

The author learns why it is best to have a four-wheel drive vehicle in desert country.

tedious. Big mobs of travelling sheep churned up the sand for many kilometres, making traction difficult. Many a time I raced over the first of a series of dunes to find my way blocked by a mob of travelling woollies. Once halted in soft sand, moving off again usually required some digging or a helping push.

I met a lot of drovers this way and often stayed with them for a week or so, gathering material for illustrated stories about their way of life. They were a fairly taciturn lot, but each had a story to tell—if you had the time, patience and skill to wheedle it out. When your car is bogged in the sand, you have all the time in the world.

Out in the flat country, around Hay and White Cliffs in western NSW and Lake Frome in adjoining South Australia, through to Coober Pedy, it seems the low-profile landscape gives rise to tall tales. Like the one about the rabbit trapper's car on the Nullarbor Plain (now *there's* flat country!). A group of trappers had decided to give the game away and had a party at their lonely camp. All around, the treeless plain rolled away to the horizon, dotted sparsely with small shrubs and saltbush. As the levels in the various bottles lowered, the rabbiters discussed how to dispose of one of their vehicles. Unregistered and mechanically well past it, the old bomb was still going modestly well and occupied a soft spot in its owner's heart. 'I hate to just leave her in this Godforsaken place,' sobbed the vehicle's owner into his umpteenth mug of rum. 'Well, let's give the old battler her freedom,' suggested one of his more cheerfully drunken mates. 'Whaddaya mean?' asked the owner. 'We'll just fill her up with juice, start her up and turn her loose.'

Everyone voted this a good idea, so the veteran's tank was filled brim full, the steering wheel lashed to the straight-ahead position and the motor started. The owner hopped in briefly to engage first gear, then jumped out, giving the old battler a last friendly slap on its rear as it set out bravely on its last lonely voyage. The group solemnly raised their glasses and drank a toast as the vehicle chugged steadily away toward the northern horizon. It was just after sundown. The campfire party continued for several hours, until all concerned were 'well away'. During a lull in the yarn-spinning, the group became aware of a steady mechanical drone, some thought growing louder, out in the night. 'Must be a train,' was one suggestion. 'No, we're too far north of the line.'

The men grabbed torches and stumbled off across the plain toward the sound. Out of the darkness came a strange apparition—the old car, festooned with shrubbery. Like so many lost travellers, it had somehow managed to travel in a huge circle, returning to within half a kilometre of camp. As the men watched, the brave old bomb suddenly dived out of sight into a blow-hole several metres in diameter. There was a prolonged crashing and smashing as the vehicle continued its plunge into the abyss, then silence. Chastened, the rabbiters trudged unsteadily back to camp to drink one final toast.

I became rather an expert on drovers and droving and convinced *National Geographic* magazine that I should do a story about droving, titled 'The Plains of Loneliness'. This involved more than a year of intermittent travel with cattle from the Kimberleys in Western Australia through the Northern Territory, Queensland and NSW to Victoria.

I bought my first Land Rover for that job—a second-hand 1954 long-wheelbase model. Mare Carter, a refugee from the American-way-of-strife, had come into my life by then. We had some exciting moments, including a night 'rush' of hundreds of cattle through our camp! Fortunately, we had our swag among some large boulders, which split the stampeding, wild-eyed mob around us.

We spent months at a time on some of the great stock routes, living a similar existence to the drovers. We ate salt beef and damper and drank bore-water tea around many a campfire, listening to and recording the yarns of boss drovers, herders, horse-tailers and cooks. We travelled the Great North Road, the Murranji, the Georgina and Birdsville Tracks in both directions. At times we imagined *we* were drovers, but our cameras, notebooks and transceiver equipped Land Rover set us apart. We were, after all, merely fellow-travellers on those distant outback roads. In my ensuing thirty years of wandering in remote places, including Europe, I learned to accept that in my trade, I would be always the stranger.

4 'A good track . . .'

'The sand in these parts is so loose, you can push a dead man underground with a forked stick.' The speaker was a boundary rider on the great Wild Dog Fence that separates north-west NSW from South Australia. I had been hearing stories about this lonely bit of countryside for some time and had come to investigate in a 1956 model Holden panel van. The first thing I discovered was that once you drove west of the Paroo River, you could bog down in dry times as well as wet.

Bogged in dry sand with his no. 2 Holden panel van. Soon after this he switched to Land Rovers.

From Broken Hill I travelled north-west to Corona homestead, which is not exactly anywhere and then pressed on to McDougall's Well, which is absolutely nowhere. I was making for Brougham's Gate in the 10 000-kilometre Wild Dog Fence. My information suggested that beyond this gate lay a journalistically untapped world of adventure, where my cameras and typewriter would run hot. It was a stark, colourful land of burning artesian bores amid red sand dunes, thick with wildlife and sparsely peopled by trappers, shooters, boundary riders, prospectors and assorted larger-than-life characters.

Getting to the gate to this wonderland proved difficult. Beyond McDougall's Well I followed a lightly defined track across claypans and dunes into the sinking western sun. Then a fearful wind sprang up, creating the worst sand and dust storm I had experienced. Within an hour visibility was down to less than fifty metres and there was nothing to see, anyway. I stopped and ate a makeshift meal inside my Holden panel van as darkness closed in. All through the night, wind and sand lashed the vehicle as I slept fitfully in the rear compartment.

At dawn, all was calm, but there was no longer any track, ahead or behind me! I tramped around the van in ever-widening circles, hoping to cut some trace of the wheelmarks I had been following, either westward toward Brougham's Gate or south-east back to McDougall's Well. For a kilometre nothing in any direction—just seemingly virgin sand dunes and claypans ankle deep in a fresh carpet of sand and dust. I lost interest in pushing further westward and concentrated on locating the trail back to the well and eventually 'civilisation' at Corona homestead, which I now remembered as being a very desirable place.

Almost two kilometres south-east from the van, I detected a sand dune deeply gouged at the crest with what had been wheel tracks. Beyond that was a claypan only lightly carpeted with new sand, where the general line of the track was visible. I trekked back to the Holden, scouting the easiest route to drive as I went. The journey was not easy, even with partly deflated tyres, due to the deep, fresh sand deposited on the dunes. Getting to the crest of each one required several attempts. I would get perhaps two-thirds of the way up, bog down and then reverse back to the claypan for a second rush. Often I had to dig out sand from behind the rear wheels before I could reverse down.

Eventually I learned to hit the clutch the instant the driving wheels lost traction. This prevented digging in and so it was just a matter of rolling back down the wheel tracks you had made partway up the dune. The successive runs packed the sand down, enabling me to gain a few metres each time.

Ultimately I would fly over the crest. But that was not the end of it. I was climbing the gentle slope of the dunes. On the other, steeper face, the freshly deposited sand was even deeper. This caused instant bogging and I had to dig my way *down* from many dunes.

I reached Corona homestead about mid-afternoon, very hot, very tired and not very happy. The squatter and his stationhands listened to my story with relish, then repaid me for the entertainment with afternoon tea, an evening meal and a bed for the night. Next morning a boundary rider in a Land Rover guided me to Brougham's Gate. I had previously followed the wrong track beyond McDougall's Well, of course.

The correct route was only marginally better. The Land Rover had to have a second go at some of the freshly crested dunes. Then the driver would run back and forth over his own tracks a few times, making a reasonably packed surface for me to follow. Now that I had a guide and towing vehicle if required, I hurled the Holden at the dunes with reckless abandon and flew over most of them first go. Thus I discovered the great secret of desert driving in conventional vehicles: reckless abandon.

All the stories I had heard about the fence country were more or less true. The boundary rider who lived at Brougham's Gate turned out to be quite a character, who filled in his spare time trapping and shooting dingoes. I did a story on him for an adventure magazine and one on his daughter for a women's publication. Her speciality was riding a hereford steer around the countryside. Then I drove north along the fence to Smithville outpost, where the boss of the NSW section of the fence lived. This resulted in a story on the headaches and hardships of looking after the world's longest fence.

Following instructions, I pressed on into South Australia to a camp of professional rabbit shooters at a place called Cananna Bore. This bore produced not only hot, undrinkable water, but flammable gas. At night, the rabbiters lit the gas flow, producing a metre-high flame, which served as their camp light. I took some night photos of the burning bore, showing the men sitting around reading by its light and later sold them to several Australian magazines. (On a subsequent trip with Mare Carter, I took a colour series of her bathing by the light of the bore; these sold around the world, including one of the more decorous shots to the *National Geographic*.) When the photos showing the burning gas appeared in America, I received numerous letters from geologists and oil companies, wanting the exact location of the bore. Now everyone knows there are huge deposits of natural gas in the area, chiefly at nearby Moomba.

My illustrated story of the professional rabbit shooters, who were making big money in those days, sold well in Australia, Europe and the USA. American *Guns* magazine featured the tale and was immediately swamped with enquiries from would-be adventurers seeking to live as professional hunters Down Under. So was the Australian Embassy in Washington and our government offices in New York and San Francisco.

They sought help from the News and Information Bureau in Canberra, who refuted the story and said it was a journalistic fabrication!

That ill-informed organisation published a leaflet for enquirers in America saying that while there was still some rabbit *trapping* in Australia, professional *shooting* of rabbits was just the figment of a certain journalist's imagination. *Guns* magazine sent me a 'please explain' and I was able to supply them with the names, photographs and signed statements of half a dozen professional rabbit shooters working along the dingo fence. I sent copies of this material to the ninnies in Canberra, asking did they think I had faked up scores of photos showing men spotlight shooting from four-wheel drive vehicles, cleaning the carcasses and loading them into mobile freezers for transport to the well-known Jack McCraith rabbit export company in Melbourne. News and Information were somewhat discomfited by their error, more so when I threatened to sue them for impugning my journalistic reputation. This had taken something of a beating a couple of years earlier when an outlandish, tongue-in-cheek story of mine about the Australian Redex Trials, submitted to a lurid American adventure magazine, somehow finished up being published by the prestigious *Road & Track* motoring monthly. The story was a compilation of the most sensational newspaper stories concerning the first two Redex Trials, under such headings as 'CROCODILE ATTACKS TRIAL CAR', 'ABORIGINES THREATEN REDEX DRIVERS WITH SPEARS,' 'GELIGNITE EXPLOSIONS TERRORISE TRIAL ROUTE TOWNS,' 'OUTBACK POLICE THREATEN TO JAIL REDEX SPEEDSTERS' and so on. Enough copies of *Road & Track* reached Australia even in those days to cause me acute embarrassment among my colleagues. Moral: if you must exaggerate, write anonymously.

My original journey out to Brougham's Gate from Corona homestead and subsequent travels up and down the dingo fence over a period of two years convinced me that a Holden panel van was not the ideal desert vehicle. The superintendent of the fence at Smithville outpost, whom I got to know well, came upon me bogged in sand on Fort Grey station near the Queensland border and remarked: 'You ought to get a medal, or get locked up, coming out here in that outfit.' He meant the Holden, which so far as I know was one of the very few conventional cars of the period (the mid 1950s) ever to reach Lake Frome via Brougham's Gate—or the north-west NSW survey post at Cameron's Corner.

It had not been lost on me that nearly everyone else in that 'corner' country was mounted on a four-wheel drive or dual-wheeled truck. There were a few exceptions: I met a VW at Smithville outpost once and a bore sinker from Tibooburra used to drive out to the fence in a massive chrome-plated Dodge de luxe. He had the habit of driving with his head out of the window, because he reckoned he could see better that way in dusty conditions. He did this once too often on the Silver City Highway near Milparinka while waiting his chance to overtake another vehicle churning up dust in front of him. A table-top lorry going the other way loomed out of the dust and decapitated him.

There finally came a time when I decided to get myself a four-wheel drive outfit. (When I got the *National Geographic* droving story commission.) In those days in NSW, the Land Rover was almost the only available off-roader, apart from war surplus Jeeps and Blitz wagons.

Nissan Patrols were about in South Australia, but the now ubiquitous Toyota was confined chiefly to far north-west Australia, appearing later in Queensland, where Thiess Brothers were to popularise them in the east. The Rolls-Royce powered Austin Champ had made a brief (disastrous) appearance, but it was soon discovered these were inclined to sink without trace in difficult conditions.

Land Rover was the obvious choice. New vehicles were in short supply and I couldn't afford one. So I bought a second-hand four-cylinder 1954 long-wheelbase utility model, complete with canvas canopy, 'roo bar and capstan winch. Registered number: BUF 154. It was going on four years old, with, surprisingly, only 45 000 miles on the clock. The owner told me he was a butcher and had used the vehicle for carrying meat supplies to his shop. There was some truth in this, but I later discovered the meat came in the form of kangaroo carcasses bought from shooters in north-west NSW and sold as pet food in Sydney. Four years of weekly trips to Bourke and environs had probably notched up rather more than 45 000 miles! Not that it mattered—I travelled another 80 000 miles in the following two years and the only major replacements were a clutch plate, universal joint on the rear shaft and a front wheel bearing.

Compared with the Holden, my Land Rover felt like a tank to drive. It was desperately slow on the highway, noisy at all times, uncomfortable in the rough. But I loved it. Off-road, I experienced the heady exhilaration of a panzer tank captain, grinding inexorably forward, crushing all obstacles. Well, most of the time. I used to practise in the Cronulla sands hills and soon found out what a Land Rover could and could not do.

I also learned not to tempt fate and do such foolish things as drive over the hard, wet sand exposed by low tide. Because, following Murphy's Law, that is when an electrical fault will leave you stranded to face the incoming tide. Luckily I was rescued by the Wanda Surf Club, who pulled me out by using the stout towrope I found in one of the vehicle's rear lockers. To this day I will not drive on tidal flats or be without a towrope in the bush.

My early journeys in BUF 154 were all joy, once the slow, boring part of the trip as far as Bourke or Broken Hill was behind me. Sand country became a pleasure to drive in and it was amazing how rarely you needed four-wheel drive, once you had it. Creek crossings up to crutch depth were no problem and a day or two of rain merely reduced my average speed. The capstan winch was mostly decoration and responsible for my abiding aversion to all types of fixed winches. To use it, you needed two people: one to steer the vehicle while the other floundered about in the creek or mud, just ahead of the front wheels, hauling the rope off the capstan. You could only go forward, when often you would have preferred to retreat—and when your submerged motor cut out, so did the winch—when you needed it most. I bought a hand winch, which I could hook on to any corner of the vehicle.

My Land Rover liked petrol so I had jerry-can holders welded to the rear corners of the vehicle. I also built a camera platform on the roof of the cabin, which provided a handy vantage point in flat country. My first major four-wheel drive trip was to Birdsville, via Cooper Creek and Betoota, on my 'Plains of Loneliness' assignment for the *National Geographic*.

Around Cooper Creek I spent a few days retracing the final steps of explorers Burke and Wills, then pushed out through Innaminka to Coongie Lakes. I had been told of a teeming waterfowl population that in good seasons inhabited the dozens of lakes set unexpectedly amid the sand dunes. Sure enough, great flocks of pelicans, ducks, herons, bitterns, cockatoos, even seagulls had my cameras running hot for days.

Back on the Betoota trail I passed Arrabury station, on the edge of a vast gibber plain the explorer Sturt named the Stony Desert. This has to be the most miserably located homestead in outback Australia. Poor Sturt carted a boat there, hoping to find an inland sea! The property is one of a string taken over last century by the legendary Sidney Kidman to form an empire the size of England and which stretched from the Gulf of Carpentaria to Adelaide. The Kidman Cattle Company survives and still controls much of the land between Broken Hill and Cloncurry in Queensland.

Betoota, which was just a pub, and Birdsville, which was not much more, provided me with further pictures and stories. In those days, the fact that you had driven to these lonely outposts was a story in itself—but now they are thick with everything from Suzukis to Range Rovers with personalised capital city number plates.

Back home in Sydney, I stayed only long enough to process my film and write my stories. Then I was ready to go again. I was firmly hooked on four-wheel touring. Mare, who had been otherwise engaged having babies up to this point, came with me on many of my subsequent Land Roving adventures.

One was to the Top End of the Northern Territory and the Aboriginal reserve of Arnhem Land. Fired by a few story ideas from Eric Worrell and others, I made up my mind to go and had everything 'organised' within a week. Mare was not so sure. Did we have enough cash to finance such a journey? In those days I had a theory that the only cost of a trip was the petrol. Accommodation was free, because we camped out. We had to eat, at home or away, so there was no additional expense there. Very simple. Of course I overlooked wear and tear on the vehicle, breakdowns, tyres, film and flashbulb costs, telegrams, phone calls, etc. But had we gone into such details, we probably never would have gone at all—like most people.

However, after one look at the map, Mare insisted we equip ourselves with a radio transceiver, so we could send and receive telegrams, in case any of the children developed hiccups or anything. It might help if we got lost or stranded, too, she pointed out. Portable car transceivers were expensive, so I bought a second-hand ship's radio, which was portable if there were two people to carry it.

The man who sold it to us was a Mr Spindler, who designed and manufactured boat transceivers. One night we drove with him into the wilds of Sydney's Royal National Park, tossed the radio aerial into a tree and talked to someone in outback NSW. (Illegally, as it turned out.) Obviously the machine worked, so we paid for it and after a lot of formalities with the radio authorities, became licensed portable radio station 8NGE (later 8NGO) and part of the great Royal Flying Doctor network.

Mare was still dubious. 'How far is Arnhem Land and how long will it take to get there?' she wanted to know. I pretended to examine a map and came up with some guesses: 'About two thousand miles, say four or five days' travelling.' Before she could ask, I scribbled a few figures on a bit of paper and said: 'Petrol for the whole trip will cost around forty pounds' ($80). At the time we had barely twice that amount to our names.

It transpired that Arnhem Land was nearer three thousand miles away and it took us ten days to get there. A couple of weeks later all our money was gone and we were glad to have the transceiver to telegram our bank manager for a loan to get us home!

The gateway to Arnhem Land in those days was the wild and woolly outpost of Pine Creek, an ex-mining and railway town on the now defunct line to Katherine and Larimah, further south. It was a rakish, down-at-heel sort of place, inhabited chiefly by refugees from half a dozen cultures and of as many colours: buffalo and crocodile shooters, prospectors, alcoholics, philosophers-off-the-rails, fugitives from justice and injustice, and assorted misfits, male and female. In appearance and atmosphere, it presented like a scene from Somerset Maugham's famous novel, *Rain*.

In the pub we were introduced to the local sport of 'bull-dogging'. Two drinkers started from opposite ends of the bar, clutching the traditional rail with one hand as a guide, rushing full pelt toward each other, heads lowered, until their skulls met with a sickening thud. The process was repeated until one of the contestants gave up, or fell to the bar-room floor unconscious. Great fun!

We met the local champ, a mechanic working on Mudgenberry station. He was a Scot who had been an RAF Bomber Command machine-gunner during World War II. A common fate in those days for gunners was having part of the top of your head shot off. This was so routine that British surgeons got in enough practice to become very good at fitting metal plates into damaged skulls. Jock confided to me that he had a plate in his skull and this was the secret of his success at bull-dogging! I'm sure the British College of Surgeons would have given a lot to have Jock's noggin back for examination.

A story that had brought me to the Top End concerned a young man who was trying to start a safari camp for hunting and fishing enthusiasts from overseas. This was located on the South Alligator River, not far from Arnhem Land. The track was quite good. The only trouble was,

there were lots of equally good side tracks, leading off through the scrub to gold mines, tin mines, prospector's camps and the hideaways of assorted non-conformers. Buffalo occasionally blocked our way, but we soon discovered these to be about as dangerous as domestic cattle.

Once we were stopped by an Aboriginal man brandishing a .303 rifle. (Everyone in the Top End in those days, men, women and children, seemed to carry a .303 rifle.) All he wanted was a lift, which we gladly gave him and his two wives and son who appeared magically from among the pandanus palms, smoking pipes! In fact, we were lucky to meet this family, because they knew the whereabouts of our safari man and guided us to his camp. Don McGregor was his name—originally from Sydney but now known to some locals as 'the white black fellah', due to his hunting skill with spears as well as guns.

He had a good set-up: a new long-wheelbase Land Rover station wagon, a knockabout Jeep, tents, canoes that could be fitted with outboard motors, conventional motor-boat, fishing, camping and cooking gear, rifles, shotguns and skinning knives. Plus an impeccable knowledge of the country, where he had lived for some years, often with the original inhabitants. All he lacked were customers. I assured Don that once my stories were published, at home and overseas, he would be knocked down in the rush of wealthy adventurers.

Meanwhile, we had to find some locals who would pose in my photos as visiting hunters on safari. It happened that nearby Mudgenberry station had been taken over by Newcastle publican and entrepreneur, Len Randall. Len had a plan to tame large numbers of local wild buffalo, then have them slaughtered under supervised hygienic conditions for human consumption. The killing and freezing of the meat would be done in an abattoir he had constructed near Mudgenberry homestead.

Len and his wife Ivy were happy to be our model tourists. Len didn't have much to do at the time, because the local bureaucracy had him on his knees. After allowing him to build his abattoir at vast expense, they had then insisted on special accommodation being constructed for the meat inspectors.

The meat inspectors wanted to go home to Darwin at weekends but as there was then no proper road, Len constructed an airstrip between the homestead and the abattoir for their convenience. Len also agreed to pay for the twice-weekly charter flights—but now there was a wrangle over who was going to pay the insurance premiums for the inspectors while they were travelling on unscheduled flights to and from work.

All this had bogged the project a full year and with 'The Wet' imminent, Len had called a halt until the next dry season. Taming the buffalo had proved the easiest part of the project. After initial mustering in from the bush, they were left for a week in a massive stockade of heavy posts and railway lines, draped with hessian. Once the buffalo learned this man-made fence was impregnable, they lost interest in trying to break out and were readily contained in paddocks surrounded by light wire fences—draped with hessian!

Len was an interesting, urbane fellow who drove his Jaguar saloon twice yearly from Newcastle in NSW to Mudgenberry station. He had a great affection for Scotch whisky. He consumed two bottles daily, neat, over ice cubes. This was for health reasons, he assured me—he had suffered since childhood with a bone problem that made walking difficult. The whisky had helped him as much as medicine over many years. He was never even tipsy.

While we sat around the table at Mudgenberry homestead, Len would regularly send an Aboriginal worker padding off across the airstrip to the refrigeration room in the abattoir, where he manufactured and stored his ice cubes. The most expensive ice cubes in the world, he told us, because to that date they were the only product from his vast investment in Mudgenberry.

Eventually we went 'on safari' with Don and the Randalls into the wilds between the East and South Alligator Rivers. There are no alligators wild in Australia—only crocodiles. Len had cherished an ambition to shoot a crocodile, so we spent a lot of time at night in the canoes, shining spotlights into the glowing red eyes of partially submerged reptiles.

Canoes are not very stable, particularly with three men aboard, armed with guns, spotlights, cameras, flashlights, bottles of whisky and vacuum flasks full of ice cubes. I did not enjoy the voyages. Len was not especially accurate when shooting, and we were all aware that a wounded, thrashing crocodile would smash our frail craft to pieces. After a few misses on successive nights, Len managed to put a bullet between two glowing red orbs that seemed to be half a metre apart (denoting a very large croc), but it was 'only average' according to Don, who skinned the carcase on the muddy river bank.

After that, we went after ducks, magpie geese, barramundi and buffalo, on different three or four-day safaris, working out from Mudgenberry homestead. These trips lasted only as long as Len's ice cubes. Then we returned to the homestead for a brief spell and clean-up before taking on fresh supplies of ice cubes from the abattoir freezer. I think the Esky had yet to be invented, so Len carried his ice cubes in half a dozen large Thermos vacuum flasks.

As supplies dwindled, he would drain water from the fullest containers and top them up with cubes from the near-empty flasks. It made a strange scene in camp each night: we would gather round a table by the light of a pressure lantern and ask anxiously: 'How much longer have we got, Len?' After juggling ice cubes from flask to flask and assessing the remaining supply, Len would answer gravely 'I think we can manage another couple of days.' We accepted his decisions without question, like survivors in a lifeboat whose captain has announced there is only sufficient drinking water for another forty-eight hours.

Len's wife Ivy was the fisherperson of the party and supplied most of the barramundi. Don speared a few with native-style spears, just to show how it is done and to give my cameras some variety. He and Len agreed there was no great skill or sport attached to shooting a buffalo, so I contented myself with photographing the herds grazing, wallowing or on the run when disturbed. I also took some portraits of lone bulls with large horns, to illustrate for overseas hunters the type of trophy heads they could expect. For these photos I went stalking on foot, because Don didn't like crashing his new Land Rover station wagon across the buffalo plains, which are not half as smooth as they appear in photos. Buffalo are generally nervous, timid creatures where humans are concerned, but an occasional cranky bull can be aggressive. So I carried some stones in a jam tin nailed to a stick, just in case. Don said this rattle would frighten off most bulls, at least long enough for me to choose a suitably solid tree to climb, or dash back to the Land Rover.

My faithful four-cylinder Land Rover utility was eventually replaced by one of the early six-cylinder hardtop models. By that time I knew the short-wheelbase models would go where the longer outfits feared to follow. But the short Land Rovers couldn't carry much, particularly if two people intended to live out of one for up to three months and travel from coast to coast.

My second Land Rover took us to what is now the Prince Regent River National Park in the Kimberleys, via the Tanami Desert track from Yuendemu Aboriginal reserve through Balgo mission and Billiluna station to Halls Creek. It also carried us across the Simpson Desert from Dalhousie to Birdsville, mostly along what is known as the English Track. This has since been used by beach buggies, modified Holdens, and all manner of safari tours, but it seemed rather hairy and lonely in the 1960s.

A rather longer excursion took us from Alice Springs westward through Papunya Aboriginal reserve, Sandy Blight Junction, Gary Junction and the Sahara Track to Wallal Downs homestead on the coast south of Broome. Don't be misled by all the place names. There is *nothing* between Papunya and Wallal Downs, a track journey through waterless country of rather more than two thousand kilometres. We carried fourteen additional jerry cans of petrol and four of water. It was only just enough for the journey.

Coming home via the just-established mine town of Mount Newman,

I foolishly listened to the advice of a WA Native Welfare Department officer whom I met in Meekatharra. He said there was a good short cut across to Ayers Rock via a route called the Gunbarrel Highway.

This started at Carnegie homestead and went just about due east to Jackie Junction. From there you went to Giles weather station and then it was more or less all plain sailing through the Petermann Ranges to Docker River Aboriginal settlement and on to Ayers Rock. He said petrol was available at Wiluna and then at Docker River, two settlements 'only' fifteen hundred kilometres apart. If you ran short, you could detour south from Jackie Junction to Warburton mission, where petrol 'might' be bought. What was the condition of this short cut, I asked. The welfare officer patted the bonnet of his Holden ute. 'I came through from Alice in one of these a few years back. It's a good track. A bit rough in parts.' I translated this for Mare, who at that stage was losing interest in Australia's wide open spaces, pointing out that from Ayers Rock it was only a stone's throw to the highway south from Alice Springs, then a mere hop, step and a jump down to the bitumen at Port Augusta. From there it was just 'a few hundred' kilometres (fifteen hundred, to be exact) home to Foxground. It did not seem politic to mention that the whole journey was around four thousand kilometres, much of it over what some people would describe as trackless desert. But I did emphasize that it would be an even longer trip if we went south to the Eyre Highway and crossed the Nullarbor.

Reluctantly Mare agreed to take the short cut and off we went. Unfortunately the track had deteriorated since the welfare officer last travelled that way. The Land Rover was not seriously challenged, in fact we rarely engaged four-wheel drive. But the going was decidedly slow, due to washaways, detours, sand, trees and termite mounds growing in the road.

We also encountered wild camels and dingoes. The camels tended to just stand in the track, blocking it—so I would send Mare ahead on foot to clear them. She had some narrow escapes, but I always had the door open for her and the motor running! The dingoes didn't block the track, but they would lope along behind the slow-moving Land Rover, for all the world like drovers' dogs following the master home. I was fascinated and spent hours trying to get photos showing how close they came to our vehicle. Without much success.

At Rebecca Creek it had been raining ahead of us and the track was blocked by a bogged and abandoned table-top truck. Its load had been taken off and stacked on the only firm ground, effectively blocking our way. To make matters worse, the packages were labelled 'High Explosives', so we didn't feel like tampering with the obstruction. Cutting a detour through the mulga and then corduroying some muddy patches took a full day. When we finally got to Docker River, there was no petrol and we had to camp there several days until a supply truck came out from Ayers Rock with the first food and fuel since the recent rains.

Altogether our 'short cut' took about ten days. It would have been much quicker to continue south from Meekatharra and then come east across the Nullarbor. The Eyre Highway was not sealed then but at least it was a graded road. Never mind. I enjoyed the adventure and still relish the welfare officer's masterly under-statement about Len Beadell's now famous Gunbarrel Highway—'A good track. A bit rough in parts.'

5 Champagne motoring on a lemonade budget

A few more years rolled by, misspent financially, making the *Wild Country* television series, though I enjoyed driving 'Big Red' the Range Rover all over the Australian continent. But something was missing in my life. Every time a new-model Porsche came on the market, I lapsed into a state of deep introspection, brooding over magazine road-tests and coloured brochures sent return mail to me by the importers, Norman Hamilton, of Melbourne (Richard Cocks had gone to ground and John Newell was yet to surface as Sydney's pre-eminent Porsche trader).

Early in 1976, I became aware that life had changed down on the farm. There was no longer the sharp crackle of motocross bike exhausts from the practice track in our back paddocks. The incessant revving of modified Renault rally car engines under test in our hay shed had ceased. The night-long competitions between amplified electric guitar, wind instruments and record players had ceased. There was silence, save for the chirping of birds and the wind in the trees. 'Where are the children?' I asked Mare. 'Grown up and gone to make their own lives,' she said, a little sadly.

'Hmm,' I said.

The Porsche agency had changed hands again. Now it was located in one of Sydney's posher North Shore suburbs, under the Scuderia Veloce banner. 'Just arrived!' the sign said. 'The new 200-horsepower CARRERA 3!'

I had a look. It seemed much the same as the old 911s, but slightly broader, more squat. No chrome work anywhere to polish (the trim was all matte black, very *chic*), enormous tyres, a massive external mirror (electrically adjusted from within), power windows, headlight washers and tall, anti-neck-snap seats.

'I'll have one of those, in white,' I said to the salesman.

'Certainly, sir,' he replied. 'Just like our showroom model? With the big wheels, sunroof, sports seats, Blaupunkt stereo radio and energy-absorbing bumpers... They're all extras, you know.'

'How the hell can the bumpers be extra?' I began.

'You misunderstand me, sir,' the salesman interjected smoothly. 'The actual bumper is a standard fitting, but there is a slight extra charge if you want the energy-absorbing springs fitted behind them!'

'All right, I'll have them,' I said. 'Do you have a white one?'

'Not in stock,' the salesman replied. 'But we can order it in. Shall we go into my office and get down a few particulars?'

It was a nice office—all leather, oiled wood and carpets, with air-conditioning and an indoor plant. The salesman gave me a lot of coloured pamphlets to read while he wrote out the order.

'How much?' I asked when he finished.

'I'm afraid, sir,' he said smoothly, 'that when you add up all the extras, we won't get much change out of $30 000.'

'Strewth! I only want one!' I said. 'Five years ago, a 911E was $11 000. I reckoned this new one would be $15 000 at most.'

'So it would be, sir, except for the import duty and taxes. They amount to ninety-eight per cent, you know.'

'I didn't know,' I said. 'Anyhow, $15 000 is my best offer. I couldn't afford more than that for a motor car.'

'We could do you one at that price, sir,' the salesman put in quickly. 'Provided you pick it up at the factory.'

'Yairs, that'll do,' I said. 'Where's the factory?'

'In Stuttgart, West Germany.'

'I see,' I replied quietly, deep in thought.

'If you own and use the car continuously for fifteen months overseas before shipping it home, you can bring the vehicle into Australia duty and sales tax free,' the salesman said encouragingly.

'Uh, huh,' I muttered, deeper in thought.

There was rather a long silence, except for the hum of the air-conditioner. The salesman doodled in his order book and I counted laboriously on my fingers. 'Okay,' I said at last. 'Put me down for a white one. How do you get to Qantas House from here?'

And so it was all arranged, on the basis of $1000 deposit on the car and slightly more for two economy one-way Qantas tickets to Germany. At home, I announced to my audience-of-one in the kitchen: 'With the children gone, it's time for us to seek new challenges, new places, new faces...'

We flew out of Australia on Sunday 2 March 1976.

A German mate whose name really is Hermann picked us up at Frankfurt airport and drove us to his Taunus mountains weekender, deep in the pine forests near Wiesbaden, about ninety kilometres from the airport. Hermann had kindly offered us the use of his retreat as a base for a few weeks, while we ran the car in. Then we would set out on our fifteen-month odyssey of Europe.

We took a train to Stuttgart on Wednesday 24 March and then a taxi to the Porsche factory in the suburb of Zuffenhausen. This is a nondescript huddle of buildings down an industrial back street. Inside, the tourist car delivery centre was a different world: sequestered, quiet and plush, with lots of indoor plants, oiled woodwork, plate glass, heavy drapes and very deep pile carpet. The air-conditioning was silky silent. On the wall was a gleaming aluminium map of the Porsche export world. A svelte, English-speaking receptionist served us brewed coffee. Later, a Canadian-accented Porsche representative treated us to a fine lunch, washed down with excellent white wine of the district. A brief visit to the company car museum, a half-hour tour of the factory, then I was presented with the keys of the car—and the car, parked now outside the delivery centre.

Waiting in the customers' lounge in Zuffenhausen, Stuttgart, for delivery of his Porsche in 1976.

The remaining formality was to pay up: DM 50 000, being $15 000 in those happy days of high exchange rates on Australian dollars. This for a car that was $30 000 at home.

Of course we had to stay in Europe for at least fifteen months to be able to land the car back in Australia without paying import duty or sales tax.

But I had brought our tent, sleeping bags and other camping gear, reckoning we could live as cheaply that way in one hemisphere as another. Several Australian magazines and newspapers had offered to buy stories about our travels, also the prestigious English motoring magazine *Car*, which meant I could earn something like my usual meagre income while pedalling my new Porsche in foreign climes. Lucky the person with a transportable trade!

The only instruction that came with the car was a mild suggestion from the company representative not to exceed 5000 revs in any gear until the running-in oil had been changed at one thousand kilometres. And I was warned to make sure the steering lock was engaged when leaving the vehicle parked because if I didn't and the car was pinched, the European insurance company might refuse to buy me another one! It was time to change the oil after just a few days motoring out from Wiesbaden along the nearby Rhine and Mosel rivers, getting the feel of the car and learning to remain calm while driving on the wrong side of the road!

With his new Porsche Carrera, hours after picking it up in Zuffenhausen.

During the next few weeks and several thousand kilometres, I got to like my new 200-horsepower Porsche Carrera, particularly when I was able to do as many kilometres per hour on the unrestricted autobahns. Mare liked the car, too, but spent much of those early weeks practising her German in the shops. Hermann *loved* the Porsche and spent every minute he could riding with me. In overtaking situations (you encounter a lot of these in a Carrera 3), he liked to be my 'eyes', having a better view ahead from the left-hand passenger seat than I had behind the wheel, on the kerbside.

When he learned how fast the car would accelerate, Hermann would begin shouting excitedly: 'Take him. Take him!' the moment we came in sight of any vehicle travelling ahead.

He believed the car was invincible and his enthusiasm occasionally outstripped the Carrera's ability. Responding to his exultant cry of 'Take him!' I several times drew out to find myself faced with an oncoming Mercedes, BMW or fellow Porsche at a combined closing speed of around 400 km/h!

On the autobahns Hermann considered that the number three outside passing lane was reserved for Porsches, Mercedes and BMWs. (European law however says the third lane is for overtaking and you should return to lane two or one after completing your overtaking manoeuvre.) But

Hermann would have none of this. Every time we moved into the third lane to pass someone, he would shout excitedly: 'Stay in this lane! This lane is for Porsches! If they won't get out of the way, keep your lights on and blow the horn! Take them all!'

Eventually we farewelled Hermann and the Wiesbaden area and headed south toward Switzerland. It was now mid April, with snow still deep on the high alps and occasional light falls along the way. For the rest of the month we toured southern Germany, Switzerland, Austria and the Dolomite country of north-eastern Italy (narrowly dodging the 1976 earthquake disaster).

It was too cold to camp, so we over-nighted in cheap hotels and pensions. For bed-and-breakfast for the two of us, charges ranged from $12 down to $4. Prices were the highest in Germany and Switzerland, where double rooms with breakfast tended to be about $15. (This was when an Australian dollar was worth almost four Deutschmarks—in 1989 it buys scarcely 1.5 DM.) The standard European breakfast is coffee and rolls, with butter and jam.

We usually made do with a picnic lunch—bread, salami, cheese, fruit—either beside the road or munched while we wandered around cities and villages, looking at the sights. For a dollar each, we ate well and healthily. A bottle of wine added perhaps eighty cents to the cost of a meal. Occasionally we did the same thing in the evening (sundown 8 p.m.), rather more lavishly, beside the road or in our hotel room. But usually we made dinner our one daily restaurant meal, at an average of $10 for the pair of us! Alas, those days are now gone forever and European costs are generally equal or higher than at home.

6 Into the midnight sun

Paris in the spring. A brand new three-litre Porsche Carrera. A long-haired travelling companion. Money in your pocket, time on your hands, the radio playing, roof open to the sun. The Boulevarde Peripherique sweeping down toward the Seine. Notre Dame drifting in the buttery morning haze downstream. Ah, such is the stuff of dreams!

Everything was as described—and more. The Boulevarde Peripherique, which circles Paris, is about the busiest road in the world. The five lanes going in our direction were choked with traffic, mostly trucks. They were moving very slowly, with frequent stops, belching clouds of black smoke and creating a mind-numbing din.

Naturally, being a Porsche, we were travelling in one of the outer passing lanes. Which was a pity, because the wick in our three-litre two hundred horsepower motor had gone out. Mare was out the back, pushing, while I steered. Our four warning flashers blinked at half-second intervals as we manoeuvred, ever-so-cautiously, toward the comparative safety of the kerbside lane—from which we eventually escaped down an exit ramp to the comparative suburban calm of Port d'Ivry. Mare was sweating from her exertions, I was in a nervous sweat...and our two hundred horses slumbered on in their rear stable, unmindful of the frequent spurring of the starter motor. The only redeeming feature of the whole wretched scene was that the road was level.

Mare's prowess with the French language eventually got us winched aboard a table-top rescue truck. By a stroke of luck, the driver was a Porsche enthusiast, who took us to the garage of the Porsche Balsa Racing Team, in the suburb of Maisons Alfort. Monsieur Balsa fiddled with the electrics and the fuel injection system for about five minutes and all was well. No charge and we were again on our way.

We had been ten days in Paris, in a cosy 55 francs a day pub (the Chatillon) in the southern suburb of Port d'Orleans. At least, it was 55 francs until monsieur the owner caught sight of my Carrera parked down the road. Then he insisted we move into a 75 franc room, giving us some cock-&-bull story about the cheaper room being already promised to someone else. Still, it was a nicer room, with private bath—and monsieur was a pleasant bloke, amusing us daily at breakfast with a little ballet he performed with our table, which he used to spin deftly around until it surprisingly stood firm on its uneven, rickety legs.

I had a bit of luck in Paris: most of the great Louvre art gallery was shut for alterations. An inveterate culture bug, Mare was not so pleased. But we did see the Eiffel tower—and by mistake (I swear) in a major theatre, a pornographic film which had just won the 'Golden Phallus Award' at Amsterdam's international skin flick festival. Artistic in places, but weak on plot.

So far as the motorist is concerned, Paris makes Sydney, London or even Rome look like a quiet country town. We sensibly used the underground Metro suburban train network, where you never wait more than two minutes for a train to arrive on almost silent, rubber-dampered wheels. The Carrera remained parked outside the Chatillon for ten days, getting the sulks—probably why it gave us trouble on the Boulevarde Peripherique when we left.

Our intention was to make our Scandinavian trip strictly a camping expedition, which was just as well, because the cost of hotel accommodation was astronomical. Another source of early misgivings were the Norwegian speed limits: 80 km/h on the open highways, down to 30 km/h in town centres. And *everyone* in Norway obeys the speed limits!

We never got out of second gear during our first two weeks in southern Norway. The good news was the scenery, which really is just as you see it in the tourist brochures. Mountains plummet down to the sea, along coastline indented with uncountable bays and coves, the clear, millpond water dotted with thousands of islands, from backyard-size to several hectares. Pine forests clothe the steeper slopes, but every usable bit of arable land was under crop: mostly fodder or potatoes—and often, to our delight, strawberries. In fact, after pine logs and spuds, I think strawberries must be Norway's major rural product. They (and hazel nuts) were the only relatively cheap item we found in all Scandinavia.

Though picturesque, southern Norway was too closely settled for my bushwacker taste. Camping was possible only in the organised grounds, which teemed with summer visitors. It was July.

Once we got about two hundred kilometres north of Kristiansand, the country was not so closely settled. Every few minutes we passed great rivers tumbling out of pine forests beneath awesome, white-capped mountains. Inviting dirt side tracks led to idyllic campsites with plenty of wood lying about and secluded little beaches for sunbaking. Despite the crush of traffic on the main roads, we rarely had trouble finding complete seclusion from other campers. Free of the crowds, we were able to average around 80 km/h on Norway's northern roads. You may think this rather slow for a Porsche Carrera—but Norwegian roads are so narrow and tortuous, the average Australian driver would have a nervous breakdown. Any serious error of judgement puts you into a solid rock cliff face or down a mountainside into a fiord kilometres deep. On the main 'highway' north of Odda, for example, much of the bitumen road is too narrow for two big vehicles to pass and you spend a lot of time backing up out of the way of oncoming trucks and caravans.

We crossed the famous Jotun-Heimen 'Opplands' by a series of lesser dirt roads that eventually linked us with the E6 highway at the crossroad town of Dombras. This major route links Oslo in the south with Hammerfest, the world's most northerly city. We met only a few local vehicles on these unsealed back roads. Eventually we reached Trondheim, the seaport 'gateway to the north', where Norway slims down to an average width of only 100 kilometres. It became my favourite Norse town, with lots to see and do among its shops, markets, museums, parks and waterfront. If you have the money to afford accommodation and meals, I recommend a couple of days in Trondheim. At the fish market on the town wharf I improvidently bought two fillets of fresh red salmon to grill on the campfire. When I heard the price, I considered having them stuffed and mounted instead!

At Trondheim I noted we had travelled 2300 kilometres from Kristiansand but were still barely halfway to our goal: Hammerfest and Nordcap. I had grown used to European distances being puny by Australian standards, and was somewhat taken back. Particularly when I worked out what petrol was likely to cost for the round trip. Undaunted, we pressed on, after stocking up our cupboard at vast expense. Despite the language barrier, shopping is no problem in Scandinavia, because just about everything is sold in self-serve supermarkets. Usually Mare and I try to master the basics of the language of the land. But in Scandinavia we gave up, apart from learning the standard phrase-book pleasantries. It was just too hard—the Nordic languages bear little resemblance to other European languages. Also, we detected a rustic hesitancy among the Norwegians to communicate with foreigners, even via a smile. It's an isolated country and the people live rather sequestered, rural lives, almost monastic during the long, dark arctic winters. Their reputation for seeming stolid and uncommunicative with strangers was often reinforced when two Australians tried the cheerful 'How are you, mate?' approach.

It has to be said that Norwegians (and Swedes) have a 'drink problem'. Officially, alcohol is regarded in Norway and Sweden somewhat like pornography is in Australia. Its sale is strictly regulated and rather frowned upon. Bottle sales are confined to government stores, which are few and far between, even in cities. Many country towns seem to have none. Liquor stores are usually down a side street, sombrely decorated, with draped windows and discreet sign-writing, rather like funeral parlors or 'adult' book shops. In the very few pubs and bars, wine or spirit drinks are depressingly expensive. The (exclusively) government-brewed beer is cheap, but its alcohol content is only two or three per cent. Anyone trying to drown their sorrows with beer in Scandinavia would have to swallow a bathtub full.

So most people turn to the hard stuff, which gets them smiling quicker, until they start brooding about what it's costing them. Then they relapse into depression, requiring further large doses of cheer. A nasty circle, which results in a lot of public drunkenness throughout Norway and Sweden. The atmosphere is akin to Australia in the bad old days of the 6 o'clock swill (for the younger reader: when hotels used to shut at 6 p.m. and at midday on Saturday).

North of Trondheim, we left most of the holiday motorists behind. The countryside became steadily wilder and more sparsely settled. After about 200 kilometres we passed the village of Grong and entered what I reckoned to be the wild north. The country was so rocky and precipitous, I kept saying things like 'I wouldn't have believed it if I hadn't seen it,' and 'How did they get this road here—and why?' By comparison, Australia's alps are a billiard table.

We followed rivers, lakes and fiords all the way, this being the only practical route for a road between the awesome, looming peaks. Around almost every bend we came upon magnificent campsites that in Australia one would happily drive several hundred kilometres to enjoy. Foaming rapids, long, deep trout pools, glassy lakes, level ground right to the water's edge, often with a sand or gravel beach. Pine and birch trees for shelters in clumps and forests, with plenty of dry firewood lying underneath. Magnificent drinking water, wild strawberries, cloudberries and blueberries growing everywhere. These we ate raw or stewed up to make a sort of jam to spread on thick wholemeal flour pancakes tossed in a pan above the campfire.

The only other campers we encountered during the ensuing weeks were dyed-in-the-wool fishing types, tricked out in yellow plastic thigh waders, landing nets, spinning and fly rods, chewing on usually cold tobacco pipes, under peaked leather and fur caps. They were intent of eye, stolidly silent and so obsessed with flaying the water they rarely noticed us.

The nature of the country can be judged from the fact that some days we would break camp, travel only thirty or so kilometres and find such an out-of-this-world site that we would promptly stop and pitch our tent again! This continued for the next 2000 kilometres. Most days the sky was blue and the sun shone down strongly.

Just north of Mo I Rana, a sizeable port, we climbed into high tundra country, above the treeline. The weather was bleak; windy, with drizzling rain. All around were snow-capped mountains. The road, unsealed in places, was wet and slippery, burrowing unexpectedly through mountains via narrow, poorly lit, dripping tunnels—in which sheep, goats and sometimes cattle were encountered!

When I stopped to take photos, I had to be quick about it, for fear of freezing solid. 'By cripes,' I said to Mare. 'If it keeps getting colder as we go north, things are going to be crook in Hammerfest.' She looked at me frostily, turned the car heater up to DE-FROST and said icily that it wasn't *her* idea to come to this outlandish place and what was the *point* of driving to the world's most northern city, anyway? There didn't seem to be any answer to that, but the road was too narrow and slippery to turn around, so we pressed on.

Where the road crossed the Polar Sirkel (their spelling), we stopped, like everyone else, to photograph the sign and a cairn of rocks. There was a rather crummy roadhouse selling cafeteria-type snacks, postcards and souvenirs. After a freezing ten-minute stint of photography, we

staggered inside this establishment for coffee and cherry cake. A lady who rode a BMW bike with 'A Woman's Place is Everywhere' written on her helmet, and whom I had snapped outside, turned out to be an Australian. She was doing the same as us, on a slightly reduced scale, on her tax-free BMW, bought in Germany at half the Australian price.

We came down out of the cold on to the shore of Saltfjorden, near the picturesque fishing ports of Rognan and Fauske. It rained fitfully, but there were patches of blue sky northward. Some optimistic farmers were forking just-cut green hay on to the long drying racks that are typical of northern Scandinavia. A small ferry took us across Sorfolde Fiord and we camped in a pine forest between mountains so steep you had to bend at the waist to look up at them.

Another vehicle ferry took us across Tyskfjorden, a voyage of about ten kilometres. These ferries have to be taken into consideration when estimating the cost of Norwegian motoring. Along the coast road between Bergen and Trondheim there are at least ten ferry rides. Toll is also charged for some of the dozen road tunnels along the route. Many are badly lit, if at all—we heard of one new Volvo written-off in a collision, deep inside a mountain with a cow!

The industrial port of Narvik, the only centre of any real size within the Polar Sirkel, is rather like Wollongong–Port Kembla on a bad day: all smog and belching smoke and shunting locomotives. This is the exit port for Sweden's rip-roaring mining town of Kiruna, located above the world's largest known deposit of iron ore.

Still further north, we camped on Balsfjorden, in the midst of what has to be the most spectacularly beautiful scenery in the world, despite heavy cloud cover. Next day the sun came out in a sky blue from horizon to horizon. The weather continued thus for a month. Shorts and singlets were the only clothes we wore much of the time, less in secluded camps. The sun was strong enough to have tanning effect from about 3 a.m. until 9 p.m. and dipped below the horizon for only an hour each night. Even at midnight, there was enough natural light to read a book or newspaper. On the last day of July, near the outpost town of Oksfjord, south-west of Hammerfest, we climbed a small mountain and gazed on the sun at midnight, floating just above the misty horizon. Above us, the weak, yellow sunlight turned to fire a permanently snow-capped peak that rose 1166 metres above the fiord.

Next day, we made camp on the banks of the famous Alta salmon river, about twenty kilometres inland from the little seaport of Alta. Craggy mountains reared on all sides, their slopes dark with pines. At the river and lake edges, silver birches made a line of bright green. The Alta seethed over rapids dark and mysterious, kilometres long. There were sandy beaches and islands, some accessible by wading. Walking trails led through the forests to open tundra, complete with grazing reindeer, elk and moose, wildflowers, cloudberries and blueberries. The few other camps in our vicinity belonged to obsessional anglers, flaying the river all through the endless days.

'They're crazies, these blokes, they never catch anything,' I told Mare. We were sunbaking on a patch of grass in front of our tent, watching an elderly fisherman methodically casting and retrieving a spinner.

'He seems to be catching one,' Mare said, lifting her brown shoulders slightly and shading her eyes to watch the old man.

He was, too. I stood up and watched in amazement as he wound in and netted the biggest fish I have ever seen taken out of a river—a salmon he weighed on a spring scale at nine kilograms. Nine kilograms! Right outside my tent. I got in the Carrera and started the motor.

'Where are you going?' Mare wanted to know.

'I'm going into Alta to do the shopping,' I said.

'Well, we could do with a loaf of bread and some. . .'

But I didn't hear any more. I was on my way—to buy a rod and reel and spinners and landing net. Even a fishing licence, if I had to. And bread—just to be on the safe side. Women are funny about shopping lists.

7 Downhill all the way

My fishing outfit cost 165 kroner. Rod, reel, line, lures, net and licence. I would have happily paid double. If that old duffer could pull a nine-kilo salmon out of the water at my doorstep, why not me? I suggested to Mare that if I caught too many fish, we could set up a roadside stall.

'Maybe you should get your line in the water, before you plan too far ahead,' she pointed out.

'I wasn't editor of *Outdoors* magazine for five years for nothing,' I responded.

We lived on tinned beans for the next few days, though I flogged the water for several kilometres upstream and downstream of our camp. No fish came my way, but I developed a relationship with a moose that slept on an island in the middle of the river. At first he sprang up, startled, and trotted off into the trees. Later, he would just lift his head and watch disinterestedly as I cast and retrieved my spinners from the bank in front of his resting place.

We were in an area that is part of Lappland's 'corner country', where the borders of Norge (Norway), Suomi (Finland) and Sverige (Sweden) meet. The Lapps are separate people from the three nationalities just mentioned. They are small, button-eyed folk with short, bandy legs and are found wherever there are reindeer.

The Lapps' traditional lands are mostly north of the Polar Sirkel, sweeping eastward from the Norwegian coast across Sverige and Suomi to the Russian border. Their situation seems comparable to that of the American Indians or Australia's Aborigines. They have been pushed around by national and state interests and are now the bemused recipients of assorted paternalistic assistance from three governments. This seems to have resulted in some demoralisation. The standard of living of many Lapps is below that of other Scandinavians.

Tourist publications detail the generosity of governments giving the Lapps the sole rights to herd reindeer and fish the inland lakes. But I never read anything about the Lapps getting a share of the proceeds of the sale of the iron ore from Kiruna, which is smack in the middle of their traditional homeland.

The Lapps tend to live in sub-standard houses on the outskirts of towns. Their physical presence cannot be ignored, due to their extraordinary and colourful national costume which they wear all the time, not just on festive occasions. This gear consists of a blue smock, worn by men and women, wildly splashed with red and silver embroidery. The men favour brightly worked sashes and the women have similarly gay bonnets, or a sort of jester's cap of many, drooping points. Their reindeer skin shoes curl up quaintly at the toe.

Reindeer to the Lapps are what kangaroos are to the Aborigines. No part of the beast is wasted. The basic product is meat, but the Lapps also dry and mount the antlers, for sale to tourists. Tanned hides are another popular selling line, plus reindeer-leather slippers and boots. All these items are sold at roadside stalls, where the Lapps erect their traditional tepees, to catch the eye of approaching motorists. Most of these tents, identical with those of the North American Indians, are canvas, even plastic, rather than the traditional reindeer hides.

On August 5, I got up soon after sunrise and began throwing spinners into the river. It was around 2 a.m. No luck, so I tramped back to camp, where I was surprised to find Mare up and about, with fire going and the billy on the boil.

'What would you like for your birthday?' she asked.

'A dirty big salmon,' I said.

'There are no fish shops around here,' she responded. 'But I do have this cake.' So she did—topped with a thick layer of tube cream, masses of fresh strawberries and a thoughtfully modest array of candles.

We were belting along the shoreline road beside Altafjord toward Hammerfest. Eventually the bitumen surface changed to newly graded earth and the road climbed tortuously inland, through mist-shrouded, inhospitable mountains. After a while there seemed to be no trees, only wet and glistening rocks, gravel and the typical crouching shrubs of the tundra region. Suddenly, we were on an undulating, gloomy plateau, reminiscent of the scrubby backblocks of far northern South Australia. But wet and boggy, instead of chalk dry.

As we progressed, the country became more and more like the moonscape territory around Coober Pedy. The road was finely corrugated, like tide-rippled sand. The Carrera didn't mind this surface at all, but I stuck to a modest 100 km/h, mindful that the road was wet and one slip would put us off into the donga, where we would bog to the door handles. There seemed to be water everywhere, in the form of countless tiny lakes, mostly about living room size, all linked and fed by creeks meandering through the soggy tundra grasses. There were mounds of snow on the higher ground. The cloud ceiling was about as high as an Aussie rules goalpost. Under that, little mists of fog drifted about and there were occasional showers of rain.

Every so often we saw herds of reindeer, but when I slithered to a halt and jumped out, armed with assorted cameras, the animals disappeared into the mist. It was now late afternoon and I felt ready to camp, but we had landed in one of the most Godforsaken places I have seen—and I've seen some. The landscape seemed to be composed of rocks and mud, over which the mists swirled weirdly. It looked like Hollywood's version of Transylvania, with Frankenstein's monster about to lurch down the road.

Mare remarked with some force: 'You've landed us in some Godforsaken places in our time, but this is rock bottom...it can only get better.'

Half an hour later we came to some settlement, composed of a dozen or so mean houses straggled along a river in the semi-shelter of a rock bank and some wind-battered trees. In a tiny clearing among some low scrub, we found a place for our tent. A sizeable slab of concrete and assorted burnt wreckage indicated there had once been a building on the site. I parked the Carrera on the level cement and went to gather firewood while Mare put up the tent. Mare *likes* to put up the tent—provided I don't help.

Strangely, it hadn't rained in this favoured corner of the country, so our camp was pleasant enough. I had a cheery fire going when Mare finished with the tent. Then I got on with my usual chore of inflating our airbeds with the Carrera's electric air compressor (intended for the spare tyre, which is stored in collapsed state, moulded into the petrol tank, under the front bonnet). While the tiny compressor putters away, I zip together our matching Paddy Pallin 'Hotham' sleeping bags, to make a snug cocoon for two. Working as a team, each doing our appointed tasks, we usually have camp completely set up in about eight minutes.

We reached Hammerfest at noon on a Saturday. The sky was blue, the sun shining and the townsfolk out and about in shirtsleeves, even shorts. Hammerfest is a sizeable port, about the size of Albury on the Victoria–NSW border. The harbour was crammed with large fishing trawlers, pleasure craft and tankers. Sailors' wives were airing their offspring, old folk dozed on benches around the fountain, and blue-jeaned student types lay around on park benches and lawns, strumming guitars, singing and tossing empty beer cans about. The streets were crowded, like late Saturday morning all over the world. About every twentieth unattached male, young or old, was visibly drunk. The skyline was dominated by fish canneries, warehouses and oil refineries.

We drove out of town a few kilometres and picnicked on a headland above a snug bay. Down at the water's edge were a few houses and a fish cannery. While we ate, a string of reindeer came along the road, their bells tonging musically.

I had in mind to take the ferry to the island settlement of Honingsvag and drive the remaining forty or so kilometres to the famous Nordkapp, goal of most tourists who get as far as Hammerfest. So we motored a further hundred rather rough kilometres to Repvag, which is strictly nowhere, except that it is the ferry embarkation point: to find we had missed the last boat for the day.

This gave me to think: what's the point of taking a fifty kilometre voyage, just to drive for half an hour across an island to a cliff called Nordkapp, and return? The most northerly *mainland* point you can reach by car in the world was just thirty kilometres up the road, so we went there, instead.

Kafjord, where the road ends, is hardly your resort town. But it gave us a nice sense of satisfaction standing on the most northerly point in the world that you can drive to unaided by bridges or boats.

Two days later we drove through Norway's outpost town of Kautokeino, crossed the north-west tip of Finland, where we then took a river ferry and came ashore in Sweden's most farflung northern outpost, Karesuando.

This is a neat but spread-out little town, with a hotel here, a petrol station there, and half a dozen shops, some here and some there, even a porno-shop and 'live show' in a canvas marquee on a vacant block close by the police station. (Shades of the Klondike—or early Coober Pedy!) But no bank where money could be changed. Luckily our cupboards were full and we had filled the Carrera's tank on the other side of the river in Kaaresuvanto, using the last of our Finnish marks. We proceeded south to the big mining town of Kiruna, about the size of Wollongong, but ultra modern with some astonishing examples of avant-garde architecture. Most tourists come to Kiruna by plane, then take a bus to the mountain and lakeside outpost of Abisko. This is the start of the great Royal Trail, undoubtedly the finest walk in the world, along which you may trek for several hundred kilometres south, as far as Tarnaby, near the Norwegian border, below Mo I Rana.

With a suitable supply of Swedish kronor, we spent the next two weeks wandering leisurely south through the mountains. Picturesque, but not a patch on Norway. The country is much more fully utilised, making it difficult to find suitable camping places, except in organised parks. These are fine, but expensive—and from July to September they tend to be booked out well in advance.

On our southward journey, we explored almost every road westward into the mountains, from Kiruna down through Gallivare, Jokkmokk to Arvidsjaur. The roads were excellent bitumen, but many were not worth the trouble, after Norway. The landscape consists of rocks, pine trees, lakes and rivers, with very little soil or grass or any suitable campsites.

We frequently drove more than a hundred kilometres through *uninhabited* country, searching in vain for a place where we could get the Carrera off the road and pitch our tent!

By far the best area was the country westward of Jokkmokk, which was also the most pleasant town we found in all northern Sweden. A side road follows lakes and rivers westward for 120 kilometres to the Lapp village of Kvikkjokk, in a truly out-of-this-world location among snowcapped peaks and lakes, with a large river cascading right through the town. There were boats, seaplanes and helicopters for hire at Kvikkjokk, or you could just go bushwalking, like most visitors. Along the (bitumen) road were perhaps half a dozen places to camp, all within a stone's throw of lake or riverfront. Better still, at the settlement and seaplane base of Arrenjarka, about fifteen kilometres before Kvikkjokk, there is what must be the best situated and set-up camping centre in

Mare gets friendly with one of the locals in the Lapp town of Jokkmokk, northern Sweden.

the world. Another westward road out of Jokkmokk leads to the fishing village of Karats. The road parallels a broad river. Between road and river is a narrow swathe of pine forest, into which you can drive and camp. Plenty of firewood, cloudberries and blueberries in season, with reindeer and elk to keep you company. A pamphlet I got in Jokkmokk claimed the river is the fishiest in all Sweden. Maybe it is, but I flogged the water with every spinner I had for five days and caught nothing. But you ought to see my muscles!

In Stockholm we stayed a week at the waterfront camping ground in the suburb of Angby. By day I played chess in the central *kultur huset* or watched the girls in adjacent Sorgels Torg square, while Mare did the rounds of the art galleries.

Apart from its drunks, Stockholm is a magnificent city, full of beauty and contrasts. Everything is either very expensive or free. You can practically live in the central Kultur Huset, with its free exhibitions, libraries, art galleries and recreational facilities. These include magazine and newspaper reading rooms, with lounge chairs and head-sets for listening to the stereo records of your choice. Also child-minding centres, chess-playing areas (boards and pieces provided, indoors and outdoors), several cheap (by local standards) cafeterias—all looking out on to Sorgels Torg square, with its fountains and arcaded shops.

The city is full of parks, where musical groups and assorted entertainers put on free concerts daily throughout summer. The new architecture is as eye-catchingly beautiful as the waterways and islands on which the city is located. If you don't like avant-garde living, there is always the fantastic old town of Stockholm, just a short bridge walk away on an island in mid-city. Or there are umpteen ferry tours (one hour to one day), plus as many galleries and museums, folk and natural-history and naval, among them the famous *Vasa Boat*, the salvaged warship that sank in Stockholm harbour five centuries ago and was lately retrieved almost intact from the mud. Much as we liked it, we couldn't really afford Stockholm. After a week of commuting via the underground rail service from Angby camping ground, we shot through.

We drove down to Helsingborg and boarded a ferry bound for Denmark's major island. The voyage took one hour. Ashore at Helsingor, we didn't hang about, brooding, like Hamlet a few years earlier. Instead, we motored to Kobenhavn, where we camped a few days. A great city, with matching prices, where you find little printed messages under the windscreen wiper, saying: *Do not park here again or you will be towed away. Signed: The Police.* The famous Tivoli Gardens turned out to be a sort of combination of Luna Park and botanical gardens, dotted with expensive restaurants and poker-machine halls. Quaint at night with its coloured lights and a brass band playing Glen Miller's old tunes, plus Stan Kenton, *live!*

We drove across the island via Roskilde, visiting a waterfront Viking museum. At Lejre, we walked about a recreated Iron-Age village, complete with student types living the simple life, tending primitive breeds of wild sheep and pigs. Another ferry took us across to a second Danish isle on our way to Odense. There was a two-hour queue for this trip, which took one and a half hours. After camping near Odense we toured mainland Denmark (Jutland) for a few days.

It's a pleasant country; the Danes are far more alive and doing and happy than the Norwegians or Swedes. Danish camping grounds are unbelievable (free camping in this crowded land is impossible). Hot showers and hot-air blowers for your hair; washing machines and drying tumblers; gas or electric community kitchens; heated dining and recreation rooms, with reading matter; car washes; kids' play areas; restaurants; shops; outdoor dance floors with juke boxes! But forget the notion of boiling the billy and singing around a jolly campfire.

The thing I remember most about Denmark is that its highest point is only a hundred metres above sea-level! We ended our Scandinavian tour at Flensburg, where we crossed back into Germany, with the Carrera

8000 kilometres older than when we drove ashore at Kristiansand in Norway.

Back on the autobahns, we managed to circumnavigate the scruffy, naughty sailor's city of Hamburg, but somehow took a wrong turn and fetched up going via Amsterdam to France. (Our ultimate goal was sunny Spain, where we intended to winter.)

Amsterdam (named after the original dam across the Amsel river) turned out to be a sprawling not-so-large town, intersected by more waterways than Venice, many of them tree-lined, with few tall buildings. Most business houses are modest structures of no more than six to eight floors. The major form of public transport is via (almost) silent tram, plus buses. In line with the rest of Europe, there are no bus or tram conductors; you just buy your time-stamped ticket from a machine on the vehicle. The ticket entitles you to ride anywhere for an hour, changing vehicles as required.

Everything in Amsterdam and Holland is organised on similar lines, based on common sense and compromise. This is the most densely populated country on earth, so they've had to work things out.

Thus, if there is nowhere to park cars and people are leaving them all over the footpath, you don't ban the practice, you legalise it—with just a few little rules. This flair for compromise, this oyster-like ability to turn any irritating particle of grit into a shiny pearl, acceptable to everyone, makes Amsterdam a place of surprises. The city looks like the world's biggest, neatest and best-kept middle-class suburb—but it is at the same time a racial melting pot and the drug and pornography capital of the world. All these potentially gritty problems have been deftly glossed over and sugar-coated until they seem offensive to no one.

Just as footpaths are available for car parking, whole villages and recreation centres have been established for drug-freaks and assorted dropouts. There is even a government provided club-house and *annual grant* to the Amsterdam chapter of Hell's Angels! The Ladies of the Street have been brought in off the footpaths and placed in nice little decorated shopfront rooms, where they display fetchingly in their native habitat—without getting in the way of old folk going to church or the kiddies coming home from school. Thus a trade normally regarded as a blight on the community has been transformed into a tourist attraction, proudly advertised by the city elders. Postcards depicting the ladies in their windows are sold at tourist bureaus and most newsagents.

We left Amsterdam full of admiration for the Dutch and their way of life (particularly their ability to speak English!). But I wouldn't want to live there. No amount of ingenuity can create wide open spaces.

8 Out of the frying pan

It was May 1978. Rain drummed on the rusty iron roof of our hundred-year-old homestead. The creeks were up and flooding. Above the roar of the deluge, I could hear water dripping into buckets strategically placed around our kitchen.

'Going to be a long, hard winter,' I volunteered, stirring what was left of the fire in the sodden grate. This cheerless prediction brought no response from my melancholy long-haired mate. She just stared out into the sheeting rain. A field mouse, driven in by the storm, ran across the rickety wooden floor. I threw a gumboot at it. The impact sent a tremor through the building. Two glasses toppled from the shaky dresser and smashed on the floor.

At that moment the rain eased, allowing a clear view across the yard. Outside the hayshed, my white three-litre Porsche 911 Carrera glistened brightly, cleansed of its usual coating of dust and cowdung. There was a long silence, broken by the sound of water dripping into buckets.

'How much would a new roof cost?' asked Mare.

'More than we have,' I responded. Then, sensing the mood of the moment, I added: 'But this rain won't last...' A clap of thunder rolled down the valley, rattling the windows. A torrential downpour reduced the Carrera to a blurry white shape against the dark of the hayshed.

'What is that car worth?'

Caught unawares, I replied with less than my usual caution. 'Not less than $30 000.'

'Then we'll have a new roof. Better still, a new house,' said Mare. Her voice had a steely quality.

Owning a three-litre Carrera that is worth every cent of $30 000 is one thing. Selling the vehicle for that amount is another. Since importing

Pondering how to attach a grass rake to the 911E Porsche.

the car into Australia following our two-year European safari, I had fallen into the habit of having the Carrera serviced by the John Newell organisation in the Sydney suburb of Bass Hill. While idling around Mr Newell's shop, I noted that second-hand Carreras like mine usually had a price tag around $36 000.

Cheerful salesmen assured me that if ever I wanted to sell, my car 'has to be worth over thirty big ones'. Which seemed reasonable, if they were going to offer it next day at $36 000. But when the time came, young master Newell approached me carrying a gun. Truly. It turned out to be an airgun, which he was using to chastise birds that showed scant respect for the Porsches on offer in his outdoor showroom. But I was suitably intimidated.

'Please, sir,' I stammered, tugging my forelock. 'May I now have my thirty big ones, for this?' I indicated my white Carrera.

Gun crooked in arm, country-squire fashion, Mr Newell surveyed the car with studied indifference. 'It has everything,' I said encouragingly. 'Electric roof, seven and eight inch wheels, Blaupunkt radio . . .'

Mr Newell peered reluctantly into the cabin. 'No air,' he said shortly. 'Cars these days must have air. It means $2000, pricewise.'

'There are Recaro sports seats and three of Marchal's biggest driving lights,' I countered.

Mr Newell took a second glance inside the cabin. 'Forty-eight thousand kilometres!' His voice expressed deep shock. 'We prefer cars with around 20 000 at most. I had no idea . . .'

And so we settled for $27 000. Mr Newell wrote the cheque with the nonchalant air of a man who did that sort of thing every other day. By chance, a few months later I met the new owner of my car, who said he paid $35 000 for it.

My bank manager was delighted to receive the $27 000 and promptly offered to loan a matching amount toward my new house. When this transaction was formalised, I went shopping for a suitable 'owner-builder' type vehicle.

Eventually I settled on a 1973-model Holden one-ton truck. These were in great demand at the time and hard to get. I paid $3500 for mine, on what was definitely a sellers' market in 1978. My one-tonner was a cut above average, boasting a limited-slip diff and Michelin tyres. It had the standard 202 motor and 'four on the floor'.

To build a house, you must first have a level site. Foxground is not very level, so I made a second purchase. This was a thirty-year-old Ferguson TEA tractor, fitted with 'dozer blade, brush slasher and carry-all. The Holden and the Ferguson proved excellent machines and did their chosen work well. Being a truck, the Holden was uncomfortable. When empty, it tended to spin its rear wheels on loose gravel or wet surfaces. So much so, in fact, that if you drove unladen on to level, wet grass or clay, you stayed there, spinning the wheels and going sideways. Unladen on bitumen, rear-axle hop made traffic light sprints futile and vigorous cornering was apt to become exciting. However, three or four bags of cement on the rear tray made a world of difference.

Then my good friend Robert Besson, then the Sydney Bilstein importer, turned up at Foxground for a day's picnicking among our resident wildlife. He was accompanied by Herr Bilstein himself, fresh from der Fatherland and anxious to meet a wombat. This was easily arranged, but unfortunately the wombat chased Herr Bilstein and would have bitten him if I had not stopped the animal with a flying tackle. Herr Bilstein was so grateful, he insisted that my Carrera should be fitted with a set of Bilstein shocks. On learning that I no longer owned a Porsche, he ordered that my 'Helldunvuntun' be shod with Bilsteins. (Herr Bilstein did not see the Holden one-tonner and I imagine he thought it was some sort of sportscar.)

Anyway, the truck soon became probably the only such vehicle fitted mit der famous high-performance Bilstein *Gasdruck Stoss-Dämpfers*. The result was nothing short of sensational. The one-tonner's handling was improved enormously. During tests, Robert Besson flung the vehicle around suburban corners at speeds that made my jaw drop—not from fear, but amazement. Axle tramp disappeared and the Holden easily out-

handled all but the most serious opposition on tortuous roads such as the famous Kiama Bends.

Unfortunately, its bench seat remained singularly uncomfortable, particularly for the passenger, who didn't have a steering wheel to hang on to. Mare put up with this for about six months, then bought herself a Honda Accord hatchback.

During the construction of our new dwelling, which is my version of a Catalan farmhouse, I was enthusiastic about my Holden one-tonner. Inspired by the magic the Bilsteins had wrought, I fitted quartz headlights, deluxe pressmatic radio and a sporty exhaust (the old one disintegrated.) But with the house completed, I became aware something was lacking in my life—a fast, exciting, comfortable car. Enthusiast that I was, I could not pretend that driving a Holden truck was fun. It rattled, and the abominable bench seat jounced me like a cocktail shaker. I began to eye Mare in her Accord with envy.

Then, in the mail, came a package from Stuttgart. It contained a small stainless-steel plaque with the Porsche emblem and my name engraved on it. No explanation. An article of mine about our European adventures had recently appeared in *Christophorus*, the Porsche house magazine. Perhaps this was part of the payment? I put the plaque on a ledge above the desk in my new study. As luck would have it, I was trying to finish my umpteenth travel book, so my gaze fell on that plaque frequently as I crouched over an obstinate typewriter. I began to daydream. I no longer needed a truck. I should have something rather more comfortable, more...ah...civilised. A little faster, too—perhaps of the sporting genre.

I put a 'For Sale—$3000' sign on the one-tonner and left it in our Wild Country Park customer's parking area. Months passed. Eventually a kindly neighbour took the vehicle off my hands—for $2000.

Driving in the Accord to our local farmer's coop for a few bags of kangaroo and wombat food, I suddenly saw red. It was a Ferrari 308GTB, going very fast along the Princes Highway. I had never liked Ferraris, but at the time, this one seemed highly desirable. I went home and browsed through some old English *Car* magazines.

Every one had something about Ferraris in it, usually red ones, written by my old friend and fellow-journalist and ex-Apple Islander, Mel Nichols. He made them sound, well, interesting. Porsche's latest introduction of the period, the 928, did nothing for me—and the 1979 range of 911 Porsches were disappointing, watered-down versions of my beloved three-litre Carrera. For once, my loyalty to the marque wavered. Surely there could be no harm in *looking* at some Ferraris? Red ones.

9 Into the fire

When the *Who's Who* people ask for a list of my hobbies, I shall include 'reading the motoring classifieds in the *Sydney Morning Herald*'. I have done this for many years, spending most of my browsing time among the P for Porsche columns.

With my new-found interest in red motor cars, I ventured further afield, into the unknown world of F for Ferrari. It proved challenging territory.

Inspired by the breathless prose of English *Car* editor Mel Nichols, I was agog to sit in and perhaps drive my first red motor car. (At this stage, I assumed all Ferraris were this colour, because Mel's adventures in the hills of Tuscany below Modena were invariably accompanied by pictures of red vehicles. While sitting at a roadside bar near Firenze early in 1976, I had seen him go by in a very red prototype 308GTB.)

In order to have a yardstick against which to judge 'pre-owned' offerings, I first visited the showrooms where new Ferraris were being sold. In addition, I contacted the Sydney importers, then Maranello Concessionares.

No one took me seriously. Obviously, new-Ferrari salesmen had an image of what potential customers look like. Anyone with cowdung on his boots who asked technical questions simply didn't qualify. New-Ferrari sales staff do not expect to be asked questions. Because they don't know the answers, I suspect, but somehow they manage to convey that you are a money-grubbing little sneak for enquiring about such things as the cost of servicing per year. The only thing I found out on the showroom floor was that 308GTB Ferraris don't have a glove box.

This happened when I asked a salesman where it was. I was sitting in the driving seat and he reached in disdainfully through the passenger window and pressed a button in the facia where one would expect a glove box to be. A little door fell open, revealing a massive array of fuses! I think it was news to him, too.

Such was the impression I made on the Ferrari sales staff, I did not even score a coloured pamphlet. Eventually the Maranello people gave me a black-and-white leaflet, which was a reprint of an English *Autocar* roadtest of the 308GTB. It was not entirely favourable and contained a wealth of technical detail: how to find the boot, which is concealed in the engine compartment, under a zippered plastic cover, where you would normally expect to find the spare tyre, which is under the front bonnet, where you would expect to find the engine...

Thus armed, I went forth in search of a suitable 'pre-owned' Ferrari. A red one. On any given Saturday, the *Sydney Morning Herald* vehicle classifieds are but lightly peppered with used Ferraris. On a good day there may be three or four. Often there are none. The first GTB I looked at seriously was red in colour and belonged to a dealer on Parramatta Road. Let us call him Ron. When I first rang up, Ron explained the car was his very own personal means of transport, the apple of his eye. Maybe it was, but later it transpired he had traded the vehicle only a few weeks earlier and now here it was for sale!

In marked contrast with the purveyors of new Ferraris, Ron gave me his undivided attention. 'This car is immaculate. Look at the duco. Not a mark or scratch. Never been dinged, you can see. Mechanically it's faultless. In fact, it's virtually brand new. Only done 19 000 miles. Original tyres.'

'What year model is it?' I enquired.

'Late '77,' said Ron.

'Could I see the compliance plate?'

'Doesn't have one, doesn't need one,' said Ron smoothly. 'The owner ordered the car privately, picked it up at the factory and shipped it back to Australia himself.' Black mark, Ron, I thought.

Cars ordered from Australia *do* get a compliance plate. On the other hand, anyone roaming around Europe who buys a second-hand (or tenth-hand) car does *not* get a compliance plate.

'Dry-sump lubrication...very good,' said Ron when he lifted the rear engine cover. Another black mark, Ron, but not necessarily the car, I mused. Cars ordered from Australia (then) came with a conventional wet sump—European delivery cars came with a dry sump, which is more suited to the extreme northern hemisphere climate.

As well as I was able, I looked underneath the car. It is very hard to look underneath a Ferrari 308GTB, due to its close proximity to the ground. But I could detect plenty of engine and/or transmission oil. And at each corner of the car there were further leaks from wheel bearings and balljoints.

Not encouraging in a car described as 'virtually brand new' but not necessarily fatal. 'Might we go for a drive?' I suggested.

Within a block of Parramatta Road, Ron had been through four of the GTB's five gears, revving each one out to a puny 2000 rpm. 'These cars have terrific torque,' he explained. 'Feel the acceleration, even in top.' (If Ron had known about 5th, we would have been in that.) He was right, I suppose. The car surged forward in fourth from 30 mph to 40 mph before the next intersection stopped us. (The MPH speedo was another flaw in Ron's story. Australian delivery cars were marked KPH.)

Eventually Ron let me drive. Within minutes, even in the suburban situation, I could understand what Mel Nichols had so frequently been on about. Here was a magnificent car! Once you got the hang of it, it went like stink, relentlessly sure-footed and confident, securely stuck-down on the tightest corners.

The only trouble was, this one hesitated noticeably about halfway through the rev-change, gasping for fuel or breaking down electrically. It did the same on sharp suburban corners, so I guessed the problem was most likely connected with the four dual-throat Webers sucking and roaring just behind me.

These niggling faults aside, I was vastly impressed. Here was a car that obviously wanted to and could go!—even if it wasn't quite as represented, leaked oil and hesitated under pressure.

Back in the yard, while Ron spun a web of words, I found a lot of little things that worried me. The electric window lifters were erratic, like the air-conditioner—and the radio was dead. The seats, handles and knobs within the car seemed worn, in marked contrast with the immaculate exterior finish of the car. The spare wheel was smooth and the road tyres, too meaty for 19 000 mile 'originals', were unevenly worn, indicating camber and alignment problems.

Ron became evasive when I asked who had been servicing the vehicle since it arrived in Australia. It was at this point he admitted to owning the vehicle only a very short time, during which service had not been required. Ho hum.

Sydney is a relatively small town and within a few days I was able to locate the gentlemen who had been servicing Ron's GTB during its previous ownership. 'There are better 308s around,' I was told guardedly. 'That one used to be blue . . .' Confronted face to face with this information, Ron didn't miss a beat. 'Yairs, it has been resprayed. A really beautiful job. A Ferrari has to be red.'

Several Ferraris later, I made the acquaintance of Laki Harris, who had for sale his own, personal 308GTB Ferrari. I should have met him sooner and saved myself much anguish and humbug. Laki Harris, it turned out, is the Sydney afficionado of Ferraris. He not only knows them and loves them but also fixes them. Laki is a top automotive wiz who did his training on Lamborghinis and now runs his own Ferrari specialist workshop. His family background is Greek, he mostly wears blue track suits and joggers, and is never seen off duty without a cigar in his mouth.

When not tending Ferraris in his Darlinghurst (Sydney) workshop, Laki Harris can be found holding court under the sun umbrella that shades the footpath tables outside the Cosmopolitan Hotel at Double Bay, his 308GTB parked handy at kerbside.

We met as a result of his advertisement in the Saturday *Herald*. Great was my surprise to observe that Laki's Ferrari was silver! I was soon to learn that it was not only its colour that set this car apart from all the others I had inspected.

Laki Harris's Ferrari turned out to be very much as represented. It was immaculate within and without and its history was easily verified. The silver GTB had arrived in Australia as Maranello's demonstration car and had passed from them to Laki after a year and some 10 000 kilometres. Since then it had been meticulously and lovingly maintained, with consummate expertise.

Laki took me for a demonstration drive out through Double Bay during the afternoon peak-hour traffic. Then I gingerly drove the car on to

Watsons Bay. As well as could be judged under the circumstances, the vehicle performed magnificently. But surely it hesitated under fierce acceleration and on tight corners? 'That's a fault of GTBs,' Laki told me. 'You see, the engine sits sideways and the Webers are designed to ride north-and-south, like they do in the Lamborghini. They sometimes get a bit starved for petrol on cornering, but not enough to affect handling. You get something similar on acceleration, which I can fix by altering the float levels...but then you can get flooding problems if you stop on a steep hill.'

Everything else on Laki's car worked and worked well, including a boosted stereo system that could drown even the Ferrari's mighty wail. When Laki put the car up on the hoist, the underside looked shipshape and immaculate. Over a period of several weeks, I spent considerable time in Laki's workshop, examining and re-examining the silver GTB. One does not rush into a near $40 000 car purchase.

I learned a lot about Ferraris during those visits. Contrary to popular opinion, a clutch replacement can be done at the roadside—which is perhaps just as well, because Ferrari clutches often need replacing. Your average silvertail Ferrari owner can get rid of a clutch in less than 5000 kilometres. Competent drivers such as Laki Harris expect at least 20 000. However you look at it, this confirms the Ferrari legend: the cars are not cheap to run, even well driven. (I noted that Laki was gentle with the clutch and minimised changes by staying in the highest gear, confident the immense torque of the motor would achieve what only high revs can do in lesser cars.)

He had an engaging honesty about the price of Ferrari ownership. 'Top quality costs top dollar...as simple as that,' he explained, waving his cigar and reminding me of assorted Damon Runyon characters. Service, Laki pointed out, depended on how much travelling you did. For me, he judged 'two or three services' (at around $200 apiece) and 'one big one' (at around $1000) each year. That included replacement of minor worn bits and pieces, but any major part would of course be extra. The 'big' annual Ferrari service is interesting. Fellows like Mel Nichols never bother to mention it when describing their breathtaking Ferrari jaunts into the Tuscan hills.

But it seems that about once a year or at least every 20 000 kilometres, the entire rear suspension and whatever has to be dismantled, lubricated and reassembled. This being the way Enzo Ferrari designed it! The consequences of not having this work done are too dreadful to contemplate.

The 'big' service usually involves a new clutch while they're at it and many expensive hours adjusting the Webers and the timing. What it doesn't have four of, the GTB308 has two of: two coils, two distributors, two contact breakers, two fuel filters, two timing belt tensioners and so on. The front bank of plugs and one distributor are entirely out of sight and seemingly inaccessible. But Laki assured me that with the aid of mirrors, 'timing the dizzies' is not too tedious. However, it all costs money—in round figures $1000, provided nothing serious is found to be amiss.

Noting the look of terror in my eyes, Laki offered the comforting advice that provided they are regularly and properly serviced by such as himself, Ferraris in fact give little trouble. Except for wearing out the occasional clutch. Thus, apart from $2000 or so each year, there is nothing to spend by way of maintenance! (This was in 1978, when a dollar was a dollar.)

Despite its complexity, lack of glove box and projected running costs, Laki Harris's 308GTB was a very desirable motor car. The bodywork was fibreglass, so rust was not a spectre. But I did hear that paint-crazing, under the hot Australian sun, was one reason the latest GTBs were coming here in metal bodies. My suburban drives in Laki's and other Ferraris on offer convinced me the GTB is among the fastest and most 'stuck-down' cars available.

The most disconcerting thing about Ferraris was the way their owners drove everywhere in fourth gear, avoiding gear changes and high revs. Perhaps they drove in mortal fear of wearing out the clutch? More likely, the sort of people who can afford Ferraris prefer the peace and quiet of high gears. The GTB will certainly out-accelerate most opposition, regardless of what gear it happens to be in.

I noted also that any sort of bump or hollow in the road caused the alert Ferrari owner to brake sharply. All this made me wonder if Laki's Ferrari 308GTB was really suitable for country roads, particularly in the wilds of Foxground.

There was only one way to find out. Soon after dawn, Laki and I headed off from his workshop through the deserted Sydney streets, heading south. Most enjoyable, with the needle close to 250 km/h several times.

The heater worked, the radio-cassette player boomed and the electric windows slid up and down on command. My only disappointment was the way the car bottomed, even at low speeds, on bumps a Porsche and most other cars could take at any speed. At a railway level crossing on the Princes Highway just north of Kiama, we proceeded at a cautious 30 km/h and the resulting crash was alarming. I know this spot well, most cars don't bother to slow down at all.

The one-and-a-half kilometre gravel road in to our Foxground empire was in unusually bad condition, but Laki managed it without mishap, although I fancy he aged visibly under the strain. The tortuous climbing private track up to our house 'Casa Simpatica' is definitely not for city boys and I daresay Laki talks about the adventure to this day. But he made it, with only a few minor scrapes in the creek crossings. Parked in our courtyard, the silver GTB looked just right. I wouldn't have wanted a red one. Even Mare admitted it looked 'stunning.'

Laki had breakfast with us and then we made the return journey to his workshop in Darlinghurst. Back on the hoist, the car was still clean underneath—no oil anywhere. We parted on the note that if my bank manager was agreeable, I would buy the silver GTB.

That kind gentleman greeted me with the news that the government had that day announced its $18 000 depreciation limit on cars. Money for 'luxury' vehicles was going to be tight, he said—and for the moment, until the situation was clarified, there was none. It took more than a month for the financial dust to settle, during which time my enthusiasm to own a Ferrari abated.

During this limbo period, I resumed my browsing in back issues of *Car* magazine. I reread all Mel's Ferrari adventures, then came across one of his stories I had missed, under the heading 'Sheer Bliss'. It was about a modified Porsche and was the most ecstatic eulogy 'purple-prose' Nichols had ever written. Everything about the car was marvellous, perfect and even better than that. Coming from Mel Nichols, who does not generally like Porsches, this had to be quite some car.

My interest was purely academic, of course. The Porsche had been set up by Kremer Racing, of Köln in Germany, at vast expense, for some unknown enthusiast who probably owned the Bank of England. The car apparently lived in that country. Kremer had been preparing race-winning Porsches for many years, their most notable successes being in the *24-Hours of Le Mans* events.

The Kremer Porsche described by Mel Nichols in *Car* was a 1977 model of the 911 line, modified somewhat to produce 250 bhp, 0-60 mph in five seconds and 0-100 mph in 11.2 seconds. More important, through the addition of a rally suspension, including Bilsteins, whopping P7 tyres, Group 4 racing oil cooler and spoiler at front, plus a rear whale tail, this road-going Kremer Porsche handled better than a turbo. At least, thus spake Mel Nichols. He went on to say that Kremer had only prepared three such road cars. (Little wonder, as the cost was around Stg £20 000 in Germany, before tax. Say $60 000 in Australia, duty and tax paid.) Two of the Kremers had gone to America and this one was in England.

Side-tracked by daydreams of the unattainable, it was some time before I came to grips with reality. Perhaps it would be better to have a silver Ferrari in Foxground than dream about a Kremer Porsche in Yorkshire or wherever... Then in the *Herald*, I noticed an advertisement offering a Kremer Porsche for sale! There was a photo of the vehicle, very similar to one I had seen in *Car* magazine.

'Is that the Kremer Porsche Mel Nichols wrote about in *Car* magazine?' I said into the phone.

'Indeed it is,' said a voice.

'Are you the original owner?'

'Indeed I am,' came the reply. 'The car was built for me. I took it to England briefly, before shipping it home.'

'Has it travelled far?'

'Only 26 000 kilometres.'

'How much do you want for it?'

'Fifty thousand dollars.'

'Out of my reach,' I admitted sadly.

The voice spoke again. 'Would you like to try the car? If you like it, we could talk more about price.' The Silver Kremer turned up at Foxground a few days later. Despite the low-slung Group 4 front spoiler, it made it to our front gate. But at the first creek crossing on our driveway the Kremer began ploughing up gravel and had to retreat. Disappointing. Later we went for an extended test drive in the surrounding countryside and such minor problems as creek crossings were forgotten.

Egad! Here was the stuff of dreams, in solid, unbeatable, unstuffupable, super-surefooted reality. It had the thrust of a jet aircraft combined with the stability of a battleship. There seemed no other yardstick to judge it by. The Kremer simply left for dead all my previous Porsches and the Ferraris I had so recently delighted in. Its acceleration and handling were simply phenomenal. Surely no other registered road car, anywhere, could go and handle like this one? In addition, it seemed to be without vice. At cornering speeds much faster than I would have dared in the Carrera, the worst the Kremer did was begin to run wide—a situation easily dealt with by lifting off momentarily.

I liked it. The handling of my three-litre Carrera now seemed decidedly 'iffy' by comparison. That car used to get light up front when you approached 200 km/h. At 240 km/h you knew you were going too fast for more than minor steering adjustments. In really hard cornering, you were always aware that the limit was nigh and if you got it wrong, there would be great excitement. The Kremer seemed to squat lower as you went faster, cornering like a train—at any speed.

After admitting to the Kremer's owner that I liked his car, I pointed out that it was not much good if I couldn't reach my house in it. Would he give me time to construct some cement wheel-ramps over the creek crossings? A week later he was back and the Kremer made the final half kilometre up to Casa Simpatica. Then we began to talk finance.

Would he take less? The short answer was yes.

So it came to pass that a place was found for the small stainless steel plaque sent to me by the House of Porsche. It was fixed on the glove box of the silver Kremer Porsche.

10 Der Silber Schnellzug (The Silver Express)

We had 7000 rpm in fourth, which showed on the other dial as 220 km/h. 'Take the picture,' I said to Van Carter, huddled in the passenger-side rear seat, camera aimed at the Kremer Porsche's instruments.

I heard the click of the shutter and changed up to fifth gear. The needle dropped, then climbed steadily back past 6000 rpm. We had 6500 rpm and 250 km/h, with more to come. Another 500 rpm and 20 km/h in fact.

Series showing the Kremer Porsche's speedo to maximum revs (7000) in four gears and 6500 revs in fifth—equal to 250 km/h.
1. First gear, 70 km/h.

2. Second gear, 120 km/h.

3. Third gear, 175 km/h.

4. Fourth gear, 215 km/h.

5. Fifth gear, 250 km/h and more to come.

'This corner is pretty lumpy,' Van said uneasily. We were running out of straight road with awesome rapidity. What had seemed a gentle any-speed curve during our exploratory run now appeared as a rather alarming, tight left-hander. With bumps, according to Van, who knows the route well.

'Try to remain calm,' I said with pretended confidence. 'Don't take the picture yet. We'll get our 7000 rpm on the next straight.' Then we hit the first of several bumps as we went through the corner.

It was not an experience I would wish to repeat. To make matters worse, I glimpsed, far ahead down the straight, a parked white car on the verge. 'Take the picture,' I said grudgingly. We still had a shade under 250 km/h.

Sure enough it was the enemy, caught early in the act of setting up their dreaded radar paraphernalia. Most unsporting, considering it was not yet 7 a.m.

'We should've taken the other cap off,' Van said glumly. 'The extra power would've got you to 7000 before the end of the straight.'

Probably right, he was referring to the heavy metal caps that normally covered two of the Kremer's three exhaust outlets. One pipe open gives 210 reasonably quiet horses for normal motoring. Two pipes open produces 230 horses for rather more spirited and somewhat noisy country driving. Three pipes open unleashes 250 frenzied thoroughbreds and a noise that can only be tolerated on the race track. My reason for keeping twenty horses capped off in the stable during our test run had been the noise factor. The roar from three open pipes would have set the cups rattling in every bear's lair on the south coast.

Anyway. We coasted sedately past the uniformed knights of the road as they fiddled with their electronics. From their baleful looks it was obvious they had heard the noise and were chagrined at having missed out by seconds on a 'move directly to jail' booking. We decided to call it a day.

One week later, an off-duty policeman visiting our wildlife refuge with his family said cheerfully, 'We've had reports on an unidentified flying object. Silver in colour and low to the ground. We've been asked to watch out for it...' If he thought he was giving a word to the wise, he was right. I refused his fifty cents when he came up later to our kiosk for a cup of tea. Bribery and corruption in high places, if you like, but the presumably desired effect of saving me from myself had been achieved. Any future speed tests of the Kremer Porsche would be conducted in the proper place.

Well, what is it like, this unique Kremer Porsche?

Before I have my say, let's hear a few words from English *Car* magazine editor, Mel Nichols, whose test report on the Kremer appeared in the March 1977 issue, a month before the car arrived in Australia.

'I reached inside the cabin and turned the key; there was a violent shattering roar, the roar that you get from a proper racing Porsche... We were looking at times of nothing more than 5.0 seconds (to 60 mph) and 11.6 seconds (to 100 mph). Kremer had given my friend the edge he sought over the Turbo, and the Boxer, and the Countach... The engine just performs, smoothly and willingly and powerfully, stopping at 7300 rpm only because the electronic cutout prevents it going further... Where the wheel of the Carrera had jiggled in the hands, in the usual Porsche fashion, the Kremer was dead steady. Where the Carrera walked about on the road, in the usual Porsche fashion, the Kremer was positive as a bullet. The difference was quite staggering...

'The Kremer Porsche stormed on as unaffected as an express train, better even than the Carrera 3 Sport and the Turbo... This Porsche, as the miles were flung behind us, was easier to place than any I had previously driven. Sharper than the Turbo, more positive, more responsive, it swung instantly and stunningly accurately into the bends and then maintained its line with perfect balance... There was no roll, no diagonal movement under hard brakes into tight bends or under power coming out of them. Just absolute control and poise. Kremer had given my friend power; they had also given him a chassis that allowed every last drop to be used and enjoyed...

'I began using it all. All but brushing the banks under brakes on the way in, holding tight, tight, tight to the apex until the tail was almost ready to creep and then coming off that hard little pedal and back on to the throttle to open up that engine; it was as if there was no break in time at all between the hard braking and the smooth, devastating acceleration... Glorious!

'There was such a feeling of control and safety and sheer speed and pleasure that I had to yell out with joy. Oh yes, it really was that good.'

I am the first to admit that my mate Mel Nichols is inclined to purple prose at times, but he does not like Porsches and frequently says so. He prefers Ferraris and Lamborghinis.

So when he admits in print that here is a car that out-performs the Ferrari Boxer, the Lamborghini Countach and the Porsche Turbo, I take it to mean that he judged the Kremer to be a most outstanding car. The comfort of the Kremer is the same as any other Porsche. The seats, front and back, are top-of-the-range Recaros, with everything fully adjustable. Even at near-racing speeds, passengers need not fall about, provided they use their feet to brace themselves. The rally suspension is hard and mildly noisy, but none of the harshness is transmitted to the Kremer's occupants. The only problem that arises from the stiff suspension is that rather more than usual road vibration is transmitted to the car body, causing things like upholstery screws to rattle loose.

One of the nicest things about the Kremer interior is the sound system. At my stage of life, there are times when I can do without the Kremer's throaty song. The boosted Bose tape deck and radio provide concert hall volume and quality so that the music completely overshadows engine noise if required. This gives the effect of jet-aircraft travel, where you are conscious of moving at enormous speed, but hear only the sound of music.

I miss the electric window lifters of the Carrera 3, but you can't have everything. Likewise the Carrera's automatic cabin temperature control. Now I'm back to tugging irritably at assorted levers which alternately make the interior too hot or too cold, but never get it just right.

The Momo steering wheel is a joy, being small and thickly padded with leather, notched on the fascia side for positive grip *in extremis*. And it is round. The Carrera/Turbo wheel is round, but mounted off-centre, to make room for your knees. This makes the moving arc of the rim eccentric, which in dicey moments gives the impression the wheel is coming adrift. Alarming. The smallness of the Momo wheel leaves room for your knees, but obscures the speedo above 100 km/h. Well, that's all you legally need to see anyway. The centre console, which serves only to hold cassettes, gets in the way of my left leg and I am going to have it out.

Servicing of the Kremer presents no problems and is more or less stock-standard. Oil changes every 20 000 km, also plugs. The Kremer engine doesn't require any additional fiddling, tweaking or tuning, although camshaft and ignition timing and tappet clearances are slightly different from standard.

I wrote to Kremers for this information and it was forthcoming by return mail, together with an assurance that any spare parts I should ever require were readily available. The letter ended with, I quote: 'Congratulations to that car—it was a very good and high performance car, which attended much reputation in tests.'

I'm sure it did. Handling and braking remain superb—phenomenal in fact. The Kremer Porsche simply does not do anything wrong, at any speed.

When I occasionally mismanage, the front tyres protest and if I have really mucked it up, the rear begins to slide. Very smoothly and positively, with no suggestion that the car will treacherously spin, like the dreaded early 356 Porsches. Of course, this sort of nonsense rarely happens. For 99.9% of the time, the Kremer corners at astonishing speeds as if it were on rails. Your body is aware of alarming G-forces and loose objects fly about the cabin, but those tenacious giant P7s stay resolutely on your chosen path.

When the inevitable parked cement truck appears suddenly around a blind corner, blocking your way, there is never a suggestion that the brakes won't pull you up in time. Their performance is astounding. You have never really pulled up suddenly until you have done so in a Kremer Porsche. To sum up, I reckon that after many years of Porschemanship, through various model changes, I now have the absolute, ultimate Porsche.

(This chapter was written early in 1980, as a review for *Wheels* magazine. I've owned several Porsches since then!)

11 Time machine

I began absconding from home on a tricycle when I was about four years old. The habit has proved hard to break and I still do it, mostly in high speed sports cars or off-road vehicles, which I regularly assess for two of Australia's top motoring magazines, *Wheels* and *Overlander*. I did a bunk on my tricycle so many times, the friendly neighbourhood policeman who intercepted me on his beat complained to my family. My dad took the wheels off the tricycle, saying it had to be fixed. It never got fixed and I was grounded for several years.

For a while I stayed at home, making occasional short journeys by 'whipping behind' horse-drawn baker's vans. They had a small step on the back, below the door. You jumped on to this while the vehicle was in motion and the driver was up front controlling the horse. The penalty for discovery was a boxed ear or a kick in the behind. It was the age of unquestioned adult authority over children, anybody's children.

My grandfather, Caleb Carter, thought my urge to travel should be encouraged. He commissioned his second eldest son, Percival (my father), to construct me a billy cart. When it was finished, Caleb presented me with an aged, cantankerous billy-goat to go between the long shafts. My power source had a fine Ho Chi Minh beard, long curving horns, mad eyes, a powerful stench and a strong inclination to violence when harnessed between the shafts of my cart. Unless led, he tended to remain motionless or go sideways or backwards. Even when I led him the procedure degenerated into a sort of tug of war. Finally he would spring forward, knock me down and run over me with the cart.

Eventually we reached an understanding and travelled more or less amicably together—me in search of gold, Billy seeking forage and/or lady goats.

The scene of these early adventures was Golden Square, an outlying suburb of the goldmining town of Bendigo, in central Victoria. In those

pre-World War II days, fossicking was a profitable pastime. We lived in High Street, near the tram terminus and on rainy days you could find enough specks of gold in the flowing gutters of the unmade road to buy a licorice strap and an ounce of boiled lollies at the store opposite my grandparents' house. Or a brace of penny ice-creams at the lolly shop two doors away, opposite Rodda's Pub (built *circa* 1857).

Billy and I spent a fruitful year together, making regular and profitable expeditions out to the gold diggings around Specimen Hill. Here there were countless abandoned mine shafts among the hillocks of gleaming quartz (called 'mullock' heaps). Many of the shafts were uncovered and if you dropped a rock into some of them, you waited perhaps five seconds to hear the 'plonk' as the rock hit the water at the bottom. Water was scarce on the surface, however. I carried my own in a square petrol tin, plus gold-panning dish, tweezers and a small specimen bottle full of water. On good days, Billy and I would go home with enough gold to buy every licorice strap in the shop. While I was panning, I used to tether Billy among the bushes where he would browse or snooze contentedly unless he got a whiff of a lady goat wandering nearby. Then he put his tether, a long length of thick greenhide, to the test! Eventually he broke free while I was away panning in a nearby gully and either found happiness or fell into one of the open mine shafts. I never saw him again and had to pull the heavy cart several kilometres home to Golden Square. I gave up gold-panning expeditions after that.

Caleb Carter was the local representative of the Victoria Insurance Company. He insured farmhouses, sheds and fences against fire and storm damage, also haystacks and crops against rain damage (a pretty safe bet in usually dry-as-dust north central Victoria!). His beat was a big one, chiefly north of Bendigo to the Murray River, taking in such picturesquely named outposts as Wychitella, Boort, Minmindie, Quambatook, Bael Bael, Durham Ox, Kerang, Weeweerup, Gunbower, Echuca, Wharparilla, Rochester, Prairie, Tennyson and Goornong.

In those days, there wasn't a sealed road in the whole of northern Victoria (or anywhere else in rural Australia). Mostly the roads were earth, sand or sometimes gravel. They were poorly maintained and still used chiefly by horse-drawn vehicles. Motorised trucks and cars were few and far between. So were garages with refuelling 'bowsers' (tall, usually round devices with a glass fuel-measuring reservoir at the top, into which the petrol was hand-pumped from an underground tank and then gravity fed via a rubber hose into the waiting vehicle).

Grandfather Caleb was one of the elite of the district and the era: he not only had a motor car, but one of the finest and most desirable then made: a Buick coupé (*circa* 1933 or '34, I'm not sure). It was shiny black, with a three-seater all-leather bench in the driving compartment and a rear outside 'dicky' seat that accommodated two companionably or three passionately. Don't imagine this rear compartment was a luggage boot that served for passengers in an emergency. It was a proper leather-upholstered seat, with no storage space when closed. Luggage in those days was carried on the side running boards of vehicles, or strapped on the rear or roof—the concept of a covered boot was yet to come.

Anyway, Grandfather Caleb mightn't have owned the Porsche of his times (that was probably a Bugatti or somesuch) but it was certainly the Datsun 280Z of the period. During school holidays he took me on many of his working trips, introducing me not only to motoring, but quality motoring; plus camping—two loves destined to stay with me all my days. Sometimes we overnighted in a country pub or homestead, but often Grandfather just unrolled our swags beside the Buick and we slept under the stars. If it was our last night out before returning to Golden Square, we usually camped near a creek or swamp or paddock of stubble, so Caleb could shoot a few ducks or quail or hares or rabbits to take home for the kitchen (no Eskies in those days, just wet bracken fern or grass crammed into a damp chaff bag).

There were few other cars on the backblocks roads we travelled, and it was common to drive all day and never sight another vehicle that didn't have a horse in front of it. The lonelier byways were just graded earth or wheel tracks through sand.

The highways were only sporadically maintained and often deeply rutted by the iron wheels of horse-drawn wagons and drays. The best of them were heavily cambered to get rid of stormwater—not that it rained much in northern Victoria. The dray ruts were on the crown of the road, so cars avoided them by driving well down on the camber, which caused the vehicle to tilt considerably. Grandfather Caleb always drove on the right-hand side of the road, because he felt more comfortable leaning against the driver's door with his elbow crooked over the sill of the acutely angled Buick. This worried me a bit (I was a serious lad) and I was forever yelling out 'Another car's coming, Grandad!' though usually it was just a trick of the seemingly permanent mirage shimmering on the road ahead.

Sometimes I was right, but Caleb always took his time moving over to the left, leaving it to the last moment to avoid what I saw as an inevitable head-on collision. Quite often, it turned out the approaching vehicle was also on the wrong side of the road (another comfort-loving driver). No corrective action was taken and the two cars would pass for all the world as if the drivers were motoring in Europe or America! My youthful heart would be in my mouth, but looking back on it, the roads were often so wide as to be almost separate tracks and the other driver's intention so obvious, little risk was involved, particularly at the sort of speeds involved (probably only 30 or so km/h).

We met some interesting bush characters in our travels: sleeper cutters, eucalyptus oil distillers, Murray River paddleboat skippers, swaggies and other itinerants, as well as the stock clientele of graziers and pastoralists, most of whom were one-off individuals of some sort or another.

The bush didn't seem to breed conformity and I was wide-eyed and delighted with most of the contacts Grandfather Caleb made on his tours—fascination, I suppose, that led me into journalism and photography.

Bendigo city and environs had more than their share of colourful characters. They ranged from the sometimes eccentric mining millionaires who lived in stately, ornate homes amid landscaped gardens and fountains to the shanty-dwelling failed diggers who fossicked abandoned fields, doggedly searching for a lottery-sized nugget missed by earlier generations of miners. Somewhere in between was the still sizeable Chinese community, descendants of the thousands of 'Celestials' (as white miners dubbed them) who flocked to the Bendigo goldfields in the 1850s and '60s.

Grandfather Caleb regularly took me into the Chinese quarter to his favourite laundry to pick up his stiffly starched and ironed shirts, neatly pinned inside white paper parcels. Just before Empire Day (ask your parents!), we would visit Chinese shops specialising in firecrackers and come away with a huge brown paper bag full of skyrockets, bungers, Catherine wheels, Tom Thumbs and other pyrotechnic wares. Another occasion for firecrackers was the Easter parade, when the Chinese community turned out in force to carry their processional dragon 'Loong' through the streets of Bendigo, to the crash of cymbals, drums and the staccato crackle of an incredible variety of fireworks. They have done this yearly since the first parade in 1871, the old dragon that I knew being replaced in 1970 by 'Sun Loong' (new dragon).

Another ethnic experience was our regular Friday night shopping visit to the Favaloro brothers' soda fountain on Pall Mall, Bendigo's main drag. This was a magnificence of glass, mirrors, polished wood, marble tables, filigreed metalwork and hand-pumped ornately moulded silver soda fountains that gushed noisily fizzing soda-water into huge glasses containing a measure of your favourite fruit syrup. Sarsparilla was popular, but I preferred raspberry, mainly for the colour. Into this brew was plonked a large dollop of vanilla ice-cream, turning the liquid cloudy and ultra frothy—and lo! you had that unrivalled Italian-Victorian creation: the Spider! Later we would stroll down Pall Mall, licking ice-creams, to look at the floodlit Alexandra Fountain at Charing Cross. Ah, those were the days; black Buick coupé, billy cart, gold in the gutters, bush eucalyptus stills, nights under the stars on the Murray River banks, firerackers, Chinese dragons and Favaloro Spiders! Plus Wednesday afternoon matinees at the Lyric picture theatre and tram rides to Eaglehawk, Mum's home town.

Nostalgia breeds nostalgia. While mooning over those carefree childhood days in Bendigo, I found myself outside John Newell's Porsche emporium in Sydney. This brought another lump to my throat, inspired by anguish rather than nostalgia.

You see, I had sold the Kremer Porsche and later on 'Little Red', a 1976 model 911 Carrera I raced for a while, on the eve of the Oz dollar crash in 1987, and had the galling experience of seeing its value (and that of new Porsches) soar to a price plateau far beyond my financial reach. While pressing my nose against the window, the better to see the latest range of Master Newell's imports, I noticed someone gesticulating at me from within. At first I thought he wanted me to stop breathing on his nice clean window, but it turned out to be Dale Goodman, ace salesman and his employer's left-hand right-hand man, if the location of his office is anything to judge by.

'Ah, gudday Jeff, long time no see,' Dale began smoothly. 'What colour is it to be this time?'

'I'm not buying, just looking,' I admitted glumly. Then the Master himself sprang out of his office, all smiles and handshakes.

Jeff Carter in Germany. (Photo: Mare Carter)

At the Great Table after XJS-V12 Jaguar tour of Rutherglen wine area.

Phoning home from the Mazda RX7 Turbo at Eden, NSW. (Photo: Jennifer Maclean)

The 928S4 on Victoria's Great Ocean Road.

Camped with the Mazda RX7 Turbo, south of Eden, NSW.

The Kremer Porsche, then Australia's fastest road car, on the move in and around Foxground (5 secs 0–100 km/h; 11.2 secs 0–160 km/h).

Trophy corner on the mantle of the Great Fireplace at Foxground.

An interesting road near Grenoble, France.

Preparing for the Scandinavian tour in the 3-litre Carrera.

Camped not far from Hammerfest, the world's most northerly town.

The author's birthday on the Alto River, Norway, with cake decorated by Mare. (Photo: Mare Carter)

A high section of the road to Hammerfest—in summer!

The 3-litre Carrera with mountain ponies in Andorra, Spain.

Bottom left: Running the bulls during Easter celebrations in Paterna de Rivera, Spain.
Bottom right: Photographer Jacqueline Lampe, my fellow traveller to Kakadu and the Kimberleys.

Cameron Sinnamon running, shooting and surveying feral donkeys on Kuranjie station. Over three years, some 20 000 were culled. (Photos: Jacqueline Lampe)

Putting the four-wheel drive Subaru through its paces in the high country around the upper Murray River. (Photo: Jennifer Maclean)

A spot of bother while trying to climb the Pathfinder over a log.

Competitors in the 1988 banjo-picking championship at Tamworth, NSW.

Lolita and the 2.7-litre Carrera Porsche near Tumut, NSW.

Jennifer and the Range Rover near Dargo, on Victoria's high plains.

Camel-driver Jim Lowe, encountered during the Murray River journey.

Tourist paddlewheeler on the Murray, upstream from Morgan.

Donald Campbell's Bluebird on Lake Eyre.

Re-living childhood memories in Bendigo with a 1988 model Porsche Carrera loaned by John Newell. (Photo: Jennifer Maclean)

The author at the Great Table, playing with his model Porsche.

Author, 911 Club Sport and baguette in rural France.

Van browsing in a ceramics shop in Capileira,
in the Alpajar district of Granada, Spain.

Van conducting Rosinante in Spain.

View of Capileira,
Granada.

Titling at windmills in La Mancha. (Photos: Van Carter.)

Bull-baiting near the Manchegan town of El Toboso, where Don Quixote encountered the 'princess' Dulcinea.

Porsche in pine forest, near Wiesbaden.

Jeff and his son Van inside the Hotel Sonne.

Outside the Hotel Sonne in the town of Offenburg, West Germany.

Hermann Richter at home.

Porsche outside Hermann's hideaway.

Porsche car museum, Zuffenhausen, Stuttgart.

'What are you doing with yourself these days?' he enquired warmly.

'Writing a few pieces for *Wheels* and a little bit of this and that,' I countered. 'One of the stories I had in mind was a nostalgic yarn about Bendigo, the town I come from . . .'

The Master and Dale exchanged glances. 'We don't normally loan cars,' Master John began. 'But you can borrow our demonstrator if you like,' Dale completed the sentence. 'It's the latest 911 Carrera, your favourite model, runs on unleaded petrol and costs around $130 000. We'd be interested in your comments.' An offer not easily refused, but I retained my cool and said 'What colour is it?'

'Black', answered Dale.

'You don't have a nice white or silver or red one?' I enquired further.

'The car is black,' Master Newell countered firmly.

'You're not related to Henry Ford?' I asked.

That rekindled his smile and he said cheerfully, 'Jeffrey, just take the car and try not to put any marks on it.'

So it came to pass I found myself whizzing down memory lane one March Friday afternoon in a 3.2-litre powered fantasy in gleaming black, putting out 231 horses despite the catalytic converter and capable of 240 or so km/h given the right circumstances. There were all sorts of gadgets to play with, some optional extras, including electric sunroof, Piranha anti-theft system, a magnificent Porsche-designed quadrophonic sound system, electrically adjusted driver's seat, powered windows and rear vision mirrors, integral air-conditioning, central locking system, high-speed windscreen washer jets blasting out silicone removing solution, etc., etc. Plus, most important, a Whistler radar detector.

This gave me a Friday afternoon safe against the dreaded on-coming mobile squad, who set the Whistler blipping intermittently at least two kilometres before I sighted them. This was in the notorious Goulburn-Yass area, where the smarter police leave their gear off until they sight a likely target, such as a black Porsche. In which case you are gone, with or without detector, unless you recognise them first and get immediately and heavily on the anchors. On Saturday morning, the Whistler saved me three times, twice in NSW against on-coming mobiles and once in Victoria near Rutherglen against a concealed car parked in a ditch among trees on the right-hand side of the road, facing toward me. Luckily a dead straight road and at least two kilometres warning.

On my way to Echuca, I detoured from the Murray Valley Highway via Barmah, a town I used to visit regularly in the old days with Eric Worrell, when he was catching tiger snakes for the serum laboratories. (Eric caught the snakes and I took the photos.) A bunch of local car lovers came out of the pub to admire the Porsche and challenge me to bush-bashing speed trials in the nearby Barmah Forest. With Messrs Newell and Goodman's best interests at heart, I declined—though I should mention that Porsche 911s are quite good bush cars, provided you don't care about stone chips and scratches.

At Echuca, once Australia's second busiest port after Sydney, I found things very different from Grandfather Caleb's day. I suppose the wool bales from pastoral properties on both sides of the Murray still go via rail through Echuca bound for Melbourne, plus other farm products including redgum and other timber. But Echuca today looks more like Disneyland than a lusty, dusty inland river port. Every second building is a museum, wax-works, arts and crafts centre, refurbished coach-house, restaurant, tea-room, gallery, souvenir shop, hotel or motel. They have even tizzied-up a defunct brothel as an attraction for the hordes of local and overseas tourists who throng the streets (most on foot, but many riding dual 'fun' cycles or various horse-drawn vehicles). The surviving paddlesteamers carry only one cargo: tourists. It was all pretty well done, I suppose, but I lingered only an hour for snapshots, then headed off in search of some more authentic reminders of how things used to be, back where I come from.

That evening, I happened into a small pub on the Murray Valley Highway in search of a bottle of dry white wine and directions to a quiet camping place on the nearby river. The bartender had never heard of dry white wine in bottles and was offering me a cardboard carton of moselle when the publican, drinking with mates on my side of the bar, intervened.

'Wouldn't get asked for anything like that around here in months,' he told me, digging into the back of a cabinet and triumphantly offering me his entire stock of the product I sought: a bottle of Queen Elizabeth riesling. I accepted it gratefully, plus his complicated directions to a quiet little beach on the Murray.

This turned out to be the venue for a water skiing convention with literally hundreds of tents up and downstream. Eventually I found relative seclusion, but it was hardly the sort of camping I recalled from Grandfather Caleb's day. Next morning I pushed on through the sleepy little town of Gunbower, which didn't seem to have changed much, then on via Kow Swamp (where I angled briefly for redfin and bream) and Cohuna to Kerang, which bills itself as 'The Duck Shooting Capital'. Explorer Major Thomas Mitchell discovered and named the area in 1836 while charting the course of the Loddon River. Nearby are the famous Reedy Lake ibis rookeries and assorted swamps that provide breeding grounds for all manner of wildfowl.

The angry wasps'-nest buzz of the Carrera's motor put some magnificent flocks of birds into the sky and I thought I had some great shots—until I found there was no film in the camera.

That was one thing I didn't care for about Master Newell's demonstrator 911: the sound of the motor. My two previous cars, the famous 2.8-litre Kremer and 'Little Red', the 2.7 Carrera, wore rally exhaust systems which produced a very satisfying roar. And black isn't the ideal colour for photos, either, because every splattered insect shows up as a stark blemish. Another little quibble might be the lack of a rear spoiler on such a fast car.

Putting my trust in the Whistler detector and hoping the Victorian police road patrols weren't too active on Sunday morning, I gave the Carrera its head while making south toward Bendigo. Around 200 km/h the car exhibited the typical non-spoilered Porsche 'wanders' in a slight side wind. Approaching 240 km/h, which I suspect is its maximum speed, a less seasoned Porsche pilot might become decidedly nervous. The tail gets light, allowing the rear end to wander slightly, requiring tiny steering corrections that can worry an imaginative driver and render hitchhikers mildly hysterical. (My chance passenger at the time was a Ms Jenny Maclean, who was later to accompany me on several safaris and take some of the photos in this book.)

Bendigo today is a fine, sprawling city, with most of its architectural wonders, public and private, carefully preserved. Also its famous gardens, fountains, monuments and historic pottery works. But since the last mine closed in 1954, it has been forced to go the way of Echuca and adapt to tourism. There's nothing wrong with this and they've done it very well, but I found my boyhood landmarks mostly blown away by the winds of change. Golden Square is all paved—no chance to fossick for gold specks in the gutters now. Specimen Hill is surrounded by neat kerbed and guttered suburbs. The store where I bought my licorice straps and boiled lollies is gone. Rodda's Pub survives, repainted and modernised. The family home, so grand when I was young, seems small and down-at-heel, with a *bus* shelter right outside it. The trams no longer come to Golden Square, although a couple ply around the city centre as tourist attractions.

Favaloro's soda fountain is gone, the Lyric picture theatre is closed and now it is an ice-cream parlor and take-away. Only a few remnants of Chinatown remain, including a joss-house, plus a shed housing Sun Loong and the head of old Loong, the temple guardian lions, drums, cymbals and other colourful ceremonial items. The Chinese dragon is still a feature of Bendigo's annual Easter procession. One mine, the Deborah, survives as a tourist attraction. Landmarks like the majestic town hall, the ornate, almost rococo Shamrock Hotel, the Gothic Sacred Heart cathedral, the Victorian mansions and public buildings, the gardens, ferneries, statues, fountains and old stores and pubs with their decorative cast-iron balconies are all still there and well maintained.

But now they seem lost in a plethora of new architecture and a suburban sprawl of neat brick houses, svelte motels and jouncy take-aways. The magic places of yesteryear have been overshadowed by progress and made self-consciously anachronistic.

Of course, my chances of enjoying a sequestered ramble down memory lane weren't helped by arriving in Bendigo on the Sunday of Victoria's Labour Day weekend! That soured my view a little. Amongst others, there were *three thousand* visiting firefighters in town for their annual convention. Needless to say, there was absolutely no accommodation even as far afield as Ballarat and Echuca! Eventually the helpful manager of the Gateway Motel at Eaglehawk did some phoning around on my behalf and found me a room in Boort, one hundred kilometres north-west of the city of my youth.

Nice little town, Boort, with a lake and a rather good take-away food bar. No restaurant, except in the motel—but it's closed on Sundays. Never mind, the manager passed on to me a few interesting snippets of local history. Boort is Aboriginal for 'smoke on the hill', which was the first sight the original inhabitants had of the new owners. The early white settlers experienced hard times during drought years. Once the lake dried up, homestead tanks ran dry and residents were reduced to drinking the water from their leech bottles. Leech bottles? Yes, every household had one, usually a screw-topped glass jar full of water and wriggling leeches, which were put on infected wounds. Presumably they strained the water before drinking it.

The closest I got to the land of my early childhood was near Eaglehawk, where my dear old Mum was raised. At Sandhurst, there is a recreated town of original nineteenth-century buildings and assorted memorabilia, including a working eucalyptus distillery and a country garage like the ones where Grandfather Caleb used to fill up with Plume or Golden Fleece petrol. However, I learned one thing during my 2400-kilometre high speed journey down Memory Lane; you can't go back, even in the latest model Porsche 911 Carrera. Nice car though, with almost the same magic as that old black Buick.

12 Turbo to Eden

It was night on the Princes Highway, just south of Moruya. I had been on the road a few hours, bound from Sydney to Eden on the far south coast of NSW. The Maxda RX7 Turbo I was driving for the first time was to my way of thinking a lively little handful, but I was getting the hang of it and enjoying myself greatly.

The mobile police around Bateman's Bay are notoriously diligent, so I travelled with uncharacteristic restraint. Once south of Moruya, I grew less cautious. I fell in behind a green Ford Cortina for several kilometres, travelling a sedate 80 km/h along a section of winding road. Perhaps a kilometre behind me, a set of headlights popped occasionally into view, getting no closer. When it was safe to do so, I overtook the Cortina and watched its headlights dwindle rapidly away to nothing in my rear vision mirror. A few minutes later, with no sign of any following headlights, I thought to give the RX7 its head. Nothing outlandish, mind you—but there was no chance the Cortina would ever see me again.

Some half dozen kilometres before Bodalla, I caught a brief glimpse of distant following headlights in the mirror. No way it was the Cortina. I slowed immediately to 100 km/h. Rule one of fast night travel: when suddenly you see following lights where there were none before, get legal in the shortest possible time. After two or three kilometres the lights approached within a few hundred metres and stayed there. We proceeded thus in tandem for the final kilometres into Bodalla. A 60 km/h sign came up and as I slowed, the dreaded blue flashing lights came on behind me. I pulled over, just short of the 60 km/h sign.

The police patrol car halted close behind me. I turned off the motor and headlights, flicked on the cabin light, lowered my window and waited. A uniformed patrolman strolled up and said affably: 'Blowing the cobwebs out of it, were you, sir?'

'I don't quite follow you...' I began.

'You're not going to stand there and tell me you haven't been exceeding the speed limit,' the patrolman cut in sharply.

'I don't believe so. . .'

'Look driver, when you overtook the green Cortina, you just disappeared. We've had to drive at speeds up to 180 kilometres per hour to catch up with you. So don't just stand there and tell me you haven't been exceeding the speed limit.'

'*Tell him you're sitting, not standing,*' hissed Ms Maclean, but I thought better of it.

'Your licence, please sir.'

And so on. He conferred with his fellow officer, who had strolled up to look at the Mazda after making a computer rego check, because patrolman number one came forth with: 'Not your car, sir?'

'No, it belongs to the Mazda company.'

'Testing it for speed, are you sir?'

'No, no. Just taking it down to Eden for some publicity shots.'

The patrolman slapped my licence gently against his palm. 'I'm giving you back your licence, sir. Treasure it and remember it can so easily be taken away from you.' He turned and strolled back to the patrol car and I drove southward past the famous cheese factory and through Bodalla. At sixty kilometres per hour.

What led to this interesting encounter? I was making another of my trips down Memory Lane for *Wheels* magazine, revisiting some of my stamping grounds of yesteryear in today's newbreed vehicles. Why Eden?

When I finally did a permanent bunk from Melbourne, World War II had been over fourteen months and I was eighteen years old. With my swag slung across my back, I began hitchhiking along the Princes Highway, bound for Queensland. My swag, an ex-army duffle bag, was rather ungainly, because amongst my other things it contained a portable typewriter, no small item in those days.

Petrol rationing was still in force and there was little traffic on country roads. Progress via thumb was slow, most lifts being only ten to thirty kilometres, with often an hour or more in between. It took me several days to reach the seaside town of Lakes Entrance, where the bitumen ended. I had never been so far from home before, even with Grandfather Caleb. The enormity of what I had done came home to me as I sat on the sand amid the roar of the surf, staring across the turbulent entrance to Lake King down the hazy, spumed infinity of Ninety Mile Beach. The previous nights I had spent under bridges and inside hollow logs and for a while I considered dossing down among the sand dunes. But the weather looked threatening, so I walked back into Lakes Entrance and discovered Whiter's camping park.

Here was luxury undreamed of, including cold showers, pit toilets and little roofed eating shelters with sturdy plank tables that served the likes of me as more or less dry beds during the memorably long, wet night that followed. Next morning, under clearing skies, I observed a vision splendid: a most fetching young female motorcyclist, camped alone nearby. In those days, motorcyclists were not common and female riders were virtually unheard of. I was intrigued, but of course much too shy to make any approach.

Later that day, somewhere near Orbost, I sat disconsolately on my damp swag beside the muddy highway. It had been two hours since the last passing vehicle, going in the wrong direction, of course. The only bright spot on the horizon was a widening patch of blue to the northeast, where I was headed. Bellbirds chimed intermittently in the dripping eucalypt forest. Otherwise there was leaden silence.

Eventually I detected a buzz, growing louder. Then a moving object appeared in the distance, meandering across the road as it approached, dodging pools of water. It was the lady of the motorcycle. Going my way. I wasn't game to try thumbing her down but managed a hesitant, friendly wave, expecting her to speed past. Instead she pulled in and said cheerfully 'Hop on!'—I stood dumbfounded, unable to believe my good luck. The lady lifted her goggles and parked them on her soft leather helmet, revealing almond-shaped deepest blue eyes. 'Fere are you goink?' she asked in what I later discovered was a Scandinavian accent.

'To Queensland,' I mumbled, hugging my swag to make it look small.

'So am I,' the lady responded, reaching back with each booted leg in turn to kick down the pillion rider's two footrests. 'Hop on!' It was a small bike, unsuitable for a passenger my size, but it would have been uncouth to refuse the invitation.

After various adventures lasting some weeks, we fetched up at the fishing port of Eden on Twofold Bay. To a young writer hoping to emulate Ernest Hemingway, here was a lusty, frontier scene of rich characters and epic potential almost beyond belief. Wild men and small ships risking the ocean's darkest moods in search of elusive harvests of fish and sharks. There were trawlers, large and small, scavenging the sea floor with purse-seine nets; longline boats fishing thousands of hooks at a time for snapper and sharks; tiny barracouta boats hand-fishing short lines with barbless hooks and red cloth lures in the frenzied shoals of sharp-toothed, dangerous 'couta; salmon and mullet fishermen, rowing their nets in an arc out from beaches and hauling their catch into the shallows, as the fishermen of the Mediterranean had done for more than two thousand years before them. Here was opportunity beyond my wildest dreams. I had to stay in Eden and write about it. Besides, I was nearly broke.

We camped for a while in Quarantine Bay until a herd of goats ate most of our belongings and chewed holes in our newly purchased army disposals two-person tent. So we retreated a kilometre south to Fourter's Beach on Shadrack Creek, an absolute paradise of a spot to this day— but mosquitoes drove us out.

Eventually we fetched up in the backyard of the Hotel Eden (now the Great Southern Inn), under the patronage of a Canadian expatriate, one 'Spider' McCarthy, a professional card player, who ran a small game nightly in his flat, close by the disused horse stables. Jobs on the fishing boats were hard to get, but a succession of friendly skippers allowed me to voyage with them, in order to gather material for the stories I was writing. Finally I got a job on a trawler and was lucky enough to be aboard when the fish were really plentiful. (The crew weren't paid a wage, just a percentage of the value of the catch.)

That early brush with Eden helped establish me as a writer and I owe the place a debt of gratitude. Which is no doubt why I've returned there so many times. In the mid 1950s I made a score of visits, gathering material for a series of illustrated articles under the not very original title 'East of Eden'. These eventually appeared in book form.

I began coming back again in the mid 1980s at the wheel of my red 2.7 litre 911 Porsche Carrera. Driven by nostalgia and a pressing yen to recapture the magic of my youth, I was accompanied by a young person, then aged nineteen, ironically named Lolita. Alas, as I had found on my journey to Bendigo, scene of my early childhood, you can't go back. All I found was a handful of ashes.

When I mentioned the Eden story idea to *Wheels* editor Robinson, he suggested I give Porsches a rest for a while and try the Japanese alternative. 'Let's face it,' he said. 'Few of our readers can afford Porsches and although the RX7 Turbo isn't cheap, at least it's not completely over the horizon.' I had to admit he had a point—even at $56 000 the Mazda was only half the price of a Porsche 944 Turbo.

When I reported to Mazda headquarters, a lady disconcertingly named George showed me what at first I thought must be the wrong car. 'No, no,' I said. 'I'm not here to pick up a 944 Porsche, it's supposed to be . . .'

'A Mazda RX7 Turbo,' Ms George put in cheerfully. 'And it is!'

I took a second look and of course she was right, but during my subsequent travels in the RX7, a lot of people made the same mistake. So Mazda are on the right track, style-wise. You can even kick the front and rear body panels and they turn out to be resilient plastic, just like on the 928 and 944 Porsches. There the comparison must end, because although I have owned and driven Porsches for twenty-five years, they have always been 911s.

I had picked up the Mazda RX7 Turbo at Mazda headquarters at Caringbah, in Sydney, not far from my old Mum's place at Grays Point, so I called in for her opinion of the car, before setting out on my jaunt to Eden.

Her first reaction was: 'Oh, dear, you haven't bought another one of those Porsches? What are the children going to do for shoes this winter?'

'It's not a Porsche and all the children have grown up and left home,' I explained. 'It's a Mazda and only costs half as much as a Porsche.' That impressed her. 'And I haven't bought it. It's just on loan.' Now she was downright pleased, but refused to get in, on the grounds that she didn't think she would be able to get out, having regard for previous experiences in my various Porsches.

She had a point: the Mazda RX7 Turbo is really a young person's car (if there are any young persons who can meet the price tag). It cries out for the sort of people you see in Coca Cola and similar television commercials. Because although at first glance it looks like a Porsche, it somehow lacks that marque's elegance, subtlety and maturity of design. You expect anyone driving a Porsche to have a few grey hairs, because it is so obviously a car designed for the rich—and you can't usually get rich before forty. Whereas the RX7 is a car for the video-clip generation, unmistakably a spunky conveyance for upwardly mobile leadfoots.

When it came time to pack my gear into the RX7 ready for my trip to Eden, I was delighted with the comparatively enormous capacity of its rear luggage compartment, once the backs of the tiny rear seats had been folded flat. Access was a breeze, via the huge lift-up rear window, activated by key or a lever in the cabin.

In went my swag, tent, sleeping bag, various boxes of cooking utensils and food, plastic five-litre water bottle, assorted overnight bags, camera case, tripod, Esky, spare boots and wet-weather gear—all with room to spare and very little on top of anything else. (There's nothing so frustrating to a photographer as having to dig under other gear every time you want to take a picture.)

Once in the driver's seat, which was snug but spartan and adjustable only fore and aft and for rake, the cabin seemed crowded at first. Rather like a wrap-around space module, with the roof very close, a large, almost intrusive steering wheel, and a bulky centre console, full of gadgetry and sprouting a stubby gear shift. Facia instrumentation was good, though, no matter where you placed the adjustable steering wheel. I sat and played with the gadgetry for a while, cruise control, air-conditioner, etc., while raising and lowering both windows via buttons in the armrest of the driver's door, adjusting the left- and right-hand rear vision mirrors with a dinky device in the centre console, switching suspension damper system from normal to sport via adjacent buttons, operating the electric sunroof by pressing buttons in the ceiling console, raising and lowering headlights with a knob on the steering column. This is a rather disquieting experience, the lamp covers being huge ugly rectangular objects that make you think for a moment you are driving a front-end loader rather than a sports car. (They turned out to be distracting at night, making the judging of corner apexes difficult.)

Lifting the front bonnet of the RX7 Turbo can also give cause for alarm. It may be a triumph of engineering, but the turbocharged twin-rotor Wankel fuel-injected engine with air-to-air intercooler and goodness knows what else, producing 133 kilowatts at 6500 rpm, is a pretty tight fit under its 'aggressive' air-scooped lid. I vowed that if ever the car stopped or failed to start, I would phone Mazda and/or the NRMA without so much as touching the bonnet release knob, located under the fascia near the driver's right knee.

My first hours at the wheel produced mixed reactions, beginning with disappointment, ranging through consternation to exhilaration. In roughly that order. My initial experience of turning sharp low-speed corners in the RX7 produced a degree of alarm. This was going down through the S bends to Mum's place at Grays Point. Travelling faster than was prudent, I gave the wheel a yank a bit before the first apex, right foot still planted, expecting to produce some understeer—and instead the bloody thing turned straight in toward the curb! Talk about low-speed responsive steering! I lifted off abruptly and was further consternated by the ensuing lurch (transmission snatch, I think they call it) which nearly caused a problem. Thank goodness no one was watching. Maybe I was rattled by the rev-warning buzzer, which at that early stage was just an inexplicable noise to me, because as usual I had not read the driver's handbook. Ah yes, the Mazda RX7 Turbo talks to you quite a bit, via a penetrating meep-meep if you get out and shut the door with the exterior lights still on.

A few hours later, when I was driving on my home territory between Kiama and Ulladulla, exhilaration finally came my way as I got the hang of RX7 piloting. It was dark then but I know the road well. For a while I had been telling my voice recorder I thought the Mazda rather skittish in the handling department, flitting all over the road like a water-beetle, particularly on lumpy bitumen. But the fault turned out to be mostly mine, not the car's. The power steering is amazingly light, almost unduly responsive (in my opinion) and without any road feel. So I was forever nervously twitching the wheel, just to make sure I was still in touch with the bitumen. Result: a somewhat erratic and worrisome progression until I became confident the car was on and not floating above the road.

Once you get the hang of it, the Mazda RX7 Turbo is a very fast, exhilarating, safe, fun car to drive. If you so desire, you can get it slipping and sliding every which way, always under control, imagining yourself on the race track, the crowd applauding your skill, the timekeepers scarcely able to believe their stop-watches. Ah, there's the rub, as Hamlet once bemoaned. Because all this drama can be induced at only moderately fast speeds. A glance at the RX7's speedo while cornering is often disappointing. You feel you are going like hell, on the limit, drifting, surely at supercar speed. But you are not. You may be progressing faster than most other vehicles on the road, certainly other Japanese sport cars. But you are no challenge to the supercars of Europe, which can corner much faster than you before they even begin to under- or over-steer or drift or whatever. Which is fair enough—the cheapest of them cost over twice the price of the RX7 Turbo.

After my lucky escape from the Moruya police, we overnighted at Narooma, stocking up in the morning with my favourite shellfish at Vicki's Oyster Supply down near the marina on Riverside Drive. I first met Vicki over twenty years ago, when she was among the top competitive NSW female surfboard riders and I was writing and illustrating a book on east coast surfing. We renewed our acquaintance when I discovered she had turned her talents to oyster farming. Vicki thought I had bought another Porsche when she sighted the RX7 Turbo, which she pronounced 'stunning'.

On to Mystery Bay, where the Mazda proved it is not a bad bush car by getting me along the rough track to Corruna Point, one of my favourite hideaways. For a late breakfast of bread and butter and shellfish, which I opened with my trusty oyster knife beside a rock pool above the tiny secluded beach. Then to the National Trust protected town of Central Tilba, well worth a few hours of anyone's time, for a fill of unleaded fuel, Devonshire tea and a photo session of the RX7 being admired by customers of the Dromedary Hotel. The countryside around Central Tilba, Tilba Tilba and south beyond Couria Creek is about as picturesque as it comes. Any photographer, painter or admirer of rural quaint would find it 'worth a journey' in Michelin Guide parlance.

I detoured to Bermagui, once the stamping ground of world-renowned big-game fisherman and author, Zane Grey—and me, somewhat later, when I was producing seafaring yarns for assorted illustrated Australian magazines. Like Bendigo, Bermagui has grown since I was last there, into a sort of Holidayville, but retains its fishing-port core, replete with waterfront market and motley fleet of commercial and private craft tied up at the wharf or anchored nearby.

The run down to Eden from Bega was very fast, over an excellent section of the Princes Highway with plenty of passing lanes, some long straights and a few sets of tight bends which the RX7 disposed of most precisely. We camped just south of the town, probably for the last time, at idyllic Fourter's Beach on Shadrock Creek. The new owner had a variety of earthmoving machines at work, preparing the way for a million dollar 'face-lift', encompassing a marina, powered and sewered van sites,

Porsche, tent and Lolita camped near Eden, NSW.

swimming pool, everything hot and cold, a sea wall with footbaths and recreation lawns, etc. Marvellous for jetset holiday-makers no doubt. But I preferred the beach as it was and don't think I'll be back. Too many new amenities and old memories to cope with.

In town I looked up old friends, including Jack Warren, brother of Billy, now dead, with whom I fished for salmon many years ago and whose exploits were recorded in one of my books on the NSW coast. Barracouta are almost unknown these days, Jack told me, plus a number of other once common species. 'Time was you could walk across the Bay on the backs of the salmon,' Jack recalled. 'They'd net so many, the price would drop and they weren't worth icing down and sending to market...' Perhaps the profligacy of those days spawned today's reduced fish numbers, I suggested. Jack didn't think so. And so we yarned about 'the good old days' and how things aren't the same any more.

Down at the waterfront, things did seem much the same, except now there are two wharves and some of the boats are bigger and of space age design. But the fish were still being swung ashore in (plastic) baskets and the yarns and badinage I overheard took me back to the 1950s. The town had changed and grown, particularly since the coming of the Japanese woodchip mill, a contentious development. Now there are supermarkets and boutiques in the main street, the Hotel Eden has an up-market name, and there is a defunct skating rink near where the stables used to be. Quarantine Bay no longer has goats, but modern holiday cabins, boat launching ramps and a weigh-in station for amateur big-game fishermen. Ben Boyd's old Seahorse Inn has been restored into a modern holiday accommodation resort. There is a good bitumen road to the woodchip mill (guided tours each Thursday) and nearby Boyd's lighthouse tower, built of Sydney sandstone in 1846, never quite finished and never lit.

Boyd was an irascible adventurer and one of our most colourful historical characters, and visitors to Eden should ask for literature about him at the local information centre. Don't fail to visit the Killer Whale Museum, because the history of Eden's whaling industry is a unique, almost unbelievable story that happens to be true. Although Eden is sited in a most idyllic location, it is named after an early Secretary for the Colonies.

To sum up my Mazda RX7 Turbo experience—I liked it. Point to point, the RX7 is not a great deal slower than the European supercars. Which means it is about the only sports car to consider unless you are filthy rich. Mind you, I don't know anything about its reliability or longevity, or cost to maintain once things begin to go wrong or wear out. But I suppose you could just go out and buy another one and still have spent less than the price of the cheapest Porsche.

13 Home on the range

What did the 1987 Range Rover Highline have in common with a 308 GTB Ferrari? No glovebox. There the comparison must end, though the RR's aluminium V8 did produce a satisfying growl at maximum revs. But I much preferred the Ferrari's singular wail. On the other hand, the RR was the final winner in the glovebox test, because it had a sizeable lidded compartment on the transmission hump.

My return to Range Rover took place during a 1987 safari to Victoria's wildest mountain country, where my father used to take me on trout fishing and deer hunting trips during World War II. My father's name was Percy, but I (and later my kids) called him Pop. He lived for his fishing and hunting, sustained in his job as production engineer in a wartime factory by the prospect of regular hunting and fishing expeditions. For weeks before each trip, he would spend every night preparing his fishing tackle, guns and rifles, regaling me with yarns about giant trout, big-horned deer and beagle packs. Real Hemingway-style 'Up in Michigan' stuff. I was just into my teens and as girls were *verboten* in those days, I readily succumbed to the substitute lure of rod and gun.

It was 1944. Wartime petrol rationing made it difficult to get away any distance from Melbourne, but luckily Pop's factory was supplying equipment to the Yanks and they had plenty of petrol. Plenty of everything in fact: grog, ammunition, cigarettes, silk stockings...and most the amazing vehicles, called Jeeps. These were something entirely new on the local scene and from our cargo-cult viewpoint, their ability to climb around in the toughest country was miraculous. When the first Chev Blitz wagons arrived, we gaped like Neanderthal Man confronted with Concorde.

Pop was delighted with the Yanks, because they could take him where he wanted to go—and the Yanks were delighted with Pop, because they needed a guide to take them into our huntin' and fishin' country. Pop had done it all before, the hard way, in late twenties and early thirties Chevs, Fords, Whippets and 'bull-nose' Morrises. Now he was in his element as expert local guide, in charge of a convoy of Jeeps and sometimes a Chev Blitz wagon. He knew property owners on both sides of the Dividing Range and was always welcome, because he was one of the Old School and always did everything right. Meaning he always asked permission to enter a property, always left gates as he found them, never littered, never did anything stupid with fires, never cut fences or caused any form of damage, always presented himself to the homestead to say farewell and offer the landowner a share of his fish, rabbits, ducks, quail, hares or deer meat.

One of his favourite venues was centred on what is now Eildon Weir. We used to go via Healesville, Buxton and Taggerty, cross the Rubicon River to Thornton and then make our way by various bush tracks to fish the Delatite, the Big River, the Howqua or the Goulburn near Jamieson. It was big, steep, virgin country that tested even the Jeeps. After storms, fallen trees blocked the tracks and had to be chopped out of the way (no chainsaws in those days). To my young eyes it was a wilderness without parallel: rushing streams below soaring mountains clad with tall eucalypt forests, with small clearings here and there, usually around a tiny split-log cabin or corrugated iron hut, with smoke rising from the frogmouth fireplace.

Our chief quarry in the Eildon country were rainbow and brown trout, which Pop and his mates pursued relentlessly with spinners, flies or bait, depending on season and conditions. By way of diversion, or when supplies were low, Pop would organise a hare drive. Armed with twelve-gauge shotguns, the party walked in line about fifty metres apart across tussocky grazing land, blasting down the luckless hares as they bolted up from cover and ran ahead of the line. If foxes were in evidence, Pop would take me, a whistle and rifle up on to a high ridge or clearing. There we would sit with our backs against a tree or log while Pop blew his homemade tin whistle, imitating the plaintive squeal of a rabbit caught in a trap. Eventually a fox would come trotting confidently up the slope until it fell with a bullet in its head.

Occasionally we stalked deer in the forests on the upper Howqua and Jamieson Rivers, but without dogs, these forays were mostly unproductive. I was glad, because although I enjoyed the excitement of sneaking through the trees and undergrowth, I did not relish the spectacle of large animals dying.

In the Dargo area, which we reached via the town of Sale in the Gippsland district, it was a different story. Pop knew a number of graziers in the area who owned packs of beagle hounds. Half a dozen or more dogs, and their handlers, would be transported in a blitz wagon or a

trailer to a likely starting point in the dense forests out from the outpost town (a store, pub, sawmill and perhaps a dozen houses, as I recall). Then Pop, the strategist, would work out his Plan of Campaign.

When this had been fully discussed over mud maps, Pop and another Jeep pilot would take the shooters along forest trails, dropping them off at intervals along high ridges. Later the beagles were released and when they picked up the scent of a deer, they set the forests echoing eerily with their baying. As the dogs got closer to their quarry, the mournful baying changed to an excited yelping. The hope of the hunters was that as the deer doubled back and forth along the gullies and slopes trying to elude the dogs, it would come within sight and range. Sometimes this happened. Sometimes it didn't—and occasionally the marksman only wounded the deer. This usually meant a long trek, following up the dogs, hysterically noisy at the dragging heels of their maimed quarry. Pop's rule was that any wounded animal had to be followed up and killed, no matter how long it took. It was high adventure for young Carter, but after I had seen one or two deer killed, I was always on the side of the hunted, not the hunters. To this day, I loathe the sound of a pack of baying hounds.

The author as conservationist.

With all this in mind, I suggested Victoria's high country when the editor of *Wheels* magazine asked me to have a drive of the latest Range Rover. I set off from Sydney one Friday arvo in June.

As I sped effortlessly and luxuriously down the Hume Highway toward Victoria, it was immediately obvious that the 1987 Range Rover Highline was a much nicer conveyance than 'Big Red' *circa* 1975. It was rather like travelling first class on an international jumbo jet, surrounded on all sides by luxury: warm air, soft music, subdued lighting, lots of buttons and knobs to press, pull or slide, all experienced with little sense of motion, as in an aircraft. I half expected a steward to arrive with a tray of drinks. The velour lined seats, adjustable every which way, are truly luxurious, with drop-down central arm rests (also adjustable) and a full tilt-chair mechanism that is difficult to describe but delightful to experience. There is deep pile carpet under-foot, easily removed to reveal rubber matting for muddy days. The door sills are walnut capped with electric windows (the fastest I've encountered) and, wonder of wonders, when you open the doors, 'puddle lamps' concealed in the lower sill come on, so that at night you can avoid stepping into water, mud or a lurking cow pat!

After a Vietnamese meal in Yass I reached Albury in time to learn from the late television news that another arrival was bad weather, in the form of rain. Further south, where I was bound, it was snowing. Maybe I would get lucky, I brooded as I began my nightly skirmish with sleep. At Benalla next morning, my luck was out. Drizzling rain from leaden skies, with cheerful radio news-readers telling me of sleet and snow along the Dividing Range from Eildon to the Dargo High Plains. Lacking the imagination to change my plans, I pressed on.

To Mansfield, via the Midland Highway, then more excellent bitumen through steadily rougher country to the delightful mountain town of Jamieson, crossing the Delatite and Howqua Rivers on the way. The RR fairly sailed along through the steady drizzle, happy as Larry, devouring the increasingly twisty wet bitumen sure-footedly. Yes, the cabin still seems to lean gently when cornering, but apprehension gives way to confidence when it becomes obvious the four driven wheels aren't going to budge off line until you do something really adventurous.

At the Howqua Bridge crossing, a gravel road beckoned me upstream. After half a dozen kilometres, it began to deteriorate and twist and wind through the trees, following the course of the river. Ah, here was a taste of the old days. Then low and behold, a fine homestead behind an imposing gate, with a sign announcing 'Howqua Dale Gourmet Retreat—entry by prior booking only'. Not at all like the old days! They accommodate twelve guests only, on a full board basis, for a minimum of two days, and are very proud of the high-class meals and wine served in the dining room.

Up river another dozen kilometres, over a tortuous, single lane track, very wet and muddy, to Fry's Crossing, where I had several times camped and fished with Pop. It was a comparatively slow but effortless trip for the RR and despite several deep gutters and mud-bogs, I think a cup of tea sitting in its saucer would have survived on the lid of the transmission hump glovebox. There were three groups of campers near Fry's, all making the best of the wet conditions around large fires, assisted by warming beverages, mostly bottled.

At Jamieson, darkness overtook me and I was obliged to camp ignominiously in a public park a few kilometres out of town toward Kevington. It was raining heavily and I was glad of a shelter shed where I could brood on my misfortunes. While thus engaged, I recalled sighting a cosy pub back in Jamieson—and had there not been a sign in a side street saying 'Restaurant'? Always the investigative journalist, I drove back to Jamieson. The pub was quite large, but made cosy by a huge roaring log fire beneath a mantle bedecked with dog traps and other indigenous machinery and memorabilia associated with hunting, fishing, goldmining and grazing. Stuffed deer heads stared glassily from the walls at drinkers, diners and pool players.

Eventually I stumbled out into the sheeting rain and splashed my way a hundred metres to the restaurant, located in an English-cottage style building under some large oak trees. Once inside, I knew my luck had changed, for I had discovered a proper restaurant: 'Watson's of Jamieson', presided over by engaging, inimitable Milton Watson. My advice is: if you're ever in Jamieson, don't miss a meal at Watson's. The building is interesting, a replica of the 'Shere Inn' in England, built by one Alan Macgillycuddy Figgis from mud bricks made on the site and stone from the nearby 'Star of the West' goldmine at Kevington.

On Sunday, it took me the whole day to drive little more than one hundred kilometres to my next camp, not far past Walhalla, a historic mining centre. Yes, I did stop to take a few photos and once I had to chainsaw a fallen tree out of my way.

But this is one helluva twisty road and what with rain and fog, there was only one way to travel: very slowly! It was child's play for the RR, no test at all, but with blind hairpins at about one-a-minute, I wasn't going to test its cornering abilities. What the day did prove was the excellence of the RR's power steering, which gives plenty of road feel, despite its lightness. The journey was tedious in the extreme, but effortless physically. What possessed people to make tracks into outlandish country like this? The answer is gold. Just about every settlement from Jamieson to Walhalla and north-east through Dargo to Omeo and beyond was pioneered by miners. And there's still gold in them thar hills, some people claim... It was a great road, though, particularly the first section to Gaffney's Creek, where the road parallels the Goulburn River and provides easy access to countless camping sites in small clearings among tall eucalypts. No facilities, of course (who needs 'em!) but plenty of firewood and excellent trout fishing within micturating distance of your tent or van.

I camped in a deep gully and spent the night listening to the wind rage like an express train through the trees on the ridges far above me— and the steady patter of rain on my tent. Next day at Maffra, a sizeable town which had suffered extensive storm damage during the night, I replenished my supplies and headed for Dargo via Briagolong and Culloden on Freestone Creek. Another helluva road, as tortuous as the creek it follows. Picturesque, but so heavily forested, there are few possibilities for camping. At Cobbannah, I got on to the mostly bitumen road linking Bairnsdale and Dargo. The country opened out considerably and between rain squalls I glimpsed magnificent vistas of broad cleared valleys below forest clad ranges. Also a few brace of emus.

Dargo is still basically a store, pub and sawmill. Serious drinkers should play it safe and BYO, because the pub is inclined to be shut when you need it most. By contrast, the store is just what you would expect of a high-country outpost, complete with genial, helpful proprietors— plus a slow-combustion stove, very welcome on a cold, wet June afternoon. Armed with a detailed map prepared by the Victorian Mountain Tramping Club and purchased at the store, I set out for the pioneer goldmining field at Happy Valley, in the Wonnangatta-Moroka National Park. This had been the scene of some of Pop's deer-hunting expeditions, long before the creation of the park. The gravel and earth road follows the course of the Wonnangatta River and is called Crooked River Road for obvious reasons.

Miraculously, the rain cleared for an hour in mid-afternoon and I was able to grab some photos of the magnificent countryside. Further on, bad weather closed in and I was halted for a while by a landslip that was being cleared away by a bulldozer. A cheerful road ganger told me that if I wanted to give the Range Rover a good test, I should take the road fork ahead to Mount Grant, where there were seven ford crossings of the Wongungarra River.

'The first is the deepest,' he told me. 'If you get across that, you'll have no trouble with the others.' Hmm.

'Has this rain brought them up much?' I enquired.

'Naa, I shouldn't think so,' he replied casually.

The bulldozer driver thought otherwise. 'I'd have a good look first, mate,' he advised. 'I hear there was a fair bit of rain upstream.'

Late in the afternoon I took the Mount Grant fork and drove about six tortuous kilometres to Randall's homestead. A short distance further on, I was confronted with the first, deep ford. The light was falling, but as far as I could make out, the crossing was aptly described and would be a very good test indeed for the Range Rover. Some startled cattle plunged into the water and tried to get across ahead of me, then thought better of it and thrashed away downstream. I peeled off my boots and jeans and waded in until the most sensitive portion of my anatomy recoiled from the icy touch of the swirling dark water. Dumb animals often show good sense, I mused—and retreated to dry land like the cows.

Back on the Happy Valley Road, I crossed Kingwell's Bridge and went on to the National Park and a good camp on the banks of the Wonnangatta. It was almost dark and raining, but with the aid of my trusty chainsaw, I soon had a roaring log fire going and used its light to put up my igloo snow tent. Next day I drove on and fossicked around the Happy Valley area, exploring boggy side-tracks to old mining ruins and motoring off-road here and there to confirm that the current Range Rover will go anywhere the original version would. Which means it can match the performance of any off-the-shelf four-wheel drive—while its occupants enjoy total comfort.

I didn't indulge in any macho-style shenanigans, being content to climb up and down extremely steep, slippery slopes, flounder through deep bog holes, plough across river sand and clamber over submerged mossy boulders while fording various creeks. In low range with the central diff locked, the RR does incredible things in third and second gear. I can't imagine ever having to use first, unless I had a heavily laden trailer or a large van in tow. The suspension seems perhaps even softer than before. Which means the vehicle squirms and wriggles in an almost sensuous manner while easing itself over the most difficult terrain. It's an uncanny experience to enjoy a luxurious ride over rough terrain that would have you banging your head and falling about in more basic off-road vehicles. The sensation is rather like riding in a sedan chair on the back of an elephant (no, I haven't, but I bet I'm near the mark). Very comforting and satisfying.

At the end of the day it was still raining, so I gave up trying to get further scenic photos, camped for the night, and returned to Dargo next morning. The pub was still shut. On the winding narrow road to Mount Hotham it began snowing and again I was glad of my chainsaw when a fallen tree blocked my way. It was a narrow, tortuous section of road cut into a mountainside, where the alternative would have been to reverse several kilometres before finding a suitable place to turn. Not a pleasant prospect in steadily falling snow, with a hike of some forty kilometres back to Dargo as the only other possible alternative if no help came along. The Tramping Club map is correct in stating: 'This alpine road is dangerous in winter.'

When I connected with the main road to Mount Hotham, it began snowing in earnest and for a time I had doubts I would get through to Omeo. There was no movement at the ski resort and all I saw were several parked cars beside the road, buried in what turned out to be a further twenty-centimetre fall of snow. With the central diff locked, the Range Rover ploughed steadily along in second gear high ratio, only sliding twice when I became too confident and tried to drive at twenty-five kilometres per hour when I should have been doing no more than fifteen. Visibility was at times barely more than ten metres and I confess I did not enjoy the experience or have any inclination to stop and take pictures (largely from fear of being rammed in the back by another idiot like me, who would have been better advised not to travel).

After an hour of this, the snow eased below Cobungra and I sped toward Omeo and a late lunch of hot pasties beside a pot-bellied stove in a roadside cafe. Not much can be said of Omeo, except that it is not my idea of a destination resort. It does have some shops, pub and garage.

It had been my intention to travel via Benambra and Suggan Buggan down to Buchan and Orbost, before returning home via the Princes Highway. But continuing rain and gloomy forecasts made a return via Albury seem more prudent. Never mind—all things happen for the best in this the best of all possible worlds, as Voltaire's character Pangloss once said.

Taking refreshment in the beergarden of the famous Ettamogah pub near Albury.

The road over the Dividing Range to Mitta Mitta is a beauty for any touring motorist who wants to get away from it all, particularly if he or she likes camping, fishing, tramping, photography, sketching or painting. I had forgotten this, not having been in the area for some twenty years. The way is tortuous in parts, but the surface good and no problem for conventional vehicles. There are plenty of side tracks for the off-roader. Mitta Mitta is an attractive little town at the beginning of the bitumen that takes you eventually to the Hume Highway. As a civilised stopover, it is infinitely more desirable than Omeo.

The sealed run down to Tallangatta didn't take the Range Rover long, despite its meandering course, and was a good test of the vehicle's main-road handling. Which I can only describe as faultless, though the slightly disconcerting body squirm takes a little getting used to. The only thing I didn't like about the 1987 Range Rover was the plastic front spoiler fitted with driving lights. It served no useful purpose and would be a damn nuisance in the rough. I vowed that if ever I owned a Highline, I would have the contraption off.

Footnote: On the way home, just north of Albury, I stopped for refreshment at the Ettamogah Pub. I swear I had only one glass—but do you know, when I left and glanced back at the building, its walls seemed all awry and I fancied there was a truck parked on the roof!

The pause that refreshes. Outside the Ettamogah pub. (Photos: Jennifer Maclean)

14 Cornered!

A Dobermann, standing on its hind legs, joined me at the bar, a two-dollar bill in its mouth. Deftly the barmaid removed the note with one hand, using the other to place a bag of potato chips between the animal's jaws. 'That's another bag I owe you,' she called after the dog as it trotted to a corner of the room and began eating. Thus I learned that chips are a dollar a bag in Wanaaring, a lonely outpost town in far north-west NSW—to Dobermanns anyway.

'You have some interesting customers,' I ventured.

'Yairs, I suppose,' the barmaid responded. 'Name's Sheeba, but everyone calls her Jaws... Eats anything.' She glanced out the window. 'I reckon that sheep's more unusual.' A large woolly ewe was standing in the middle of Wanaaring's dusty main street. 'Chases cars,' the barmaid intoned laconically.

Sure enough, a battered ute rattled past and the sheep took off after it, bleating aggressively. No doubt about it: I was back in the land where I belong.

How came I to Wanaaring? Exploring down Memory Lane again, this time in a Nissan Pathfinder.

One of my early stamping grounds was the Corner Country of north-west NSW, plus the adjoining territory in South Australia out to the Birdsville Track and north into Queensland beyond Cooper Creek to Betoota and environs. Much of the area consists of stony desert and red sand dunes. The 10 000 kilometre Wild Dog Fence bisects this huge tract of arid land and was the subject of some of my book and magazine yarns.

I have fond memories of that wild territory, where most of the characters I met loomed larger than life and indelibly inscribed themselves

Sheeba the Dobermann buying potato chips from the bar of the Wanaaring pub.

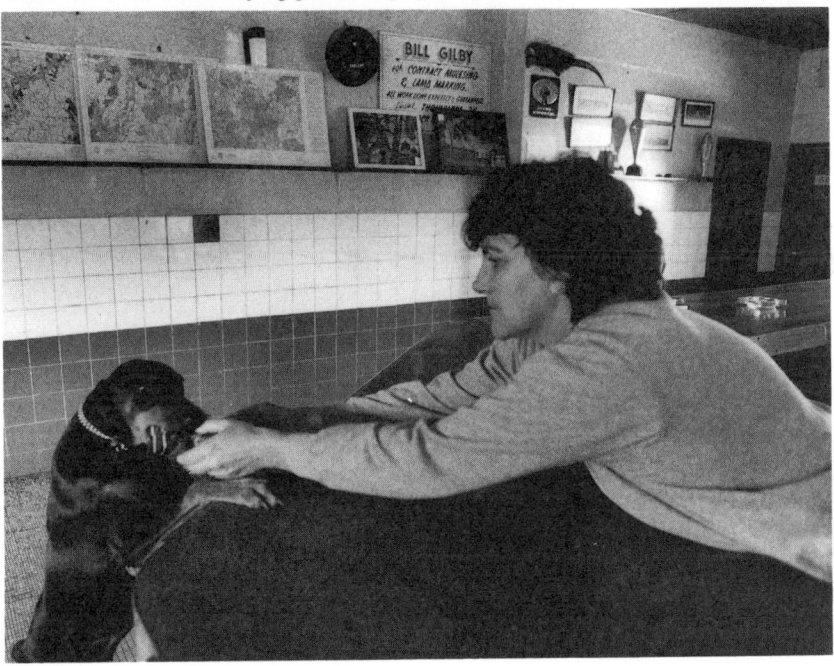

on my memory. Lately I've often wondered if such colourful characters still peopled the backblocks, or had they been swept away by the winds of change? The old tracks?—highways now? And the ramshackle pubs?—gone, replaced by motels? When the editor of *Wheels* told me he had a Nissan Pathfinder for me to try out, I grabbed the chance to revisit the Corner Country.

After stowing my swag, rations, camera gear, etc., and a couple of twenty-litre jerry cans for extra fuel, I punched the Pathfinder over the Blue Mountains to Bathurst, followed the Mitchell Highway to Nyngan and then the Barrier Highway as far as Wilcannia on the Darling River. It was pension day and the town seemed to be inhabited entirely by Aboriginal people, apart from the shopkeepers, hiding inside from the midday sun. A fill of petrol, a quick take-away snack and I said goodbye to the bitumen.

The graded road to the opal-mining town of White Cliffs was in good condition and the Pathfinder whizzed over most of it at 100 km/h, ironing out corrugations and ruts to give an impressively comfortable ride. Indeed, during my entire 4000-kilometre jaunt, the Nissan Pathfinder rode as softly as most family cars, even on the roughest tracks or while off-roading over sand dunes, gibber plains or crossing steep, sometimes rocky creek beds.

White Cliffs, where a wizened, bearded local character spent a lot of time assuring me he wasn't a mirage, didn't impress me. But then I've spent a lot of time in Coober Pedy, a far larger, livelier and more colourful polyglot town.

Never mind: there was a pub, store, post office, information and craft centre, hospital, cafe-cum-laundrette, caravan park and limited accommodation at the pub or the unlicensed Family Inn. Plus an interesting solar power station and the usual underground opal showrooms and walk-in display mines.

Like Coober Pedy, White Cliffs probably grows on you the longer you stay. I didn't—and sped off toward Tibooburra. Another generally excellent graded track across the barren and forbidding landscape for some 140 kilometres to the Silver City Highway, camping overnight in a dry creek-bed on Pulgamurtie station. Again I was able to average 80 km/h when on the move, between stops for photo sessions. Where are the horror tracks of yesteryear? The Pathfinder breezed along the dry sandy creek-bed to my first camp in first gear high-range four-wheel drive. Next morning I caused the Pathfinder to climb the steep bank of the creek and clamber over some deeply guttered terrain in low range four-wheel drive, just to see what it could do. The result: in first and second gear it seemed as unstoppable and comfortable as a Range Rover, giving a similar squirming, undulating ride. I came away convinced the

Pathfinder would take me anywhere I might reasonably wish to go in an earthbound vehicle.

The highway to Tibooburra was in good nick, having been recently graded. At the tiny outpost of Milparinka I paused long enough to confirm that fuel and refreshments are available. A modest improvement since the days of Charles Sturt, who was marooned by drought nearby for six months, in 'a landscape which never changed but for the worse.'

The explorer had with him a boat, in which he hoped to cross the fabled 'inland sea'. The grave of one of his party, James Poole, is close by.

Tibooburra, NSW's remotest town, to my great delight, seemed not to have changed since my last visit some twenty years ago. The first thing I saw was a rabbit hopping across the main street! Still just two pubs and a gaggle of venerable buildings that look like the set from the cowboy classic *High Noon*, all tucked into a boulder-strewn landscape straight out of a spaghetti western. Some 'improvements' are slotted in here and there: modern houses, a new school building, post office and police station, plus some motel accommodation and an office of the NSW National Parks and Wildlife Service, which administers nearby Sturt National Park. There are new faces, too, but some of the old-timers I knew still survive, including Jos and Barry Davie, proprietors of the historic Family Hotel (*circa* 1888)—famous, amongst other things, for the Clifton Pugh mural in its bar.

The Olde Worlde custom of paying cash prevails in most Tibooburra establishments, so I was surprised to see the Bankcard emblem displayed outside an emporium offering unleaded petrol. All went well as the jovial, jokesy pump attendant and his dog filled the Pathfinder's tank. Then consternation when I produced my trusty plastic Open Sesame. 'Ah, well now mate, I can't handle them things,' the attendant admitted. 'You'll have to wait till the boss gets back.'

'When's that?' I enquired.

''Bout an hour, he's gone home fer lunch.'

So I returned an hour later, to discover the boss was hardly more familiar with Bankcards than his servant. Eventually we sorted things out, after destroying half a dozen sets of forms in the much-abused and misunderstood Bankcard imprinter.

At the National Parks office I learned there is now more or less a highway to once remote and inaccessible Cameron Corner, where the NSW-Queensland border meets that of South Oz. When informed that I wished to test the Pathfinder's ability to climb red sand dunes, the NP representative suggested I drive north along the highway to Warri Gate and then follow the Wild Dog Fence on the Queensland side to Cameron Corner.

Soon after leaving town, I began sighting red kangaroos and emus by the score, the first I had seen since leaving Sydney. Hawks and eagles were also much in evidence, often feeding by the roadside on carcasses of 'roos killed by passing vehicles. They were slow to take flight when I stopped to photograph them and when they took to the air, circled fearlessly above me. An astonishing change from 'the good old days' when eagles were declared pests and shot on sight. It seems that nowadays they realise they are protected and are losing their fear of humans.

At Warri Gate I drove a car's length into Queensland, then followed the fence track westward into the lowering sun. The going was relatively easy, across claypans and over low red dunes, with occasional dry creek crossings and deviations around rocky jump-ups.

After some fifty kilometres I passed Toona Gate and the dunes became steadily higher, requiring a fair turn of speed to get over in two-wheel drive. (There are two ways of traversing dunes: you rush them in two- or four-wheel drive, relying chiefly on momentum—or you churn slowly up and over in second or third gear, low range four-wheel drive. When there are a lot of dunes, you soon get sick of the second method and the first is usually the more successful anyway.)

Flying over the crests of sand dunes while blinded by the setting sun is a good way to have a head-on collision (not uncommon along the Wild Dog Fence), so I made camp amid some mulga and whitewood trees. Not long after sunset, I was sipping a mug of billy tea and tending my customary chunk of eye-fillet steak as it sizzled with some garlic in the pan. Since entering Queensland, I hadn't seen a 'roo or emu, I mused. Apparently the gun still rules in this state.

Next morning at Fortville Gate I nicked back into NSW and sampled the last seventeen kilometres of the highway to Cameron Corner and found it suitable for any conventional family car. Kangaroos and emus were evident before I was out of sight of the fence, and the country, ungrazed by cattle or sheep for more than a decade, looked in better shape than the adjoining Queensland territory. At the famous corner marker I joined a queue of three other vehicles to take the obligatory picture and sign the visitors' book.

From the border to the Strzelecki Track the dunes come thick and fast and grow steadily bigger. Experienced drivers can pilot conventional vehicles through, but might have problems in hot weather when the sand is really 'running'. Rain would quickly stop ordinary cars. Once more outside the Sturt National Park, I saw little wildlife, but it was around midday, when kangaroos tend to lie up in the shade, out of sight. I did see one large bull camel, striding purposefully along a sand ridge. The road surface was generally good and the Pathfinder breezed along in two-wheel drive, slowing abruptly to a crawl at the frequent gutters and dry creek crossings.

After about seventy kilometres of due west travel, directly crossing scores of magnificent red sandhills, which lie north and south, the track veered north and ran mostly between the dunes until joining the famous Strzelecki Track near Merty Merty homestead. This route follows Strzelecki Creek upstream to where it (sometimes) flows *out* of Cooper Creek near the outpost of Innamincka. If you think that's odd, remember the Cooper is the only creek in the world with two large rivers as its *tributaries*—the Thomson and the Barcoo.

That doyen of cattle drovers, Harry Redford, pioneered the Strzelecki Track last century when he walked a large mob of stolen cattle overland from Queensland to Adelaide. The Track today is a fairly easy run in cool, dry weather, apart from frequent washaways and crossings, plus some sand, that occasionally make you glad you have four-wheel drive. It is scenically pleasant, with plenty of coolabah, river gums and other trees along the way to ease the eyes and provide shade and firewood. Ideal for camping, but don't forget to carry your own water.

Don't go near the Track during or after rain! At such times, proceed west from Merty Merty about fifteen kilometres to the Moomba Gasfields Highway which runs from Lyndhurst in the south to Innamincka. Warning: the section north of Moomba from the Gidgealpa turn-off to Innamincka (some sixty kilometres) can be impassable after rain—so get advice at Moomba before proceeding. At Innamincka, which I recalled as one derelict building and a large bottle heap during my last visit twenty-five years ago, I found a thriving general store (the Trading Post) with post office, a pub offering limited motel-style accommodation and a *canoe hire* centre.

Upstream and downstream along the Cooper from Innamincka are various monuments to members of the ill-fated Burke and Wills expedition, which finally came to grief nearby. The storekeeper warned me that firewood was scarce at these popular tourist attractions, so I finally set up my tent on the banks of the Cooper a half-kilometre downstream from a location sign-posted as King's Marker (John King was the only survivor of the four-man party returning from the Gulf of Carpentaria). Other travellers had preceded me, but there was adequate firewood after some scouting. The Cooper was up and running well after recent falls of rain in south-west Queensland. Pelicans, ducks and other wildfowl floated on the swirling, opaque water. Countless white cockatoos and pink galahs squabbled in the branches of the coolabahs and river gums lining both banks of the stream. Close overhead, a variety of hawks circled fearlessly—watching out for scraps, I suspected, rather than natural living prey.

I sat at my lonely campfire, enjoying the silence and occasional nightbird call, mindful of the changes to our once forbidding outback.

Due to the combination of vastly improved roads and vehicles, backblocks travel today is mostly fast, safe and comfortable. The biggest challenge is no longer 'getting through' but dodging other vehicles and trying to find a place unmarred by the remnants of other camps.

Next morning I returned briefly to Innamincka, where the storekeeper suggested a day trip to Coongie Lakes might be photographically rewarding. A day trip—it used to be a three-day expedition! The lakes were full, he said, and teeming with birdlife. I set off early, crossing the Cooper causeway (which was running briskly) without problems, after locking the front hubs and engaging four-wheel drive. The run up to the lakes was easy, except for a few gates and some rough patches in the final stanza of the 115-kilometre journey.

Beyond Kudriemitchie outstation, I followed the north-west branch of Cooper Creek to the lakes, a twenty-kilometre journey I would not recommend for conventional vehicles. Had I but known, the alleged grave of Charlie Gray, a member of the Burke and Wills expedition, was close by Kudriemitchie, near Lake Massacre, and I would like to have visited it.

Some years ago I wrote a book called *In the Steps of the Explorers*, in which I pointed out that John McKinlay, sent to look for survivors of the Burke and Wills expedition, did *not* discover the body of Charlie Gray here (as generally accepted), but those of *two* unknown Europeans.

Apart from the discrepancy in numbers, McKinlay wrote in his diary that the body later thought to be Gray's was a bare skeleton and 'appeared as if it had lain in the grave some years'. King had been dead only a few months. Interesting how these furphies become part of our folklore.

After photographing the idyllic scene and prolific birdlife at Coongie Lakes, I was back at Innamincka just after sundown, in ample time to ferret out another good campsite on the banks of the Cooper. Had time permitted next day, I would have hired myself a canoe, because the idea of gliding quietly along the famous stream, snapping birdlife or just enjoying the solitude seemed appealing. Instead, I refuelled and pressed the Pathfinder along the southern boundary of Sturts Stony Desert to the Nappa Merrie crossing on the south side of the Cooper. Which had been closed for several weeks and was still running at a metre and a half. So after lunch and snapshotting a few pelicans, I sped south to Tibooburra, noting that road signs along the way are all still in miles!

It rained half the night in Tibooburra, making the excellent graded earth road to Wanaaring decidedly sticky next morning. Luckily, after about forty kilometres of four-wheel drive slogging and sliding, the road changed to bone dry and I bowled along at speeds up to 120 km/h. Following my canine encounter in the pub and a quick call on old friends, the Skinner family on Wanaaring station, I pressed on to Bourke, along a not-quite-so-fast stretch of graded road, where I encountered the bitumen that led me back to Sydney.

15 Costa brava (rugged coast)

Inside a pub at Horsham, Victoria, on a wet June afternoon, ten macho-looking blokes, most with Zapata moustaches, sit drinking lemon squashes at a long table near the bar. Enter your servant and number three son, Vandal, having parked our 928S4 Porsche at the kerb, just outside. I order counter lunches and two small glasses of low-alcohol beer.

'That yours?' the barman enquires, glancing through the window at the lurking beast.

'At the moment,' I reply. Then I lean forward conspiratorially. 'Tell me, are the radar patrols very active in this area? You have some nice straight roads and we thought to verify the maker's claims...'

The barman holds up a silencing hand. It is his turn to lean forward conspiratorially. 'Those blokes sitting directly behind you,' he whispers,

'are the mobile radar squad, up from Melbourne. Five carloads of them, here for a few days to give the district a going over. I'd watch out. They've got no sense of humour.'

Game, set, but not match to the forces of law and order. Van and I drink and eat in glum silence, our mood further dampened by the onset of rain outside, which has dogged us since leaving the coast at Portland. Suddenly the ten gendarmes rise as one and march out.

In an attempt to turn adversity to advantage, I run after them and corner a straggler. 'Tell me, good sir, I am but a poor ignorant New South Welshman. Is it true that radar detectors are now illegal in this fair state?'

'Yeah,' he answers guardedly.

'And what is the fine for use and or possession?' I pursue.

'Don't know, the first cases haven't been heard yet. But we have the power to confiscate them and the fine for refusing to hand them over is $500.' He regards me sternly. 'You an interstate trucky?'

'Something like that,' I fence.

'Best way to stay out of trouble is don't turn it on,' the trooper warns gruffly. 'If you don't turn it on, we don't know you've got it, do we?'

'You mean your equipment tells you when someone is using a radar detector?' I enquire.

'Yep, that's right.' The trooper turns away abruptly and hurries off in the direction of his brothers in law.

I hurry to the nearest phone and speak with a Mr Mulligan, of Creative Electronics in Sydney, purveyors of the Whistler 2000 radar detector I have fitted to the 928S4 Porsche. 'Wrong!' he says stoutly. 'The Whistler emits no signal, only receives, so it's not detectable, full stop.' Reassuring news, but Van and I decide that Horsham, with five patrol cars buzzing round its environs, is not the best place to put the 928S4 through its paces, certainly not to check its claimed top speed of 265 km/h!

What is a down-at-heel kangaroo farmer from Foxground, NSW, doing motoring around Victoria in the latest 928 Porsche, price tagged at over $200 000? The simple answer is: I like Porsches. The 928S4 Van and I were pedalling around the Victorian west coast and hinterland was the Australian importer Alan Hamilton's personal transporter, plated AH 928.

Like all dyed-in-the-wool Porsche buffs, I had long refused to have anything to do with 928s. There was no way the hefty, luxurious, bulbously sensual 928 could be regarded as sporty or racy. It was a successful, middle-aged gentleman's conveyance: fast, but genteel and passive, like a big old Jag or Merc. An expensive, kept-mistress sort of car, for the well-to-do tycoon, whereas the 911 could be regarded more as a volatile, unpredictable girlfriend, independent and hot blooded—much more exciting.

Once or twice, while loitering in Master Newell's Sydney showroom, I perused some colour brochures on 928s. It seemed on paper they might perhaps go like hell, in the right hands, what with their revolutionary Weissach axle to prevent the dreaded Porsche oversteer, ideal weight distribution, impeccable suspension and brakes, powerful V8 motor, etc. However, I steadfastly refused all offers of test drives. I had an image to keep up: as the sort of fellow who preferred...ah, 911s.

Then on one memorable occasion, Mr Brian Woo, a discreet North Shore dealer in exotic vehicles, persuaded me to take a suburban spin in a 928S Porsche temporarily garaged at his impressive St Ives home, alongside a couple of Ferraris, a Maserati, a Lamborghini and suchlike. I tore off in typical fashion around the hilly, winding and tree-lined streets of St Ives, imagining myself among the bushclad hills of my native Foxground. Rocketing toward a crest, I observed what I assumed to be a continuation of my road sweeping away uphill to the right. Alas, as I flew over the crest, I perceived that my road went sharp left, while the sweeping right-hander began at a T-intersection blocked by a car waiting to turn out and a van turning in.

I was going much too fast for the left-hander, but as there was no alternative, I made the necessary motions with the steering wheel, fortunately keeping my right foot planted, as there was no time to get it off. The 928S responded splendidly, keeping on my side of the road, albeit with some tyre squeal and a final whip of the tail when I nervously feathered my right foot. It was a textbook example of how the Weissach axle can save idiots from themselves. The experience gave me pause to think about 928s. But soon after I fell into possession of the Kremer Porsche, then 'Little Red'—and once again, 911s were the only Porsches I wanted to know about.

Finally the editor of *Wheels* said to me sternly 'Jeffrey, it's time you broke the habit and tried driving a Porsche with the motor where it should be—in the front. I've arranged for you to have a week with a new 928S4. Let me know your reactions. I suggest you try Victoria's Great Ocean Road. It's scenic, has many bends and should suit you. But mind you don't fall into the sea. That coast is already famous for its wrecks.' He meant shipwrecks, of course.

So it came to pass that Van and I presented ourselves at the Melbourne House of Porsche, exchanging, temporarily, my 1979 Commodore station wagon (bought secondhand for $7000) for Senor Hamilton's 928S4 Porsche.

This splendiferous machine was explained and handed over to us by a chic lady and gentleman representing the company. Both had difficulty maintaining their aplomb as we began loading the 928's large rear boot with tents, sleeping bags, ground sheets, billy cans, frying pans and miscellaneous boxes of camping gear. It all fitted in, no trouble, including Van's large suitcase, my usual motel kit, plus camera case, tripod, overalls, wet-weather gear and so on. Access was good, via the electrically operated giant rear window hatch, which sprang up at a touch, by driver or passenger, of buttons adjacent to both front seats.

While Van, who is interested in mechanics, listened to a technical rundown on the car, I thumbed through a magnificent glossy pamphlet. This pointed out that the new Mark-4 engine has a block made of alloy mixed with silicon, giving the cylinder linings and other important bits a hardness similar to that of industrial diamonds. No wonder the vehicle costs more than thirty second-hand Commodores, I mused. The pamphlet also drew attention to the 928S4's ABS braking system, with aircraft-standard electronic monitoring systems, which means you can pull up even on ice without going sideways.

After studying a swag of tourist maps and literature, we sped off to Geelong, then on to the Great Ocean Road. This begins at Torquay, which turned out to be an uninspiring miniature suburban sprawl. At Lorne we booked into a motel and made the lucky choice of Kosta's Greek Taverna for our evening repast.

Late June is not a busy time in Lorne, so we soon fell in with the proprietor Kosta Talimantois, his elder brother Chris and their other four customers, all locals, seated close by a log fire. It turned out that Chris owns the Beacon Point Restaurant at Apollo Bay and that he and Kosta are rabid car enthusiasts. Chris pilots a Subaru Turbo and Kosta runs an Alfa-Romeo, a replacement for his previous mount, a Saab, which he said 'fell to bits' in the salty climate. Both were pleased to have the Porsche tethered outside. Kosta broke out a bottle of Chateau Neuf du Pape to go with our souvlaki and Chris produced a recent issue of English *Car* magazine, featuring a story on the 928S4. Both urged us to try in the morning to better their best time of twenty-five minutes for the forty-five kilometre run to Apollo Bay (average speed 108 km/h. We promised to consider the challenge while fending off Kosta's insistent requests for a short test drive of the Porsche. 'I tell you, my friends, I guarantee it will be veery hot when I breeng it back.' 'And maybe veery dented,' his brother Chris added drily.

Next morning we made no attempt to break any records, concentrating instead on photographing car and coast. However, I must report it's a challenging road between Lorne and Apollo Bay and no doubt a great source of enjoyment for the Talimantois brothers and other sporting motorists with no fear of blind corners, great heights and water (you are rarely more than a flick-of-the-wrist from a long plunge into the sea). We did not put the 928S4 to the test, but quickly established its potential to go from Lorne to Apollo Bay in rather less than twenty-five minutes.

Beyond Apollo Bay, the road climbs through the very scenic Otway National Park and a little further on, we took the Johanna Beach detour. You can free-camp (no amenities) behind this fine stretch of sand, provided you don't mind the constant roar of the giant breakers rolling in from the Southern Ocean. The main attraction is the sculptured green hinterland, manicured like a vast city park by grazing sheep and long-haired black Aberdeen Angus cattle. Nearby is the Melba Gully State Park, accessible from the main road beyond the village of Lavers Hill, where night excursions can be made to see the glow worms.

Further on, between Princetown and Peterborough, is the rugged, break-away cliff coast of the tourist pamphlets, grander and more spectacular than the brochure photographs suggest. The first we came to were the Twelve Apostles (we could only count seven), then Loch Ard Gorge, scene of one of the coast's many shipwrecks, the Arch, London Bridge, the Grotto, etc. In the middle of all this is Port Campbell, which has three motels, a pub, some shops and a camping ground above the sheltered beach and estuary. Not a large town, nor particularly attractive, but bigger than Peterborough, which is tiny.

Just before Warrnambool, the Great Ocean Road joins the Princes Highway, which continues to hug the coast as far as Portland. Warrnambool is Victoria's fifth largest city and apart from being famous as the home of the Fletcher Jones pants factory, offers the visitor a variety of attractions. These include Flagstaff Hill Maritime Village, a re-creation of the port as it was a hundred or so years ago when whalers and sealers were more active.

The whales, now protected, are coming back, and a viewing platform has been erected at Logan's Beach for the use of visitors who like to whale watch. Just out of town toward Portland is the Tower Hill State Game Reserve, located in a volcanic crater sheltering a scenic lake that attracts a variety of furred and feathered wildlife. A narrow one-way bitumen road circumnavigates the lake and there are idyllic picnic sites and short walks for the energetic. 'Worth a Visit' in Michelin parlance and a must for shutterbugs.

There are some fine, short, straight bitumen roads inland from the Princes Highway between Warrnambool and Port Fairy. It would have been irresponsible to check the 928's claimed top speed of 265 km/h but I can report that we accelerated (manually) very rapidly to 240 km/h with the rev-counter at about 5300 and rising steadily. I'm sure it would have climbed willingly to 6000 rpm and even further into the red, given enough road. But it was not the time or place and the heavy showers that dogged our whole trip again caught up with us. However, we did get in a couple of 0 to 100 km/h runs of 6.2 and 6.3 seconds. And two 0 to 160 km/h bursts of 14.4 and 14.7 seconds. Both Van and I were pleasantly surprised by these figures, because the automatic's slight hesitation getting off the mark and making changes does not inspire optimism.

But that five-litre V8 is deceptively powerful, sling-shotting you down the bitumen faster than you think. There is far less impression of acceleration or speed than you experience in a 911. I think this is due to the mass and sheer luxury of the 928S4— you feel that anything so heavy and comfortable can't possibly be going as quickly as a nimble, racy little 911.

Ah, but it does. Thus perceptions are proved wrong and our cherished, stubborn attitudes must change. Reluctantly I had to admit that on public roads the 928S4 was as quick as any off-the-shelf 911 Carrera.

On to Port Fairy and Portland through a mostly picturesque landscape with lots of interesting little side roads to explore, coastward and inland. We were plagued by intermittent bad weather, but with some blue sky above, it would be easy to spend several days exploring the Warrnambool-Portland coast and hinterland.

The tiny, historic whaling and sealing centre of Port Fairy was the most attractive settlement we encountered on our journey twixt Torquay and Portland. In common with Lorne, Apollo Bay and Port Campbell, it has its new developments, but much of the Olde World character of the place has been retained. More than fifty buildings are classified by the National Trust, including the Caledonian Inn, Victoria's oldest licensed hotel (*circa* 1844). Originally named Belfast, and settled by English, Scottish and Irish whalers and sealers who came over for 'the season' from Van Dieman's Land, waterfront Port Fairy still has the atmosphere of a nineteenth-century English fishing village.

Portland, by contrast, although billed as 'Victoria's oldest permanent white settlement' and boasting 'over one hundred historic buildings', presents to the visitor as a bustling, commercial centre and industrial port. By and large, history has been swamped by 'progress'. Among the listed tourist attractions are the four wool stores and the Alcoa smelter!

Trying to dodge the weather, we pushed further inland, to Hamilton and Horsham, via the Grampians National Park. Admittedly the weather was bad, but we failed to discover the Grampians of the tourist pamphlets. Maybe we took the wrong road. We were similarly unlucky at Horsham, where a combination of bad weather and the Melbourne radar squad foiled our plans to really put the 928S4 through its paces.

One thing we did discover on this detour into the wool- and wheat-belt: we were driving a great wet-weather car. The rainy conditions allowed us to test the ABS braking system, which is amazing. Slam the brakes on hard *while travelling straight ahead* in the wet and you simply come to a fast, unfussed halt, the pedal hammering audibly under your right foot. The feel and noise are intentional, so you know the ABS system has taken over and you are therefore in the very best of hands. The same thing happens on loose gravel: you just hit the brakes and let technology do the rest—provided you are travelling in a straight line.

You can certainly make use of the brakes while cornering if you are that sort of driver, but I did not care to make any definitive test of the ABS system while cornering on public roads. I imagine the best they could do would be to make the accident less serious. We also found out during the cold and rain that the 928S4's heating and demisting system is excellent. Also the electrically adjustable sports seats, radio and tape system, adjustable steering wheel and instrument binnacle, plus such appointments as the centre console tape and small-change compartment, rear compartment air-conditioning controls and the air-conditioned front glovebox!

The only thing I didn't like was giving the car back to Alan Hamilton.

16 Blast the bush!

There was a tremendous explosion. 'Whacko!' said William. 'Jolly good show!' exclaimed Maddock. 'Gosh!' breathed Len, completely over-awed. 'Great Scott, what a sight. Well done, chaps!' announced Kevin. In Maddock's diary for the day was a facetious entry, scribbled in by irrepressible Len: *'Up early to darn my socks, brush teeth, fold my washing, let off atom bomb and iron my hankies.'*

An excerpt from a *Boys Own Annual* ripping adventure story of the fifties? No. The occasion was the first British atomic bomb test in Australia, near Emu Junction west of Coober Pedy on 15 October 1953. William was Sir William Penney, later Lord Penney, British atomic scientist. Maddock was a top electronics boffin, the man who pressed the button on that fateful day. Len was Len Beadell, surveyor-explorer, the man who had made it all possible by discovering and developing the site. As Range Reconnaissance Officer for the Long Range Weapons Establishment, a joint British–Australian military organisation, he surveyed and constructed the access roads to rocket and bomb testing areas in previously trackless, uninhabited desert country west and south-west of Alice Springs. Well, more or less uninhabited. There were some people about: Pitjantjatjaras, Wailbris, Pintubis, Tjarutjas and some unidentified (by Europeans) nomadic family groups.

No matter, Sir William and his merry band were so confident of the safety of their experiments, they stood and watched that first historic explosion from a distance of just seven kilometres. Their only protective measure was to turn their backs at the instant of detonation to avoid the flash. Truly it was an age of innocence. Did anyone have doubts about the wisdom of exploding atomic bombs in Central Australia? Not in official circles, but even the happy collaborator, Len Beadell, had a momentary twinge after the fact.

He later recorded in one of the half dozen books he has written about his adventures in the bush: 'I was told that to look at the flash would be like looking at the sun itself from only a few kilometres away and I began to wonder at the wisdom of being there at all.'

The Aborigines were apparently given no such warnings, concerning flash or fall-out. Lately they have begun to agitate for compensation for injuries sustained and this may become another Agent Orange type saga, with people like blind Yammie Lester at its cutting edge.

Meanwhile, what of the indestructible Len Beadell? When I visited him in June 1988, following his retirement after forty years service with the various Weapons Research Establishments, he appeared his usual cheerful, boyish self. Mentally sharp and more active than many sixty-five-year-olds, despite a near fatal bout of hepatitis, Len seems busier than ever, writing, cartooning and riding the public-lecture circuit (743 appearances to date), tour-guiding and collecting awards for public service—including the Order of Australia. On the dust-jackets of his various books he is billed as 'the last of the true Australian explorers'. Near enough.

Back in 1947, driving a Jeep, Len began exploring the desert lands north-west of what is now the town of Woomera. He was in search of a tract of uninhabited country 2000 kilometres long and some 500 kilometres wide that would serve as a rocket firing range for the British Long Range Weapons Establishment. (The bomb-site quest came later, in 1952.) After being pummelled by German rockets during the war, England was seeking a powerful deterrent to any future aggressors and looked to its colonies for a suitable testing ground.

Canada was examined first but its climate was inhospitable and its Anglo-French politicians less tractable than Australia's under a Labor government. Australia in those days was regarded by the rest of the world as a more or less uninhabited continent, certainly its vast inland, where Aborigines weren't listed on electoral rolls and were therefore statistically nonexistent.

Len Beadell had never been in Central Australia, but was chosen for the job of exploring our remotest inland because of a combination of extraordinary if not unique qualifications. He was a surveyor and an extremely meticulous one, having learned his trade in the old school, studying and mastering astro surveying—the art of fixing a point on the earth's surface solely by star observations, without reference to existing landmarks or datum points. He had served in the army survey corps in New Guinea during the war, was used to *and liked* living and working rough—and was still in the army, a useful status for anyone engaged on what was a military operation.

The year previously, while waiting to be de-mobbed, he had worked as surveyor with a CSIRO expedition to Arnhem Land, which was still uncharted country to Europeans, requiring astro fixes to establish datum points. To accept this job, Len Beadell deferred his army discharge for a year. During the assignment he proved himself a resourceful, innovative and industrious worker, at home in the bush, with a cheerful, outgoing personality—traits valued where people are thrown together under harsh conditions in extreme isolation. He also possessed what might be called a Diploma in Improvisation, an essential qualification for outback survival.

After delaying his army discharge another year, Len signed up with the Weapons Research Organisation in 1947 and set out from Adelaide with a small crew mounted in two Jeeps and a three-tonne truck.

Their assignment was to locate a site for what the Weapons Establishment boffins described as 'a sort of rocket range'. Between what was then the rough track to Alice Springs and Lake Torrens, Len and his team laid out the site for a village, airport, access roads and launching pads. Bulldozers and graders followed and began the work of clearing and levelling. A township of prefabricated Nissen huts and workshops sprang up.

The first inhabitants were mainly Australian military personnel, but soon the British boffins and their entourages began to arrive. Officially they were scientists and technicians working for the Long Range Weapons Establishment (later the Weapons Research Establishment, the Defence Research Centre and today the Defence Science and Technology Organisation). The first British arrivals were very much establishment types, often condescendingly amused by the quaint colonial lifestyle they encountered in this outlandish desert outpost of empire.

Len Beadell got on well with them—but couldn't resist poking uncritical light fun at his employers via charcoal cartoons he drew on the mess hut walls and in his later published books. In one, titled *Blast the Bush* (published by Rigby, Adelaide, 1965), he describes how the rocket-range town he established got its name: 'Being polite English gentlemen, they had acquired a glossary of Aboriginal words... Running their fingers down the pages, the word "spearlauncher" stood out, stimulating their imagination... "By Jove! These aborigines are launching spears and we are about to be launching rockets. I say, wouldn't it be polite to refer to this place by the name for their apparatus for a similar function, and christen it *Woomera*?" It was instantly agreed that the Aborigines would certainly be pleased with the choice.'

Maybe they were, but maybe they weren't. It might have been even more polite to ask. But as Len went on to point out in his book, there were no Aborigines in sight at the time.

The enormity of the project Len Beadell undertook is difficult to portray, unless you have travelled on the ground over the area. It is mostly

sand dunes, either bare or covered in spinifex, with large tracts of mallee
or mulga scrub and here and there low, rocky ranges. The whole country
is basically waterless, hence the names Gibson Desert to the north and
Great Victoria Desert in the south. Driving over it, despite its apparent
flatness, is often harder and slower than walking, as Len's diaries attest
(twenty-five kilometres in a straight line when bush-bashing was
considered a good day's travel). The scrub is often impenetrable—and
vehicle-damaging where you can just push through—which is why Len
invented the now much-copied sloping body and windscreen protecting
rods. During the five summer months, temperatures of 50°C+ are
normal. In winter, overnight temperatures drop below zero, containers
of water freeze solid and frost can persist until noon in shady areas.
Around September, gale-force winds continue night and day for weeks
on end, sand-blasting vehicles and clogging engines. Len Beadell's first
road west from the Stuart Highway (a track then) was a 600-kilometre
sweep through the Musgrave, Mann and Tomlinson Ranges into Western
Australia, then north to the Petermann Range area and west again to
the site of what became the Giles Meteorological Station near the
Rawlinson Range. (This outpost was named after explorer Ernest Giles,
who camped nearby in 1873, the year one of his party died tragically
and gave the Gibson Desert its name.) The new track was later extended
a further 800 kilometres westward to Lake Carnegie station. This became
the modern-day 'adventurer's' route, known as the Gunbarrel Highway.
Len got a well-deserved British Empire Medal for this effort, awarded
in 1958.

Contemplating the Gunbarrel Highway near Lake Carnegie station, WA.

By then, Black Knight and Blue Streak satellite launching rockets were common sights in the Centralian skies. So were the more sinister mushroom clouds created by the series of atom bomb tests, first at Emu Junction in 1953 and later at Maralinga (another Aboriginal word, meaning 'thunder'—I wonder if they were pleased?).

Apart from Lake Carnegie station and the Warburton Aboriginal mission, there had been little penetration of the rocket range and bomb testing area by Europeans since the expeditions of Ernest Giles, John and Alexander Forrest and Colonel Peter Warburton in the 1870s. In some ways, Len Beadell had it tougher than his predecessors. They had horses and camels, which are more suited to scrub-bashing, crossing sand dunes and rocky outcrops or climbing through eroded gullies than pneumatic-tyred motorised vehicles, even the allegedly 'unstoppable' Land Rovers.

Beadell had the assistance of aerial reconnaissance (and rescue), but there his advantage stopped. Anyone who has tried to drive a vehicle genuinely across-country for any distance in the area will agree. What appears to be flat going from a distance turns out to be hatched with deep washaway gutters and rocky outcrops. Vegetation that seems sparse comes up as spinifex in seed to clog radiators hourly, or impenetrable mallee, or tyre-staking, panel-piercing, screen-smashing mulga. Inviting saltpans can be quagmires, even months after rain. From early November through March the sun can kill the waterless traveller in a few hours, or at least make life near unbearable from dawn to dusk. (Sensible travellers don't venture here in summer, but the urgency of Len's assignments left him no alternative.)

The adventures and misadventures Len enjoyed and endured during the heyday of his bush career (which totalled forty years) are recounted in his books, some of which should be required reading for anyone interested in genuine outback off-roading. His droll style and cartoon illustrations make the books a chuckle-raising good read in almost anyone's language.

On the general subject of the inland climate, Len quotes a local schoolboy's answer to an examination question: 'The climate of Central Australia in summer is such that its inhabitants have to live elsewhere.' Dealing specifically with wind and duststorms, he describes the calm before the storm and the ensuing onslaught in inimitable style: 'Whereas a piece of paper would have fallen vertically if dropped just before the storm struck, I don't think an anvil would have touched the ground a moment later.' Then: 'The sun was obliterated by a dense fog of red dirt and as midday turned to night in the space of a minute, I pressed a towel over my face in order to breathe. After four hours I began to wonder when it was going to ease as I huddled down under the windscreen. I was still wondering the same thing two days later...'

Dust storms were a common trial, like mulga-staked tyres (for which Len must hold the record), plus every known form of vehicle breakdown. Len's mechanical ability and ingenuity overcame most of these: broken axles, diffs and gearboxes, even replacing a collapsed water-pump impeller seal with the aid of a forked tree and a twelve-tonne hydraulic jack (try that beside the track a thousand kilometres from anywhere!). Unlike the early explorers, he didn't face the same dangers of dying from thirst or starvation, due to the availability of aerial supply drops. But on some of his solo reconnaissance trips, he experienced his share of hairy moments. These usually centred on impending battery failure, which threatened to prevent him transmitting the location of his breakdown or bogging. (History shows that aerial searches often fail unless pilots have reasonably precise information on the position of their target.)

Here's a typical Beadell adventure, experienced while scouting a possible track across the Gibson Desert between Giles and the Canning Stock Route. 'The trip had now become an all-out effort to get out alive. I was on my last tank of petrol, with practically no water and the heat beginning to play tricks... I noticed that the iron nails in my boots had loosened in the intense heat and the steel heels had fallen off... When I awoke just before midnight, the temperature had dropped to 38°C... It was almost impossible to keep to the observed bearing because the sandhills were worse than ever, some requiring a dozen attempts before they were negotiated, and others defying crossing altogether. Water had to be sprayed frequently on the fuel lines (to dispel vapour locks) due to the added heat caused by these desperate attempts...

'It was becoming almost hopeless, but I couldn't retrace my tracks, as on many of the crossings the vehicle had slid down the far side in a small avalanche of sand... Although the speedo indicated I had travelled forty kilometres that day, the astrofix showed that I had moved only twenty-five kilometres as the crow flies from my last night's camp... My meal consisted of a small tin of meat and a mug of water... A small drink of water served as breakfast... During one enforced spell (a heat-induced vapour lock), I opened the transmitter box and found to my dismay that in the intense heat of the cabin, some plastic parts on the instrument panel had withered to half their size and dropped out of their sockets. The packing around other dials had melted, causing the glass covering to drop on to the needles so that they couldn't be tuned and I began to wonder if the transmitter could still operate at all...'

And on another occasion: 'I had broken a front axle and owing to the long detours off-course made necessary by the loss of the four-wheel drive feature, had almost run out of petrol. The nature of the sandhills had forced me to stop in the centre of a circle 500 kilometres in diameter, surrounded by thick scrub and high dunes... I lived in that spot for three weeks... Because the battery would not last long with almost no petrol left to recharge it. . .as the days turned into weeks, I had some misgivings about placing too much reliance on the radio. . . Then, in the middle of a radio talk as to how salvage (rescue) arrangements were progressing, the battery died away. . .' Fortunately, the redoubtable Len didn't and he was 'salvaged' by a rescue party in three Land Rovers. His radio out of commission, Len guided the search party to his lonely camp by firing pistol flares at night.

In typical droll style, he recounts their arrival: 'I had made up the camp-fire so that I could give them a cup of coffee when they got in, provided they supplied the sugar and tinned milk, and of course the coffee. . .'

Some of the major roads and junctions in Len's 6500-kilometre network are named after members of his family—the Anne Beadell Highway for his wife, the Gary Highway for his son, Jackie Junction and the Connie-Sue Highway for his two daughters. The Gunbarrel Highway is the best known of his works, but for difficulty, Sandy Blight Junction is the toughest route. At least it was when I last visited the area.

Over the years, many of Beadell's roads have fallen into disrepair, while others have been periodically maintained by oil-search companies. At such times, some are negotiable by conventional vehicles, but by and large, what I call Beadell Country is best visited in a proper off-road mount, at very least a Subaru or one of the more recently introduced four-wheel drive station wagons. Len told me in June 1988 that he is hopeful his roads will soon be upgraded, as he has a dream they will help 'open up' the country (an area about the size of western Europe)—but I wouldn't count on this.

Meanwhile, fuel is still a major problem in the area. Sometimes it is available for sale at the Aboriginal communities at Docker River west of the Olgas and/or Warburton. But don't rely on these sources, particularly if you haven't troubled to obtain a permit to enter these Aboriginal lands. The only sure sources of supply are at Coober Pedy, Ayers Rock, Carnegie homestead and Laverton or Leonora. Which means you need to carry enough fuel to take you at least 1200 kilometres. Plus water, food, tools, spares, compass and good maps. A transceiver is a must, if you travel in a lone vehicle—just in case.

A number of 'adventure tour' companies now use Len Beadell's roads, so you are not very likely to die of starvation if you break down, because someone like Dick Lang or Rex Ellis or Bill King will usually be along within a day or so. But travel in the months through April to end September and *keep to the major tracks*, as this is still dangerous country, despite the comparatively heavy tourist traffic.

For the past six years, Len Beadell has been accompanying some of Dick Lang's 'Desert Trek' tours in the area, as guide and resident campfire raconteur. Prior to that he worked for a time with John Crook's 'Down-Under Tours' and the Rex Ellis organisation. So it's remotely possible to meet 'the Man' while pottering about in Beadell Country. He's easily recognisable—always wearing shorts and heavy boots without socks—and if it's around lunchtime, eating a jam sandwich. Len *always* has jam for lunch. Either apricot or tomato. Mostly tomato, which he makes himself, from 'just tomatoes, no melon', he told me. A man of simple tastes and pleasures, who could never stay *Too Long in the Bush*.

17 Full circle

Long, long ago, before the recorded history of Land Rovers began in Australia, itchy-foots like me had to get about the country as best they could. Having discovered I had no aptitude for motorbikes, the only mechanised transport I could realistically aspire to, my method was to hitchhike. Not an easy mode in those days, when the few cars travelling the countryside were invariably full of farmers and their dogs. Trucks were crammed with garrulous soldiers on their way to be demobbed, or returning drunk and disorderly to camp. Whichever, they were rarely inclined to pick up a thumb-waving, fluffy-chinned youth clad in disposal-store khakis and toting a hefty ex-navy kitbag.

I speak of the years immediately following World War II, during which time I biked and thumbed it from Melbourne to Cairns and back several times. Gathering grist for my mill, which was a 1938 model Underwood portable typewriter. On this I wrote fiction stories, which I sold to newspapers and magazines, including the famous *Bulletin* (established in the 1880s), the nation's most literary and rabid publication, still then in tabloid, newsprint form with pink, wrap-around outer pages.

The bike I speak of was not mine. It belonged to the young lady of Scandinavian descent mentioned in an earlier chapter. The cheapest bikes, ex-army Harley Davidsons, were being black-marketed for about sixty dollars in northern Queensland and Darwin. Which was why I was always making for Cairns. My weekly income was around five dollars, less expenses, but I managed to save the price of a bike several times. Then I would head north, to find myself once again broke when I eventually located an army surplus depot where bikes were available. So I was fortunate to meet the young lady, who became my fellow-traveller for half a dozen years.

Around 1948 I saw my first Land Rover and fell in love with it. Ex-American army Jeeps had been available in very limited supplies on the second-hand market for some time, but they never captured my imagination. I think they appeared too spartan, too military, with little more accommodation than a Harley Davidson bike and sidecar. By comparison, the Land Rover seemed almost sumptuous, certainly more commodious, with its high, square canvas canopy above an extended rear tray—all of a metre long! It had doors (of a sort) where the Jeep had none, and its square aluminium side panels, bonnet and wheel guards beguiled me completely. Here was an attractive but utilitarian vehicle with more than sufficient storage for one's swag, typewriter and other worldly possessions, with at least lace-down if not lockable security. Reputed to go anywhere once four-wheel drive was engaged (by pushing down a yellow knob beside the gear lever) this short-wheelbase magic carpet seemed the ultimately desirable vehicle for this young would-be motorised swagman. But how to get one?

The problem was to plague me for years. In desperation I tried a succession of jobs, ranging from hotel floor-walker (chucker out) through road mending, trench digging, builder's labouring, wool combing, cotton winding, cold-store labouring, street hot-dog selling, street ice-cream vending, chicken farming, market gardening, goat breeding, street photography and so on, fetching up as editor of a hunting and fishing magazine. Chucking out paid the best, but was inclined to have repercussions. All the while I continued to freelance stories and now some photos. But the purchase price of a Land Rover eluded me. (You had to save the full amount in those days—hire purchase hadn't been invented.)

Between jobs, I was still inclined to hitchhike north. Out of habit, I suppose. On one of these excursions I squandered forty dollars of my savings on twelve acres of virgin land a kilometre inland from the beach at a place called Grants Head, between Laurieton and Port Macquarie. I was influenced by the novelist Kylie Tennant, who happened to give me a lift while she was delivering the mail south along the Princes Highway toward Taree. She was living in Laurieton and regaled me with stories about the local timber-cutters who worked the great eucalypt forests just inland, and oyster farmers, bee-keepers, fishermen and others. It seemed a pretty romantic, exciting place, warm enough to grow bananas and other tropical fruits, yet within striking distance of Sydney.

I reckoned I might grow early strawberries on my twelve acres, once it was cleared, air-freight them to Sydney and raise the price of a Land Rover in next to no time. I paid for the land and returned home, broke, to Sydney. Where I stayed several more years without sighting my land.

Then came my Peugot and Holden panel van period, during which I built a shack on the land at Grants Head, which was later renamed Bonny Hills, probably at the instigation of developers. But nothing came

The author outside his uncompleted shack at Grants Head near Bonny Hills, around 1955.

of my strawberry growing venture, the hut rusted away and eventually I sold the twelve-acre property for $500!

Once again a young lady saved me, this time an American writer of detective pulp. Every other week Mare delivered a short novel to her publisher, thereby earning as much as the editor of a hunting and fishing magazine. Pretty soon I gave up editing and wrote pulp westerns for the same publisher. Within a couple of years we had our first Land Rover. As I mentioned in an earlier chapter, this was a second-hand 1954 long-wheelbase ute which had travelled some 45 000 miles in the hands of its previous owner, the kangaroo skin and carcass buyer. So it was no stranger to NSW's north-west 'corner country', where I headed on my earliest four-wheel drive safaris. I had been previously up and down the famous wild dog fence in a Holden panel van, spending much of my time digging in sandhills. The Land Rover was truly a revelation.

It was seemingly 'unstoppable' in dry going, sailed through crutch-deep water crossings and only stopped in mud when that substance built up under the wheel arches and physically prevented the wheels from turning. However, it did tend to lose directional stability after heavy rain west of the Darling and I developed an abiding dislike of wet-weather travel in that country. (To this day I tend to head for a high sand dune or ridge and put up my tent if rain catches me more than a day's travel from an all-weather road—my theory being I'd rather sit down in a place of my own choosing than make a forced camp in a sea of mud after slipping off the track into a hole or gutter.)

During my first two years of Land Roving, I notched up some 80 000 kilometres, mostly in western NSW and Queensland, plus a run up the Birdsville Track and a tour of the Northern Territory. The only replacements were a clutch plate, a universal joint on the rear drive shaft and a front wheel bearing. These items seem as nothing thirty years on, but the clutch gave up in sand dunes near Lake Frome, the universal snapped in the Diamantina and the wheel bearing collapsed in Arnhem Land. Such experiences taught me to carry plenty of spares and tools and caused me to become something of a bush mechanic, against my natural inclinations.

My first book, *People of the Inland*, was based on those early Land Roving years, when I encountered all manner of outback characters, including squatters, shearers, cooks, rodeo riders, professional trappers and shooters, boundary riders, drovers, truckies, pub keepers and assorted itinerants, many of them misfits and as eccentric as myself. One of my

Camped behind Seven Mile Beach near Gerringong, with one of the earliest-made Land Rovers (80-inch wheelbase).

most poignant early encounters took place in the 'corner country' near Tibooburra, where I fell in briefly with a newly married couple. He was a local station hand, just returned from his first trip to Sydney, where he had impetuously married a starry-eyed lass from the beachside suburb of Manly. They were waiting in town for the mail truck to take them to their first marital home, an outstation on fetchingly named Lake Pure, several hundred kilometres north of the Cooper in Queensland. 'It sounds loverly,' the young thing mooned. 'I love to be near the water.' Her husband coughed nervously and changed the subject. I left ahead of them and a day or so later drove past Lake Pure outstation. It was a sagging ruin, half buried by a sand dune that had built up against it. Sheets of loose roofing iron clanged in the hot desert wind, torn lengths of hessian flapped in glassless window openings and there was a constant, mournful creak from the windmill, leaning drunkenly over the collapsing, rotten stock yards. The 'lake' was a dry and dusty claypan that year, shimmering in the desert mirage. I often wondered how the young bride from Manly fared at Lake Pure and how long the marriage lasted.

By the standards of the day, there wasn't much wrong with our 1954 LWB Land Rover, apart from being deucedly uncomfortable. It always started and rarely stopped, except when fed muddy petrol pumped from forty-four gallon drums in remote places.

Even when breakages occurred (such as those mentioned), you got a few hundred miles warning before whatever it was finally gave up the ghost. Only electrical failures caught you totally unawares. Steering backlash was fearsome, but this was tamed by fitting a shock absorber between the steering rod and the front chassis. The 'adjustable' twin air vents above the dash were a great idea in those days before air-conditioning, except that the screw knob adjustment quickly filled with dust and jammed shut (in hot weather) or open (during rain). Murphy's Law.

Around 1958, a Series 2 model came on the market, in panel van form, with an allegedly bigger, better motor and other mechanical improvements, including lever controls for the front air vents. I didn't care to know about overhead valves, etc., but I liked the idea of an all-metal body, as against cab and canvas canopy—and the new quick-acting air vents were irresistible. We bought a cream coloured LWB and drove it almost non-stop back and forth across the continent for several years. Again I clocked up several hundred thousand kilometres and had only minor problems—mainly to do with rubber, as I recall: radiator hoses, fan belts, clutch and brake master cylinders, etc. Maybe another wheel bearing and a universal joint. The motor, transmission and air vents worked perfectly. I did twist off a few rear axles, but only when I fitted dual wheels, an ill-advised experiment. Which led me to the discovery that letting down the tyres is a better way of getting added traction on the rare occasions this is required.

As a matter of fact, I did quite a bit of sand driving, practising first in the Cronulla dunes, not far from what was then our home on nearby Port Hacking. Then I got some tuition from the late Mac Clarke of Andado station on the western edge of the Simpson desert, before crossing from Dalhousie to old Annandale, above Birdsville.

Sensibly, I followed the various oil company seismic tracks, but there was enough sand about to make letting down the tyres necessary once or twice. Which led to another discovery: the spark-plug pump!

Our cream LWB and I fetched up in some odd places and savoured a variety of interesting experiences. Near Arnhem Land, I fell in with some members of the shooting fraternity. They shot all sorts of things: crocodiles, buffalo...each other. One lady was wont to walk naked down the main street of Pine Creek, loosing off shots from a .303 rifle at anything that took her eye. This happened while I was in the general store. The proprietor was Chinese and his clientele were of fairly mixed origins. When I politely enquired about the hullabaloo outside, someone replied: 'That just Maureen on the grog again. More better you hang on here a bit longer. She still got a couple shots left...' Apparently everyone in Pine Creek knew how many rounds are contained in a .303 magazine clip. Another customer said scornfully 'Ah, she couldn't hit a shithouse with a handful of wheat at ten feet!' To prove his statement, he strode out of the store, jumped into a Jeep and drove off.

There were a couple of quick shots, but the Jeep driver continued on, unscathed. As if the 'all clear' had sounded, everyone left the shop. Soon after that episode, my friend Don MacGregor, a sometime resident of Pine Creek, was shot by a lady at point blank range with a .303—so they weren't all poor markswomen! Don survived and established a successful tourist camp not far from Arnhem Land.

On a subsequent trip, I went looking for the remains of explorer Ludwig Leichhardt, at first in the Diamantina country of south-western Queensland.

Half a century earlier, some harnessware and other gear had been dug out of a sand dune at what was thought to be Leichhardt's last camp. The trail proved false and I have always remembered a local man's comment on the futility of trying to find anything in that howling wilderness: 'There wouldn't have been any trace of him left after the first blow...the sand's so soft around here, yer could push a man underground with a forked stick.'

After giving up in that area, I drove the Series 2 LWB up the Tanami

Track through Halls Creek to the Kimberleys, where explorer Augustus Gregory, sent to look for the missing Leichhardt in 1856, reckoned the erratic German had fetched up. Gregory discovered a camp made by Ludwig on his fatal 1848 journey at Elsey Creek, not far from what is now Mataranka and deduced he had probably gone on to the Kimberleys and perished in The Wet, or been speared by the unusually fierce tribespeople of that area.

I discovered no trace of Leichhardt, but I did verify that Land Rover radiators were prone to come adrift about every 5000 kilometres when bashing over rough outback tracks (the mountings were later strengthened and modified).

In the early 1970s, the American *National Geographic* magazine began to help with my expenses, so I traded up to a bonzer new Series 2A LWB station wagon. Joy unconfined! I suppose it had its faults, but I don't remember any—just the splendiferous luxury of the outfit.

Seats fore and aft, doors fore and aft (swung on outrigger hinges that stopped them springing agape on to the first catch when you hit a hard bump), insulated ceiling with lights, plus external sunroof, fold-down steps, lined doors with map pockets, heavy bonnet and firewall soundproofing, softer and slightly adjustable driver's seat, no-backlash steering, improved bonnet release, bigger, better radiator (strongly mounted). . . and so on. Plus no doubt, an improved motor, transmission and suspension— items I confess I gave scant attention in the general excitement of owning my first luxury vehicle. It would probably look and feel like a truck now, but at the time, the Series 2A station wagon was akin to a four-wheel drive Rolls Royce.

About this time I had delusions of becoming an afficionado of the Land Rover marque and purchased, for farm use (we were now at Foxground) a Series 1 SWB 1948 model, the original 80-inch wheelbase job. A couple of years later, not to be outdone, my number one son, Thor, purchased a slightly younger 88-inch SWB, which he 'modified' for outback travel (wide tyres, bull-bar, long range tanks, driving lights, extended exhaust, all the usual things).

On our first two-vehicle safari, to Coober Pedy, Thor's pride and joy developed engine, gearbox and diff problems all on the one day! We left it in a shed on Anlaby station, South Australia, in the care of friend Geoffrey Dutton, who was to become literary-magazine editor of *The Australian* newspaper and later a Mudgee writer. Thor's Land Rover may be at Anlaby still.

The LWB station wagon took our family film crew (we were now making television documentaries) all over the three eastern states without missing a beat. Somehow it escaped the rigours of the desert, but it got its share of hard going from the alps of Victoria to the rainforests and deep creek crossings of Northern Queensland. It notched rather less kilometres than my earlier Land Rovers, but as Thor did most of the driving, it was tested fairly severely (he was a spare-time rally driver).

By 1973, we had the combined resources of the *National Geographic* and Channel 7 behind us, so I lashed out on a Range Rover, one of the first to reach these shores. This was surely the ultimate four-wheel drive off-roader, I thought. And still do. The Range Rover took us all over backblocks Australia in perfect comfort and never missed a beat, apart from getting its bulging radial tyres spiked and shedding minor bits like rear vision mirrors and door handles (for which there were no replacements available). It was utterly reliable and never broke anything serious, although it was the only vehicle in which I did much genuine off-roading (in search of a lost aircraft in Central Australia, finding out the true story of Gibson in the desert which bears his name, etc.). Apart from being the most comfortable and genuinely 'unstoppable' vehicle from Solihull that I had owned, the RR performed on bitumen like a sports car, recording a true mph 'ton' (160 km/h).

Those who know me won't be surprised at this story. I'm prone to wild enthusiasms, often short-lived, one recurring obsession being high fidelity music reproduction. Yes, I have bouts of audiophilemania. Recently I discovered CDs, which led to the acquisition of an expensive player, an even more expensive amplifier (made in a bark hut factory at Dyer's Crossing in rural NSW, so they aren't all Japanese), and most expensive of all, new speakers.

What has this to do with four-wheel driving? I'm coming to it. The opportunity to obtain what I considered in the heat of the moment to be the best speakers in the world came at short notice. After a high-speed dash from Foxground to Sydney, in order to audition these desirable thunder-boxes, I returned home and after five minutes' deliberation, began negotiations by phone. A modicum of haggling and they were mine, provided I brought a bank cheque that night and took them away (their owner was shifting house to Queensland next morning and the furniture van was already at the door). Fine, except that my car is rather smaller than the two speakers.

After a frantic whip-around among my farming neighbours, I borrowed a battered and mud-splattered Japanese kombi-style van, full of sheep droppings and empty corn sacks. The sun was already down, but the lights worked, so I got on my way as fast as the oriental motorised Weetbix box would carry me. I had no idea what I was driving and didn't much care, my attention focused on getting to those speakers. Once they were stowed aboard, I drove home rather more circumspectly, not wishing to damage my investment. It had been raining at Foxground and the steep, half-kilometre goat track up to my house was badly washed out and slippery. The little Jap van eventually bogged down on a steep pinch.

Foiled and furious, I tramped through the darkness up to the house and phoned my neighbour. I apologised that I was unable to return his vehicle until morning, when I intended towing it with my trusty TEA Ferguson tractor. There was a longish silence, then my neighbour said drily: 'Did you try four-wheel drive?' Thankful he couldn't see me blushing, I confessed I hadn't noticed his vehicle had that capability. 'I thought you would've known that, a man in your position,' came the laconic reply. A man in my position—how true! 'Well, thanks for telling me, I'll try again,' I mumbled. 'Don't forget to lock the front hubs first,' came his parting shot. I took a torch back with me and after rubbing some caked mud and cowdung off the vehicle, ascertained that I was in temporary possession of a Toyota Tarago 4×4. After giving the front hubs a twist, I got in and sure enough, there was the additional gear shifter I hadn't noticed due to my obsessive state over the speakers. Given the use of all its wheels, the Tarago climbed easily up to my house. Where I realised I had no one to help me unload anyway (each speaker requiring at least two strong people to lift it). Such are the penalties of blind passion.

One of my regular fellow-travellers complained recently that I never convey to her any of the 'secrets' of four-wheel driving technique. We were stuck halfway up a sand dune near Coongie Lakes at the time. As usual, I hadn't bothered to engage four-wheel drive until forced to. I got out and locked the Pathfinder's front hubs, climbed back in, pulled the correct lever and restarted the motor. We were balked at a steep angle, the rear wheels somewhat dug in. 'Surely it won't climb straight up from here?' my companion asked. 'Of course not,' I responded, backing down on to the claypan behind us. Far enough so that when we moved forward, there was enough momentum to justify second gear as we reached the foot of the dune. We sailed over in great style. 'Nothing to it,' I observed. 'I could've done that!' came the response. 'Yes,' I agreed, 'because your common sense told you it would be necessary to back down first and get up some momentum.'

That's largely what four-wheel driving is all about—common sense. You either have it or you don't. There are few secrets that I know of...except perhaps not slipping the clutch in deep water crossings, or driving out on the battery if the motor drowns. 'But common sense should keep you out of such situations in the first place,' I added, 'unless you are test-driving for *Overlander* or competing in a club event or somesuch.'

'What about real rough stuff, like boulders and gutters and ridges and logs and things?' came the next question. 'Use low range, so you can proceed slowly—and for maximum traction—keeping your wheels on the highest ground, not the diffs and sump. Again, just common sense—which might suggest it's quicker and easier to walk over such country, rather than drive...'

Early in 1987, after a long break from off-roading, I resumed my longtime love affair with four-wheel driving in general and the house of Rover in particular. After driving a succession of Japanese offerings on assorted outback safaris, I found myself once again at the helm of a Range Rover, headed for a week in Victoria's wild country, centred on the high-plains town of Dargo, as detailed in an earlier chapter. It was a pleasant experience and quickly re-established the RR's supremacy over all-comers in the off-road field. Disregarding price, of course, and assuming that like me, you prefer being comfortable to being uncomfortable, would rather go faster than slower and appreciate good handling, on and off the road.

Driving the Highline RR made me wonder if the new-breed traditionally shaped Land Rovers had been similarly improved. To my eye they looked much the same as the dear old wrist-snapping, spine bashing, noisy dust-suckers of the sixties. But I had read they now have RR suspensions, power steering and various other refinements, such as integral air-conditioning, permanent four-wheel drive, etc. Plus a *Japanese* diesel fed engine!

When the editor suggested I write an occasional feature travel story for *Overlander* magazine, the first door I knocked on was that of the venerable house of JRA (Jaguar-Rover-Australia). No problem—I could have a County 110 diesel for two weeks and take it where I liked.

I chose to take the County diesel back to Grants Head and environs, plus as far inland through the big timber country as Tamworth, where a number of banjo pickers, guitarists, mouth harpists and fiddle players were scheduled to hold their sixteenth annual country music festival. The reasons for this last decision were various: my number three son, Vandal, a bluegrass banjo picker, was going to be at Tamworth, likewise Mare, his mother, a child of the Appalachians (and I retain a mild interest in banjo music, having studied the instrument for some years, until forced to accept that, like bike riding, I have little aptitude for it). In addition, another onetime fellow traveller and family friend, Danish-born Monika Allen, had invited us to Tamworth for the launching of her book on the festival.

So off I went down Memory Lane in my 1987 version of the 1960s series Land Rovers. The general appearance of the County 110 delighted me—just like the old models, except for a few rounded corners. The seating is somewhat improved, but still gives the same general impression: spartan. Sitting up in the pilot's chair, high above the road, peering ahead over the square, flat bonnet, felt just like old times. Sure enough, within a couple of hours I had the old familiar crick in my neck I used to get driving the old models. I soon found out why they call it the 110—that's about as fast as it will go, except downhill.

The weather was hot for most of the trip and the County's air conditioner was barely equal to the task. Again, never mind, just open a window, as we did in the old days. Ah, talk of nostalgia—that really took me back! Particularly the vibration on idle of the diesel motor— like a fifties LR running on two cylinders—so much so, I christened the County 'the cocktail shaker'. But, these carping criticisms aside, I reckoned the vehicle an ideal long-range outback tourer—particularly for the adventurer who plans to do some real off-roading.

The Laurieton to Bonny Hills area had changed beyond recognition since I built my hut in the wilderness, the old wild seclusion replaced with motels and urban-style holiday developments. I discovered my old block of land, now cleared and manicured like Hyde Park, with a cream brick home and swimming pool. The once lonely, pristine beach today is entombed among caravan parks.

I fled inland through the timber towns of Kew and Kendall, making a brief detour into the state forest to pay my respects to the famous Bird Tree, a giant blackbutt some seventy metres tall. Heavy rain made photography tedious and the roads slippery but the County 110 remained sure-footed at any sensible speed. The country inland from Kendall through Lorne and Comboyne to Nowendoc is magnificent, a mixture of rugged forests and lush pastoral country, all of it steep, with rushing creeks and occasional waterfalls. The area is traversed with a network of forestry commission roads, all neatly sign-posted, but not with destinations, just the names of the roads: Campbell's Road, Moore's Road, MacDonald's Road, etc. So it's easy to get lost. I did.

Rain was bucketing down, the mist closed in and somewhere west of the Bulga Plateau, with my trusty Suunto pocket compass at home on my desk at Foxground, I got nicely boxed. Suffice to say that when I finally popped out of the forest on to a proper road with a sign pointing to Wingham, I went in that direction. Then on through steady, drenching rain to spend the night in a motel at Taree and to hell with what *Overlander* readers might think!

Next morning I drove under a blue sky to Gloucester, then explored north-west into the Woko National Park area, going via Rookhurst, which is a tiny country school, a tennis court and one house. Most of the other place names in this area are just that, so do any shopping or refuelling in Gloucester! This is truly picturesque country, with a capital P—ideal for the cameraperson, artist, walker, botanist, bird-watcher and all those seeking to refresh themselves with what Henry David Thoreau called 'the tonic of wilderness'. Canoeing is popular on the many sizeable streams, including the Bowman and Manning Rivers (you can hire canoes just out of Gloucester on the Barrington Road). Trout fishing is another possibility. There are several good free-camping sites along the Little Manning River between Gloryvale and Bretti, also upstream in the Woko National Park, which offers facilities such as good pit toilets, fireplaces and log tables.

The name Carters Road on the map intrigued me, so I drove beyond Woko to Curricabark station, then followed this excellent route high into the hills beyond Bennys Top to the Pigna Barney River. Great country! But literally prickling with *Keep Out* and *No Camping* notices, a result (speaking as a man-on-the-land myself) probably of a few idiots doing the wrong thing, such as littering, setting fires, shooting, frightening stock, damaging fences, and leaving gates open. Here and there rough tracks slip away into dense forest country where I daresay responsible off-roaders could lose themseves for a night or two without arousing much attention. Don't be alarmed if a mob of wild brumbies stampede through your lonely camp in the dead of night. Not far south-west there are plenty of state forests near Barrington Tops where camping *is* permitted, plus a multitude of fire trails to tempt four-wheel drive explorers.

After a few days of pleasant camp life, I blundered on to one of Kerry Packer's rising equestrian empires, centred on Ellerston and Glenrock stations. These isolated properties are in magnificent hill country near the headwaters of the Hunter River, below Gogs Top and Mount Royal Ranges. At Ellerston, the media magnate was spending squillions of dollars on what must be the biggest and mostest horse-breeding centre in the universe. It was not really four-wheel drive country, despite eighteen creek crossings in as many kilometres between Glenrock and Barry stations. Alas, Mr Packer does not encourage campers. The best I could do was set up my igloo tent on the banks of Ben Hall Creek, beside the road to Nundle a couple of kilometres from Barry homestead. I was entirely surrounded by several thousand goats, which were being used to clean up the neglected and overgrown pasturelands.

On then to meet Vandal and Mare at Tamworth, where we spent a few pleasant but hot days in company with about 30 000 other country music enthusiasts. Hail and rain had played havoc in the town's several camping grounds, so we were pleased to stumble on a motel cancellation for our four-night stay. After the music, the best thing I enjoyed during the festival was the motel air-conditioner (temperatures were mostly in the forties, night and day), plus the Stockman's Steakhouse Restaurant, a few kilometres south of town on the Newcastle Road. We dined there four nights in a row, in company with mostly local residents, who come regularly during the festival for the establishment's advertised main attraction: *no* country music! The food is pretty good, too—and inexpensive.

Driving home, I mused that over the years I had come full circle in the world of Land Roving, starting with their early basic post-war models and ending with their ultimate basic jet-age offering. In appearance and ambience, the earliest and latest Land Rovers bear an uncanny resemblance. I can't think of any other marque that has retained such a constant image for so long (not even the Porsche 911). With good reason, I'm sure, not out of cussedness or conservatism. It was a good basic idea in the 1940s and it's still a good basic design in the late 1980s.

18 Down the lazy river

Grandfather Caleb Carter used to take me cod fishing on the Murray, back in the mists of time. We trolled feather-tailed metal aeroplane spinners bigger than many fish caught these days. That was when the Murray waters were clear enough for the cod to see and chase spinners, before the muddy drainage from irrigation canals and burgeoning towns fouled our greatest river. Caleb fished mostly between Swan Hill and Barmah, north of Kerang—we lived further south, in Bendigo. He also took me duck shooting on Kow Swamp near Gunbower and upstream toward Echuca, then a decaying backwater, dreaming of its paddlewheeler heyday.

I can still hear the punch of Caleb's twelve-gauge shotgun reverberating through the rivergums and the splashing of his Irish retriever dogs coming out of the swamp with dead or dying teal and wood ducks clasped in their jaws. And recall the huge, gape-mouthed shining wet cod, sometimes as big as me, gasping in the bottom of the flat-bottomed boat. The unforgettable stuff of adventure for a ten year old, unimpressed by grave Prime Minister Robert Gordon Menzies' recent announcement that England and therefore Australia was now at war with Nazi Germany.

A decade after that was ended, I was back on the Murray with camera and typewriter, recording the lives of the river people: professional fishermen, ex paddleboat skippers, redgum sleeper cutters, charcoal burners, eucalyptus oil distillers, tigersnake hunters and other itinerants. Above the Hume Weir east of Albury, I photographed the removal of the old town of Tallangatta to its new site and the drowning of those buildings that could not be moved, beneath the rising waters of the enlarged Hume Reservoir. That was in 1955–56.

Further upstream, beyond Geehi, Tom Groggin and Kosciusko, toward that lesser peak known as the Pilot, where the great river begins, I recorded the lifestyles of the cattle graziers and brumby hunters of the

171

high country. The most famous of them, immortalised by A.B. 'Banjo' Paterson as the legendary Man from Snowy River, was supposed to be John Riley, of Tom Groggin station. In which case Paterson's epic poem should have been titled 'The Man from Murray River'. But Paterson never said who inspired him, and his widow Alice recalled: 'Many people claimed to be the Man from Snowy River but my husband said he had no special person in mind when he wrote the verses.'

Thus truth erodes the gilt from memory and fable. With this in mind, I wondered how my recollections of the magic of the Murray would stand re-appraisal when the editor of *Overlander* handed me the keys of the latest short-base Nissan Patrol and said: 'Try to be back within two weeks.' I doubted if this was enough time, because another legend has it that a cork tossed into the Murray near its source below the Pilot takes seven weeks to reach the river mouth near Goolwa in South Australia. Notwithstanding that a Nissan Patrol can travel faster than a floating cork, it seemed to me prudent for any delineators of the modern Murray scene to slow down to the pace of life along that great lazy river, if they wished to get the story anywhere near 'properly true', as the annihilated original inhabitants might have said.

Long aware that life's a compromise, I began my odyssey undeterred.

First compromise was to start my story below the Hume Weir at Corowa, where the river has established the sluggish, meandering 'Mississippi gait' for which it is best known. (Above the weir, the rushing, turbulent, high-country Murray is a separate story.)

According to the songs and legends of the original historians of this area, the great snake Biami dug the course of the Murray. That seems reasonable, when you look at charts of the river, which follows a most serpentine course below Albury, becoming increasingly convoluted, akin to the writhing of a great python, as it meanders across the plains toward South Australia. No wonder the course is tortuous and the pace lazy, when you consider that on its 2225-kilometre journey to the sea from the Hume Weir, the Murray drops only 192 metres. (The creek that tumbles through my farm at Foxground descends as far in a couple of kilometres!)

Below the Murray's junction with the Darling, Aboriginal historians agree that a great cod dug the river's course to the sea. Hunters snared the giant fish in Lake Alexandrina and the enusing struggle created the mess of estuaries, bays and islands of the Coorong, that confused mouth of Australia's greatest river.

No one, black or white, knows how many Aborigines lived along the Murray when the bickering European explorers Hume and Hovell 'discovered' the river near Albury in 1842. (Naming it the Hume, by the way.) But from a reading of 'our' (i.e. European) history of Australia, the indications are that the Murray and its tributaries supported perhaps the densest Aboriginal population on the continent. For example, the second white 'discoverer' of the river, Charles Sturt (who named it the Murray), recorded sighting 4000 Aborigines during his voyage of 1830. They surely represented only a small percentage of the total black population living beside that stream which was teeming with fish and wildfowl, edible reptiles and furred creatures. It seems reasonable to conjecture that from sightings of 4000, a total muster of at least 40 000 could be projected (including the aged, women, boys, girls and young children, who were rarely sighted by explorers). And Sturt travelled only half the course of the Murray, entering it via the Murrumbidgee below Balranald. So an Aboriginal population of 100 000 along the river is a reasonable guesstimate. Lest you grow weary of bald statistics, I will record only a final demographic note: the fullblood Aboriginal population along the Murray shortly after Federation was nil.

Making my first contact with the Murray at Corowa was not so much a compromise as a subterfuge. Just across the narrow wooden bridge into Victoria is the rustic village of Wahgunyah—close by is George Sutherland Smith's venerable All Saints winery—and a little further on, the town of Rutherglen. I needed cooking wine, you see. Below Corowa, I found the NSW side of the river more interesting as far as Tocumwal, then crossed back into Victoria and followed a series of lesser roads to Barmah, exploring a few of the many tracks to such fascinating hideaways as (naturally) Carter's Beach and Barmah State Forest. The latter is a huge tract of river box and redgums worth a few days of anyone's time.

Access to Barmah State Forest is from the settlement of Picola North (to the Bunyip Track and Gulf Track) or via the timber town of Barmah (to the Moira Lakes and Sand Ridge Tracks). Due to its location on a great loop in the river's course, Barmah can boast of having the only Victorian pub north of the Murray. It also has a store and camping ground, plus a distinctly rakish, last-outpost atmosphere, especially when the locals gather in that unique pub.

In the heyday of the Murray riverboats, the redgums of the great Barmah forest were decimated by loggers' supplying the railways in both colonies with sleepers. The uniquely hard, beautiful and long-lasting timber was also used in general construction work, bridges, wharves and shearing sheds, and to make furniture (the bar in the famous Ettamogah Pub is of redgum). Soon after Federation, the trees were given limited protection and today's logging is strictly controlled.

Tucked into the Barmah Forest Reserve, a few kilometres from town, is an excellent interpretive centre, run by the Forestry and Conservation Commission. Apart from the variety of historic, ethnic, ecological and geological displays, the centre offers ten different video documentaries for viewing. Two deal with Aboriginal history and trade routes, another with riverboat life. My earnest advice is don't miss the interpretive centre at Barmah. My other advice is to be extremely cautious when driving minor tracks in the forest after rain! My visit followed weeks of intermittent showers and I had some most interesting experiences in the short Nissan Patrol. You don't necessarily bog in the greasy grey clay—you just cease to go anywhere, except perhaps sideways. Or in circles!

On to Echuca, via a good Victorian gravelled road that crosses the Goulburn River, a Murray tributary, at Stewarts Bridge. During the golden age of paddlewheelers, betwixt 1865–95, Echuca was Australia's third busiest port. Around 100 000 bales of wool crossed the town wharf annually, plus a similar volume of general cargo. Customs officers cleared 800 craft annually, while Chinese, Dutch, Norwegian, Swedish, German, Irish, Scots, Canadian and American crew boozed and played in the port's eighty-four hotels and umpteen brothels. (One of the latter is preserved today, unstaffed, as a tourist attraction.) The town newspaper, the *Riverine Herald*, was published daily. The railway line from Melbourne to Echuca was extended, by a private company, across the Murray some eighty kilometres to Deniliquin, in the heart of NSW's Riverina district. Soon after, more railheads were established on the Murray, firmly anchoring NSW's Riverina to the junior colony. Settlers around Balranald, Moulamein, Deniliquin, Berrigan, Corowa and other centres in NSW thought of themselves as Victorians and supported that colony's proposed annexation of the Riverina. There was also a Riverina movement in favour of separate statehood. Nothing came of these schemes, but to this day, many folk north of the Murray think and act Victorian. Not so many years ago, the mayor of Deniliquin said to me: 'Ah, you're from up in NSW, are you?'

Strangely, the match that lit Echuca's brief candle, the railway, eventually snuffed its flame. Rival Murray railheads, on both sides of the river from Morgan in South Australia to Albury in NSW, drew trade away from the bustling, boisterous port. They eventually extinguished all the ports on the Murray and its tributaries—the Edward, the Murrumbidgee and the Darling—sounding the deathknell of the paddlewheelers and other riverboats (there were a few screw-driven craft). Now tourism has brought a revival for the paddlewheelers, while house boats and smaller pleasure craft are becoming alarmingly popular: ski boats, speed boats, jet skis and the like. House boats, some offering the height of luxury, can be hired at most of the larger Murray towns. Off-season, they are probably great fun, but I imagine in the busy holiday periods, it might be quieter and less stressful to 'relax' at home! The once tranquil Murray, particularly that stretch between Renmark and Morgan, is now one of the nation's 'playgrounds', boasting four-hundred more hours of annual sunshine than that other Shangri-La, Queensland's Gold Coast. Ah well, that's progress for you.

Below Echuca, in grandfather Caleb's old stamping grounds around Gunbower, Cohuna and Barham, I found side tracks leading down to a riverland scene that has changed little since I was a boy. No motels, hotels, clubs, poker machines, house boats, museums, jet skis, etc.—just the tree-lined river swirling lazily along its serpentine course. Here and there good natural campsites on the high banks, thankfully without the 'amenities' that draw the crowds. Generally not much firewood, though, because it's hard these days, even with four-wheel drive, to locate pristine campsites on the banks of the Murray.

For those who prefer flushing toilets and hot showers, be assured the river has plenty of first-class camping and caravan parks, rarely more than fifty kilometres apart, from Albury to the Murray mouth at Goolwa. Most with excellent on-site vans available. And there are countless motels, hotels, holiday cottages, cabins, flats and apartments. Or you can enjoy pampered luxury afloat on the new tourist paddlewheelers, such as the giant *Murray Princess*, which plies up and downstream out of Renmark. Marvellous, if you like that sort of thing. All you need is your cheque book. And the compulsive gamblers should know all the poker machines are in the clubs on the NSW side of the river, those machines being illegal in Victoria.

At Swan Hill, the river scene gets very civilised downstream to Mildura, the heart of the Sunraysia irrigation country. Like Echuca, Swan Hill has re-created a pioneer village—worth a visit, but if you miss it, there's another at Loxton. Murray Downs homestead, just out of Swan Hill on the Moulamein Road, provides another look at yesteryear. It comes complete with olde-worlde restaurant featuring spit roasts. Towards Robinvale, historic Tyntynder homestead is also open to the public. Just above Robinvale, near Wood-Wood and Boundary Bend, there are extensive state forests between the road and river with interesting tracks to lure the well-shod off-roader reader.

Camping is permitted in Victoria's state forests. One sign-posted track goes to the Murray's junction with the Murrumbidgee. But watch your step after rain and if in doubt, try reverse!

Mildura is all orange groves, vineyards and orchards, interspersed with olive groves and almond plantations. The rural landscape is distinctly Mediterranean, as is the population, while the architecture is reminiscent of Los Angeles, that other irrigated Eden on the edge of a desert. No wonder—the Canadian-born Chaffey brothers, who established Mildura, pioneered similar schemes in California. Their plan to make an oasis in the desert succeeded, but their efforts to make Mildura a temperence settlement failed. The Mildura Working Mens' Club has the longest bar in the world, at 90.8 metres! The original vineyards were not established to produce wine grapes, but sultanas and raisins, dried on racks beneath the hot Mallee sun.

Just below Mildura, on the opposite bank, is Wentworth NSW, at the Murray's junction with the longer Darling River (yes it is, at 2730 kilometres). A country town compared with Mildura, Wentworth has greater historical interest. Here pioneer overlander Joseph Hawden crossed the Darling in 1838 with the first mob of cattle brought from NSW to Adelaide, in the new colony of South Australia. He was closely followed by Edward John Eyre, Charles Sturt and others.

In the ensuing decade, overlanders bringing stock to South Australia were in frequent conflict with the Aboriginal residents of the area, who resisted the invasion as fiercely as they could, spearing a number of Europeans. This incited the indiscriminate shooting of Aboriginal men, women and children, culminating in the dreadful massacre at Rufus River, where at least two hundred tribespeople died. Ironically, many of the killings were attended by the South Australian Protector of Aborigines, Dr Mathew Moorhouse. The overlanders were not the first to slaughter Aborigines along the Murray—explorer Major Thomas Mitchell established the bloody precedent in 1836, while 'discovering' and naming Swan Hill.

Just out of Wentworth on the Renmark Road are the colourful Perry sand dunes, complete with an official Recreational Vehicle Area where off-roaders are invited to test their skills. There is a vaguely marked obstacle course for those who enjoy the challenge of de-bogging. The sandhills are as red and steep as any in the Simpson Desert but are conveniently located between the river and main road. Some good stands of shady gums are nearby, providing picnicking or camping spots. But firewood is scarce, as the place is popular with locals.

The remainder of the 180-kilometre trip to Renmark follows an earth and gravel road through inhospitable country that would be no fun in summer or after heavy rain. Real backblocks stuff, with the tiny settlement of Rufus River on the edge of Lake Victoria the only sign of civilisation. A fellow traveller told me the Hare Krishna people some time ago re-opened Lake Victoria station, but I did not investigate, as I find their chanting tedious.

Barely twenty kilometres further west, close to the South Australian border, is Cal-Lal homestead. The property was suggested as a site for the national capital because of its location at the corner of three states. All I can say is: I'm glad they chose Canberra! Great off-roading country, though. Few fences, camp wherever you can find a tree, or explore along various unmarked tracks toward the Murray. I left the main road and followed the old mail track in past Cal-Lal, popping back onto the 'highway' about thirty kilometres later in South Australia.

Renmark is a sizeable, modern Riverland town with everything—including a very large, picturesque, excellent camping and caravan park amid trees on the bank of the river. Highly recommended.

From nearby Paringa there is a not-to-be-missed detour to the colourful, dramatic Headings Cliffs and Murtho Forest. The free camping grounds are highly recommended (I even found some firewood!). No amenities, just splendid riverbank naturalness. Angove's huge and picturesque vineyard and winery are on this road, protected by majestic poplar-tree windbreaks marching over the horizon.

The Chaffey brothers pioneered irrigation farming at Renmark, before they shifted to Mildura. Today the orchard-lands and vineyards seem to extend unbroken through Berri, Barmera and Loxton to Waikerie, 150 kilometres as the river winds downstream. (Rising salt levels threaten the Riverland's future as a modern Garden of Eden, but that's another story.) The main crops are citrus, grapes, peaches, apricots and, recently, olives. Berri is the orange-juice capital of Australia and boasts the country's biggest winery, crushing 30 000 tonnes of grapes yearly, with a storage capacity of 27 million litres of wine.

There are other wineries, some producing traditional Italian- and Greek-style wines. And so on... lots of everything, including a polyglot community with a variety of ethnic clubs, paddlewheeler cruises, house boats, caravan parks, museums, zoo, fish farms, wildlife sanctuaries, every sporting facility, hire bikes, greyhound racing, even gliding clubs. A surfeit, in fact, so I went via the historic Overland Corner Road to Morgan, a comparatively sleepy, traditional-style port, where the Murray turns abruptly south toward the sea at Goolwa.

My advice is: see the Riverland (certainly Katarpko and other game reserves) by all means, but don't miss the Overland Corner Hotel on the Morgan Road. No accommodation, but you can camp nearby on the river flats, as the early overlanders did, while resting their cattle at Herron's Bend, before crossing the river. Plenty of firewood! The pub has been refurbished by the National Trust to its pristine condition (it was built in 1859). No longer licensed, unfortunately, but you can buy marvellous hand-crafted chocolates made on the premises by the lady of the house, also a fascinating booklet on the early history of the district, as told by local residents. The long-term plan is for the pub to be a going concern again, with licence and (limited) accommodation.

Life was tough in the early days along this stretch of the Murray. During the Depression of the 1890s government-sponsored communes of unemployed city folk were established between Waikerie and Pyrup (above Berri). The new settlers were given a handout, tools and some camping equipment, and were dumped from paddlesteamers in groups along the river bank and told to make the best of it. A local historian related: 'Some laboured and won; others went mad, blew their brains out or quietly hanged themselves. Women battled flies and mosquitoes, wilted in scorching summers out in the red sands. . .' Only one of the nine communes survives under its original charger: Lyrup.

The run south from Morgan to Mannum is through fairly lonely, sparsely settled country, a welcome change from the Holidayville atmosphere of the Riverland area. There are spectacular cliffs in many places, with endless billabongs and backwaters teeming with wildfowl of every description. Plenty of opportunities to free camp, or you can enjoy all amenities at places like Blanchetown. Budding anthropologists should look out for the Nildottie Cliffs near Devon Downs and Roonka stations, where the skeleton of Tartagan Man was found, plus Aboriginal tombs going back to 17 000 BC.

Below Mannum, a pleasant town, the river flows through increasingly developed countryside, via the towns of Murray Bridge and Tailem Bend, losing its identity as a river just below the village of Wellington, in the broad waters of Lake Alexandrina. Much of the landscape is now dotted with dairy cows.

Eventually I drove through a sort of rural suburbia around the lake's western shore to Goolwa and out onto Sir Richard Peninsula. This is as close as you can drive to the Murray mouth without breaking the law by off-roading across the protected, regenerating beach dunes.

My assignment completed, I quickly retraced my steps a few kilometres to Langhorne Creek, where I had glimpsed the Potts family's famous Bleasdale Cellars. I needed more cooking wine, you see.

19 The way we were

In 1983, I was outraged when *Wheels* did a comparison test of the Porsche 928S and Jaguar's XJ-S V12 and suggested the English car might be the better choice, in some circumstances. Five years later, having spent ten days and 2000 kilometres with the cabriolet version of the XJ-S, I was almost ready to agree—in some circumstances. No, I hadn't slipped my moorings (I'd just bought another Porsche!), so read on.

Fans aware of my twenty-five year allegiance to Stuttgart may well ask: under what circumstances might I consider the Coventry product more desirable? Well, if you are short of the readies, for a start. The German product costs roughly twice as much as the Jag, which in 1988 could be had for a mere $106 000 in cabriolet form. And if you prefer a sort of plush, regal progress, albeit at eye-widening speed, drifting in sequestered, club leather-armchair exclusivity, the XJ-SC V12 is your car. For nostalgia buffs, the Jag is the only choice, with its antiquated polished walnut and chrome facia, battleship proportions, soft, undulating ride, fold-down soft top, massive steering wheel and driver's doorstep handbrake. It is certainly not a car of this era. (During my brief stewardship, people kept asking: 'What a lovely old car—how old is it?' Answer: 'It's brand new.')

What was the doyen of Porschephiles doing in the anathema of Stuttgart? As usual, the editor of *Wheels*, Peter Robinson, was to blame. In his ceaseless efforts to break my Porsche habit, he chose the XJ-SC V12 for my final safari down Memory Lane. Mindful of my complaints about his earlier comparison of the Jag and the 928S, he remarked: 'This could be an enlightening experience for you, Jeffrey, provided you open both eyes.'

So it came to pass that once again I was running the heavily police-patrolled gauntlet between Goulburn and Albury, bound for the wine-producing area centred on Rutherglen in north-east Victoria. In earlier days I bummed around the district as an itinerant farm worker, stacking hay and picking fruit. Later I cut my journalistic teeth hereabouts, producing illustrated stories on the tobacco and hop growers of the nearby Ovens Valley, and profiles on identities like George Sutherland Smith, a pioneer vigneron who established the now famous house of All Saints at Wahgunyah. (In those days, his produce, mainly ports and muscats, rarely got much further than Albury, apart from occasional boot-loads sold to visiting oenophiles.)

This stretch of the Hume Highway is the *bête noire* of all Motoring Toad speedsters and the scene of continuing anguish as the radar raiders pile up our points and ravish our wallets. As usual, my trusty Whistler 2000 was riding shotgun with me, but I was keeping a careful eye ahead for those seasoned on-coming troops who don't pull the trigger until they see the whites of your eyes.

The XJ-SC V12, for all its olde-worlde charm, has mounted in its wood-veneered facia the very latest in electronic car computers. At the press of assorted buttons you can know your average speed, the elapsed time of your journey so far, your average fuel consumption, the precise number of litres per hundred kilometres the V12 is guzzling at the moment, the time—and probably your age next birthday, once you master the thing. I was explaining all this to my fellow traveller, saying something like 'Now, as I put my right foot down and we accelerate to 140, fuel consumption momentarily skyrockets...to, er...80 litres per 100 kilometres!' The shock of this sobering knowledge caused a brief lack of concentration and I failed to take my usual thirty-second interval glance in the rear vision mirror. When I did, it was full of a police patrol car flashing its headlights at me. 'Done like a dinner!' I groaned, pulling into the slow lane in front of the line of law-abiding motorists I had been passing. But the excited patrol car sped on, probably to a bank robbery or some other assignation. There is some justice after all—and, in the eyes of all the other drivers observing the legal limit at the time, one law for the rich and one for the poor.

At Yass, somewhat shaken, I pulled into a service station to allow the Big Cat to slake its thirst. But I must digress: some years ago I was tickled by a *New Yorker* magazine cartoon depicting a huge American flagship style vehicle being fuelled, the harassed service station attendant shouting to the driver: 'Would you please turn the motor off, sir?—I can't keep up with it!'

Well, at Yass the young female attendant announced the Jag was full after only a few dollars worth of unleaded had gone into the tank. Having in mind the distance I had travelled, I urged her to see if it would take more. She gave it another squirt and said 'No, it's full, sir. See, it's bubbling over.' So it was, but that meant the V12 was as economical as a motor scooter!

The Jaguar XJSC in the main street of Rutherglen.

'Try again, slowly, because I'd like the tank full,' I said. 'I'm doing a fuel consumption check.' Obligingly, she began to trickle more fuel in, pausing frequently when it bubbled up and over, seemingly full. Some ten minutes later she had coaxed another twenty litres of fuel into the tank! I imagined that with the V12's motor running, the *New Yorker* cartoon situation might have become a reality!

Foxground to Rutherglen is a 576-kilometre journey. The trip took us seven hours, including the long fuel stop at Yass, a half-hour picnic lunch, a visit to the famous Ettamogah Pub near Albury and a break for afternoon tea. So the Jag is no slouch.

This was my first experience of big-car motoring and the Jag seemed like an aircraft carrier for the first few days. I felt apprehensive when the scenery began to stream past at 160 knots or so, but eventually became confident of piloting the nearly two-tonne leviathan very rapidly indeed. My lasting impression of the XJ-SC is that it's a tractable, old-fashioned, civilised, fast conveyance. It is sometimes boring, always comfortable and often quite exhilarating, although the soft, floating ride is somewhat queasy-making at high speeds particularly on undulating highways and fast curves.

In and around Rutherglen we made frequent stops at wineries and restaurants during our seven-day bibing and dining tour. It was Melbourne Cup Weekend, but luckily the Tuileries French Restaurant at the Jolimont Winery and Cellars (formerly Seppelts) had a table to spare. We enjoyed an elegant experience.

The district wineries? A subject dear to my heart, but I must needs be brief. The best wines produced in the area, in rough order of quality and fame, are as follows: muscat of all types, including old or liqueur types; tokays ditto; ports of all types, including vintage; dry and sweet white wines; various sherries; sparkling champagne-style wines; red wines. These last require five to ten years in the bottle, so it is often hard to find any outstanding red wines ready for drinking. Cellars the serious drinker should not miss: Campbells, Stanton & Killeen, All Saints, St Leonards, Gehrigs, Chambers (Rosewood). This last establishment produces an Old Liqueur Muscat and an Old Liqueur Tokay judged by two international wine magazines as the best of their type in the world (but very expensive!). There are other wineries I did not visit or which were not to my taste—but they may be worth visiting and might please you better.

After what I fancy was four days in and around Rutherglen (one's sense of time becomes hazy on wine-sampling tours), I swung the Big Cat's helm over until her bow pointed due south, on course for the wineries of Kelly country, centred on Glenrowan.

We fetched up at Bailey's Winery, just a few kilometres out of town.

This cellar is famous in particular for its muscats and old tokays. They also market, in half bottles, a red open-wine, tasting like freshly pressed sweet grape juice, called *muscat à petits grains rouges*, which is worth buying just for the original label.

On then to Milawa and a pre-booked meal at the historic Old Emu Inn, one of my favourite Victorian country eateries. Hosts Val and Kurt Rietmann offer a variety of old-world peasant dishes such as house venison sausages mit Kartoffel (spuds), preceded by Swiss-style dumpling soup. Modest prices and BYO, which helps, mit log fires in winter. Almost next door is the Milawa Lodge Motel, where we stayed, which has its own restaurant, called La Vallette. Down the road about a kilometre is Falkirk House, where a range of a dozen or so made-on-the-farm gourmet mustards may be tasted and purchased. But Milawa's biggest drawcard is Brown Brothers Vineyard, one of the largest commercial wineries in north-eastern Victoria and to my taste, one of the best. Apart from the usual range of traditional muscats, tokays and ports, Brown Brothers make and market a palate-boggling array of dry and sweet white wines, including an excellent bubbly. They also offer a big variety of red wines, including some older vintages, ready to drink. Nearby is the not-to-be-missed Milawa Cheese Factory, offering a variety of products, including one in Tasmanian Mersey Valley style and Australia's answer to English Stilton.

After leaving Milawa, our wine bibing tapered off, which was just as well, because we were beginning to suffer sore heads. Not entirely from quaffing the local products. You see, the XJ-SC is not an easy car to enter or leave.

If you do the instinctive thing and put a leg and/or your posterior in first, you have to duck your head uncomfortably low to avoid banging it against the roof above the door opening. Even short people are prone to suffer a sore noggin while mastering the technique of getting in and out of the car. Which is to lead with your head and follow with your body, in or out. Deucedly awkward for chaps and decidedly indecorous for gals. Once seated, you make the further painful discovery that if you reach out to shut the wide open door, once again you bang your head against the low roofline. (It was pointed out to me that many Jaguar owners probably have someone to close the door after them!)

In the magnificently preserved historic town of Beechworth, we lingered over a few ales, for a change, in Tanswell's bonzer old Commercial Hotel, one of many National Trust protected buildings lining the main and back streets (where the original Ecks Brewery still stands). Once a goldmining centre and scene of anti-Chinese riots last century, Beechworth and environs are worth a day or so of anyone's time. Now the chief industry seems to be tourism, centred on history, arts and crafts, scenic tours and trout fishing. Victoria's snowfields are nearby. Lots of accommodation, modern and traditional, in what has to be one of Australia's most attractive country towns, set amid forests and mixed farmland with the alps as a backdrop in the powder-blue distance.

Not far away is rustic Yackandandah, smaller, a little deeper into the hills, sprinkled with craft shops and galleries in a setting reminiscent of an American goldrush town. Wood-oven baked bread, home-made pasties and suchlike, but nothing much in the way of a proper eatery and scarcely any overnight accommodation.

Not to worry, I had previously discovered the nearby Allans Flat Colonial Restaurant and Motel. This unique little hideaway, located in the middle of nowhere, is the nearest thing I know in Australia to provincial France. The restaurant was once the old bakery and post office, set amid spreading oaks and herb gardens above an attractive pond, *avec* rustic bridge and ducks. The four double motel units look out across fields to a line of hills. I fancy this could be the only motel in this country entirely surrounded by silence. For guests staying a few days there are shaded picnic tables on a flagged terrace and barbecue facilities nearby, above the wine cellar. Log fires in the restaurant in winter. 'Brunch' (including pancakes and maple syrup) served until 10 a.m., with midday as checkout-time. Very civilised.

Thence home to Foxground, not in record time, but very quickly and

Testing the Jaguar.

effortlessly. That is the thing about the Jaguar XJ-SC V12, I suppose—it is rather like passenger-jet travel—you get in and are encapsulated, the outside world does not exist and you are transported luxuriously and without drama to your destination.

There is certainly a sensation of speed (the scenery just whizzes past) but little excitement. In fact boredom is never far away, because this is not a driver's car—it is more an olde-worlde, elegant, luxurious form of travel. The fact that you have to steer it and occasionally press a pedal or button or push a lever is almost irrelevant. Not really my cup of tea and in fact at times I might have dropped off to sleep, but for the irritating wind-roar from the ill-fitting targa roof panels and cabriolet fold-down hood. The whole concept is not a very good idea. Getting the roof off and stowed in the boot or getting it out of the boot and back in position takes a deal of time and a toll of fingernails. I'm sure a sudden summer storm would produce a most ignominious situation. But no doubt Lord Peter Wimsey types find the whole business a ripping idea and deucedly enjoyable on a top-hole sunny day.

Eh, what, Carter? You carping, beastly rotter!

20 Gentlemen, start your motors!

By the 1980s, only fifty per cent of the Carter menfolk remained passionately absorbed in motoring and motor cars: the patriarch and his youngest (myself and Vandal). By then I had been grandfathered a number of times and was affectionately (?) known to half a dozen tiny tots as *Abuelo*, which is Spanish for 'grandfather'. We were recently established in our new Catalan-style farmhouse on a sequestered hillside in the rainforest above the pioneer cottage on Glenrock Farm that had been our home some twenty years. We being myself and Mare.

Karen was schoolteaching and raising a family in the north of Western Australia. Thor was photographing and raising a family in Tasmania. Goth was busking on the streets of Sydney. Vandal was managing a farm produce store and raising a family in the nearby town of Berry, only ten kilometres from Foxground. In his spare time he was customising and club racing a Holden Torana XU1. Somehow I fell into the role of pit crew, travelling with him at weekends to Amaroo, Oran Park and other race tracks, helping with tyre changes, keeping lap times and so on.

After a couple of seasons as second fiddle, I began to have delusions of becoming a first string myself. Van by then had a mantlepiece crammed with trophies and was the acknowledged fastest performer in the NSW Porsche Club, even though mounted in a humble Holden (somewhat modified!). So, while idling about Master John Newell's car showroom, I spied a 1975 model 2.7 litre 911 Carrera, mechanically fuel-injected, coloured red. This particular example of the marque had a well-deserved reputation as being 'competitive'. Say no more—I put down my money and drove it home.

On the concrete quarter-mile 'test strip' of the Foxground Road, Van and I established that 'Little Red', as we christened the car, could turn in a standing quarter mile time of 14.2 seconds—proof positive that the car was 'competitive' despite its age (it was now 1983). Acceleration is

Van conducting his XU1 Holden Torana at Oran Park—faster than Dad's Porsche.

The author in 'Little Red', a 1975 model 2.7-litre Carrera, at Oran Park.
Rounding the Castrol Corner before the straight at Oran Park race track.

CARRERA CATALAN

(equipo del abuelo)

FEDERATION INTERNATIONAL DE L'AUTOMOBILE

AUSTRALIA

VALID FOR YEAR STAMPED HEREON

	1983	1984 6. 2.84	1985
	N.2158 CG	N.420 EG	N420 EG

Issued to   JEFF CARTER
Approved assumed name
Born at   MELBOURNE VIC on 5. 8.28
Address   339 Foxground Road
          FOXGROUND NSW 2534

Next of Kin
Address

Special conditions

Issued at   SYDNEY   NSW on 7.9.1983
CONFEDERATION OF AUSTRALIAN MOTOR SPORT
per

THIS LICENCE WAS ISSUED
WITHOUT ALTERATION OR ERASURE

GENERAL COMPETITION
DRIVER ENTRANT
PROVISIONAL

VALID ONLY AS STAMPED AND ENDORSED

Signature of Holder   J Carter

Oran Park Nov 27th P C NSW'S First Speed Event.

22 of the 43 competitirs were members of P C NSW. I'd like to thank the
members who helped as officials for the event, you made everything work
so well with a minimum of instruction and I give fair warning now that
next year we're organizing 3 events !

Terry Furey. Comp Director

FTD ,			Van Carter	(PC)	52.51
1st Sports Cars	0-21		Rex Hodder	(Lotus)	57.11
"	"	2.2-51	Warren Riddell	(PC)	56.13
"	"	2.5-31	Graeme Andreus	(PC)	55.50
"	"	over 31	Jeff Carter	(PC)	52.87
Touring Cars	0.21		R. Storr	(NSSCC)	59.80
"	" over 21		P. Merry	(TCC)	59.65
Sports Sedans	o 2.01 plus		D. Dudley	(NSSCC)	56.56
"	"	2.01 "	Warren Wichman	(PC)	53.87
Racing Cars			Bob Whyms	(PC)	53.81

Located at: Foxground NSW 2534 Australia
              16 Km south of Kiama — just inland from the Princes Highway
Phone: (042) 34 1019

*Author's 'skite sheet'. Jeff's 1975 model 2.7-litre Carrera was the fastest road registered
Porsche of any capacity at Oran Park circuit for two years. Vandal, conducting his
XU1 Torana, was even quicker, competing in the 'sports sedans' category.*

not everything, so we tweaked 'Little Red' in other departments, setting the suspension low, fitting a location bar between the front shock absorber top mounting points, competition brakes, a smaller diameter steering wheel (to allow room for my knees while 'heel-and-toeing'), a raised clutch-foot shelf, level with that pedal, two lightweight Kevlar race seats by Sparco and full-harness, six-point safety belts. Most important, I invested in a set of Hopwood lightweight fifteen-inch-diameter mag. wheels, fitted with Dunlop racing slick tyres, eight inches wide at the front, nine inches at the rear. On race days we removed the engine air filter, to allow the motor to breathe more freely—and the spare wheel, to reduce weight.

All this took several months of weekend pottering and experimenting, during which time I applied for and obtained a Provisional racing licence, after attending CAMS (Confederation of Australian Motor Sport) lectures, having a rigorous medical test, filling out countless forms, paying various fees and acquiring an approved safety helmet.

On my first race day I provided the official Porsche Club movie-camera operator with an exciting sequence on how to spin a 2.7 litre 911 Carrera off the track while negotiating the notorious Oran Park Esses. But in subsequent meetings I redeemed myself and for two years 'Little Red' was unchallenged as the fastest road-registered Porsche of any engine capacity, including Turbos, around Oran Park race track.

This is not as impressive as it sounds, because Vandal kept improving too, and I was never able to officially better his time of 52.5 seconds around Oran Park South, although I came close with 52.8. All of which shows the importance of the driver—during our competition years, almost every Porsche on the track was potentially faster than Van's Torana XU1, but he was never beaten. (The South track has since been modified and improved and road-registered Porsches now occasionally circulate in 51.5 seconds.)

Around the end of 1985, Van and I put our racing careers on 'hold', due to financial, work and family commitments—he was now father of two and I was *Abuelo* of seven! One interesting thing our competition experience did establish was that Porsche owners take their racing very seriously. No one thought it was funny that we called ourselves *Equipo del Abuelo*, the Team of the Grandfather. Nor did the club ever see fit to acknowledge in the monthly magazine *Porsche Power* that its two top performers over several years were an irreverent greybeard and a farmboy in Berry Rural Co-Op overalls driving a twenty-year-old $5000 Holden Torana.

21 Copper country

It is night in the unlit mining town. Drunken sailors besiege a worker's primitive mud and stone cottage, kicking at the plank door and lobbing stones on the iron roof. The mob's leader shouts that he wants a light for his clay pipe. Crouched behind his assailed door, Gottlieb Keirnall knows the mob really wants his young, attractive and pregnant wife. The door begins to collapse under the onslaught. Desperate, Gottlieb flings it open, rushes out and splits the mob leader's skull with an axe.

In the town's shanty pubs, the Cornish, Welsh and Scots miners drink on, unmindful of the mayhem outside. It is long past closing time. Like the pubs, the smelting works is going full blast, the glare of its furnaces brilliant under the inky sky. Chains clank, wheels creak and giant hammers pound the ore. Hissing clouds of water vapour and smoke erupt as the huge bellows breathe ominously. There is a pervading, hellfire stench of sulphur while the molten copper runs in a fiery torrent from the great ladles. The scene is pure Dante's Inferno—men working urgently in front of the glowing furnaces, silhouetted against the glare, their tall shadows on the smelter walls dancing grotesquely like giants dangerously close.

In the dugout and shanty homes of the town, the children are sleeping, frightened off to bed with threats of 'that theer Man up to Mine' (a life-size effigy of the mythical Cornish miner Johnny Green, fixed atop the mine shears, holding aloft his drill and hammer). Every mine child knows that Johnny comes down from his perch at night, to chastise youngsters not gone to bed.

Next morning, the town crier, in long-tailed khaki coat, tall hat and red woollen scarf, ringing his bell in Market Square, awakens the town, calling: 'Oyez! Oyez! Last night a brutal *murther* by a German. Taken now in custody for trial by jury. God save the Queen! Oyez! Oyez!'

Down along the banks of Burra Creek, the butcher, baker and grocer

191

are making deliveries to the miners' dugout homes; the news about
murderer Gottlieb is shouted down flour-barrel chimneys to the Cornish
and Welsh housewives baking pasties in dark underground kitchens below.
Their menfolk are away, underground in another place, digging out
copper or feeding the smelter's insatiable fires. Tomorrow they will be
away again, even though it's Sunday, boozing in the town's rough pubs
with fellow workers and visitors from the earth's four corners.

The mine kids (those under eight and not working in the pits) are
sitting in the gutters outside Malowen Lowarth in Paxton Square or
adjoining Aberdeen or Llwchyr, watching mule teams led by Chilean
muleteers clad in gaily coloured ponchos and broad sombreros, their
immense spurs jingling, lassos draped from ornate, silver-decorated
saddles. Tonight Don Pedro Ramirez will play his guitar in the Spanish-
speaking camp out in the hills as Senora Carlotta and Senorita Inez dance
in the firelight.

What exotic work of fiction is this, lying uneasily 'twixt true tales
of adventure and humorous encounters? It is fact and I tell no lies about
this not un-typical day in the life of the copper mining town of Burra,
South Australia, in the year 1850.

How came I to Burra? In a short wheelbase Nissan Patrol, on the
instructions of *Overlander* magazine. 'There's a large blank spot on the
map, south of Broken Hill, just across the border into South Australia.
Could be interesting, or a challenge for some of our readers. Look into
it,' the editor instructed me.

Sure enough, examination of a set of 1:250 000 Natmaps revealed an
intriguingly sparse tract of country within a huge triangle cornered by
the towns of Broken Hill, Wentworth and Burra, north from the Murray
and west of the Darling. Many of the place names were accompanied
by the ominous word 'abandoned' in parenthesis, tracks were marked
'disused', and there were notations of 'numerous small sandridges'. My
sort of country. Some place names told the story: 'Dead Finish', 'Faraway',
'Worlds End', 'Weary Dam'. In the midst of all this was a large area
designated as the Danggali Conservation Park, sure sign of hard country.
(If you want to pinpoint our worst badlands, they are marked on maps
as Aboriginal reserves or conservation areas, meaning they are no further
use to white people, having been crook to start with and made worse
by over-grazing, burning, etc.)

Appropriately, the first fellow travellers I encountered were in a wagon
hauled by a team of camels. Initially, I imagined the turbanned driver
to be Afghan, but he turned out to be sun-browned Anglo-Saxon Jim
Lowe, from Goolwa on the lower Murray. Jim was travelling with his

wife Glenyse and son Simon, who were in charge of a donkey string hauling a second wagon. The trio had been on the road six months, were going nowhere in particular, and thought it might be a year or so before they got back to Goolwa. Their previous safari had been from the Nullarbor, with freshly broken camels caught on the plain, a slow walk of some 1600 kilometres.

Like so many laconic 'bushies', Jim was something of a philospher when drawn—and fresh-faced cheerful Glenyse an intelligent, articulate educator, lecturing at schools along the way on such diverse subjects as history, art, biology, geography, English, crafts and social studies. Dressed in colonial costume, Glenyse demonstrates the traditional crafts of spinning camel hair, hat and lampshade making. Jim talks to school groups about Afghans, camels, Aborigines, explorers and allied subjects while young Simon takes kids on donkey rides. The trio didn't look as if they were getting rich, but they were getting by, each doing something they liked. Glenyse had hopes of selling stories about their travels and gleaned what she could from me on the subject of freelance journalism. (I could not be optimistic, but I hope I was helpful.)

In the Murray town of Berri, I visited the offices of the South Australian National Parks and Wildlife Service to garner information about Danggali Conservation Park. As I had suspected from studying the map, Danggali consists of four adjoining run-down sheep-grazing properties, covering some 2500 square kilometres. The stations were purchased by the Federal government in 1976, when grazing ceased. Today the country is beginning to recover from half a century of depredation by sheep, goats, rabbits and other introduced livestock.

The area has ecological importance because it is home to a number of plant species near the limit of their range and provides much needed habitat for uncommon or rare native birds such as the Mallee fowl, the scarlet-chested parrot, the Major Mitchell cockatoo and the apostle bird. Danggali also provides sanctuary for more common animals such as kangaroos, which are hunted professionally in the surrounding countryside. A number of botanical boundaries meet within the park, which contains the southern limits of the desert poplar, pituri and mulga, plus the northern limit of the sand pine and various mallee species—so it has considerable botanic interest and importance.

In 1988, the authorities were not actively encouraging the public to visit the park, but permission to enter was fairly easily obtained if you: (a) expressed interest in ecology and conservation; (b) had a four-wheel drive vehicle and were totally self-sufficient in the matter of fuel, food and water, etc.; (c) agreed to camp only in the designated area; (d) travelled only on made tracks; or (e) stated that you wished merely to drive through the park *en route* to another destination.

The most convenient, shortest and safe way to enter the park is via Renmark from the south, using the special district map supplied by the National Parks and Wildlife Service office in nearby Berri. The approach from Burra via Koomooloo and Canegrass stations is twice as long and is over a confusing network of tracks where it is easy to get lost—and some printed maps of the area are a bit fanciful (one shows the 'Pepper Tree Motel', which is an abandoned hut beside a sheep yard!).

Off-roading is not allowed. The low sand dunes don't require four-wheel drive, but I imagine this facility could be handy after rain. There are no monumental geographic attractions in the park, but if you have any interest in arid land ecology or just like driving in remote, uninhabited wilderness, a two- or three-day visit is worthwhile.

The resident ranger, Mate Osborne, is a friendly, interesting and helpful bloke, once the ice is broken. A knowledgeable local, he is stationed at Canopus homestead, the only habitation within the huge park, where there are two small camping areas with fireplaces and wood supplied. No dunnies or other 'facilities'. If he has time and inclination, Mate sometimes walks visitors around the abandoned Canopus woolshed and other points of interest, including the site of a tragic small-plane crash near the homestead.

During my visit I drove alongside the station airstrip just as a single-engined Piper, smartly decorated in company colours, touched down. Being much interested in fermented grape juice, I recognised the logo at once, and as the pilot stepped down I enquired: 'You wouldn't have a decent bottle of Chablis on board? You see, we've some cooked yabbies on ice. . .'

'Nothing cold,' came the equally breezy reply. It was Tim Knappstein, from the nearby Clare Valley. Not selling the company product, unfortunately, but checking on the progress of a convoy of South Australian entrants in the 1988 Bourke-to-Blatherskite Bash, who roared through in a cloud of red dust moments later.

Canopus, by the way, was named after the star, which back in 1914 provided the original surveyors with the astro fix they needed to establish the precise location of the newly taken-up grazing run. Likewise Hypurna, next door (now untenanted).

This was always tough country, which is why so much of it now lies abandoned. Not that the pioneers weren't tough enough to match the country. Take Harry Brand, who once worked on nearby Chowilla (pronounced 'Chowla') station, in the dairy at first, then *droving* pigs to market down in Adelaide, 200 kilometres away. Harry was mustering cattle near Yartla Lake, over Menindie way, when his galloping horse plunged through a clump of dead, bone-sharp mallee scrub. A broken, pointed branch gouged out Harry's left eye. He fell, but his foot caught in the stirrup and he was dragged some distance. Harry later recorded: 'At last my foot came out of the stirrup. I put up my hand and felt for the eye, but it had gone. . .then the agony of the thing started and for some time I lay twisted up on the sand.' Harry spent that night in camp 'rolling and kicking' on a tarpaulin.

Next day, New Year's Day, under the blazing sun he was carted in the bottom of an open sulky to the outpost of Menindie. Unfortunately everyone was 'on the spree' and blind drunk, including the town doctor. Harry lay in a darkened room 'suffering agonies' for three days before the doctor was sober enough to tell him he could do nothing. So Harry bought a horse and saddle for $20, determined to ride to Adelaide. A friend led him as far as Wentworth on the Murray, 'in cruel, hot weather, tortured all the while by flies'. From there, Harry rode alone, taking nine days to reach Adelaide and skilled medical attention. Four months later, he was back on the Darling with a bullock team, 'snagging' the river for sunken logs, ready for the first paddlesteamers. This was around 1862.

During the next decade, many cattle disappeared from stations north of the Murray, wandering into the mallee scrub and sand dunes of what is now Danggali, never to return. White settlers had failed to penetrate this forbidding, waterless barrier and a legend grew up that somewhere beyond was a sort of Promised Land, where the errant cattle fetched up.

The still indomitable, one-eyed Harry Brand made two attempts to solve the mystery, the first nearly fatal. He rode beyond the point of no return into the scrub and sandhills. Man and beast suffered terrible thirst as they struggled back toward the river. By day, Harry tethered his horse Jack in what shade he could find and buried himself in the sand to conserve body moisture. The pair travelled at night, guided by the stars, Harry walking and leading Jack, who had knocked up and 'lost his intelligence'.

Harry's journal for the final day of his marathon records: 'I knew that water would have to be found, but ahead appeared nothing excepting dense mallee and porcupine (spinifex) and low down, a red ball of fire, the sun.' Luckily, that morning Harry had stumbled into a fencers' camp. After vomiting up most of the water he was given, he pressed on, arriving home at his property on Wigley's Flat near the Murray around midnight, to find his wife 'in a terrible state, thinking we were lost and lighting fires as beacons for us'. The women of the west!

Typically, Harry had a second try, in cooler weather, this time accompanied by a neighbour and carrying plenty of water. After riding a few days, they broke out of the mallee scrub onto 'rich plains waving with geranium and spear grass. . .through what appeared to us like paradise...and we saw mobs of cattle...in grand condition...that appeared to be some of those which had got away many years before... Water was lying about everywhere in pools.' The Promised Land at last! Of course it was not—there had just been a run of good seasons. But soon Harry and others took up the country for grazing and the stations of Pine Valley, Morgan Vale, Oakvale, Mutooroo, Postmark, etc., were established. Some are now abandoned and form part of Danggali Conservation Park.

West from the park toward Burra, you wonder how the remaining stations survive. City-bred travellers could be forgiven for complaining of what rock climbers call 'exposure', while driving across these seemingly endless plains of loneliness. In dry times, much of the landscape is completely bare. The best of it has patches of low scrub, spinifex and saltbush, with occasional dry sandy creeks and low stoney ridges. A great place for newchum adventurers to experience 'the real outback', only a short drive off the bitumen linking Burra (and Broken Hill) with Adelaide. (But you wouldn't want to live there, as the American pioneer whose family had been scalped by Indians in the Mojave desert once said.) If you enjoy dry camping in splendid isolation, with nought to savour after the sun goes down but 'the glory of the everlasting stars', stay a day or so in this stark landscape, where the far horizon comes down to your boots in every direction.

The town of Burra today is easily identifiable with the pioneer mining villages of the 1850s described in the opening paragraphs of this tale. There were originally half a dozen independent neighbouring settlements, including Redruth (Cornish), Llwchyr (Welsh), Aberdeen (Scottish), Hampton (English) and the company-owned Kooringa—all known collectively as 'the Burra Towns'. A shepherd, Thomas Pickett, discovered the Burra copper lode around 1845 and received $40 for his trouble from the syndicate that floated the Burra Monster Mine. Cornish and Welsh miners flocked to the burgeoning settlement, which became Australia's first industrial town.

By 1851, there were 13 kilometres of underground workings at the mine, some of them deep. Depth measurements were traditionally in 'fathoms' (about 1.8 metres). At Wallaroo Mine, south-west of Burra, miners worked as deep as 405 fathoms, nearly 800 metres! In its heydey, during the 1850s, the Burra Monster Mine employed 12 000 men, some of them boys as young as eight years.

The traditional underground 'crib' lunch of the Cornish miners always included pasties, based on minced potatoes, swedes, turnips and mutton, baked inside an envelope of hard pastry. The test of a good Cornish pastie was that it should survive a fall of at least five fathoms without shattering!

Mining ceased in 1877, but the Monster re-opened in 1969 as an open-cut, ceasing operations finally in 1981.

Apart from the mine's closing, little else has changed in Burra these past hundred years. Many of the old stone houses and public buildings survive, trimmed with lacy, white painted wrought iron, fronted by manicured lawns and formal gardens. Everything in the town is spruce and neat as apple pie, as the Welsh and Cornish people used to say. The great open-cut is a lake now, surrounded by the remains of the engine houses, powder magazine, chimneys and other mine structures, some being restored as part of a great open air museum. 'That theer Cornish miner', Johnny Green, still holds aloft his drill and hammer, atop a tall chimney near the ruins of the old smelter. The dugout homes along Burra Creek are no longer tenanted, but the miners' cottages of white-washed rubble in Paxton Square (*circa* 1849) remain in use, as tourist accommodation.

There is still a Market Square, complete with elevated, circular brass-band rotunda (for the Sunday concerts, look you), five pubs and four churches, all mint 19th century. Ducks swim on the tranquil waters of the *mere*, beneath willows, elms and larches, a picture in autumn when the yellow and russet leaves fall. There are caravans and tents now in Olde English Park, where the children scamper over neat lawns to feed ducks and swans. Nearby, under the verandahs of the Paxton Cottages, swept and scrubbed regularly by the tidy householders of Burra, visitors browse among the craft shops.

Tourism has replaced mining as the district money spinner, but this will always be a mining town, in spirit at least. As I am the product of another mining town, Bendigo, perhaps I'm biased, but I found Burra the most pleasant Australian country village I've visited in a long while. (My grandfolk were Cornish and Welsh, I confess.) Not just for its beautifully preserved 19th-century architecture (the town is on the Register of the National Estate), but for its friendly, relaxing, leafy ambience. Burra has preserved a life-style, as well as its buildings. Paradoxically, though it is unabashedly geared to tourism, the town has retained its dignity and avoided the crass commercialism of such 'olde worlde' tourist traps as Sovereign Hill. No carriage rides, convict floggings, rented gold pans, clicking turn-styles or pay windows and not a motel in or near town. The folk of Burra haven't changed a thing to pander to popular tastes, but sensibly and sensitively applied themselves to authentic restoration. Full marks to all concerned. The only other town I know that has done likewise is Beechworth, in north-eastern Victoria.

All pubs offer accommodation and there is an excellent caravan park, but I stayed in one of the self-contained Paxton Cottages, operated on a non-profit basis by the town council. And at the town bakery, traditional Cornish pasties well able to pass the five fathom test...

When night comes in Burra, there is drinking to be done in the pubs as always and now a fine restaurant overlooking Market Square.

The younger children are abed early, still fearful 'that theer Cornish miner' may have come down from his perch and be abroad in the darkened streets. But hush now, the town is sleeping...only you can see the ghosts of the past, among them poor wronged Gottlieb Keirnall, sent to Van Diemen's Land and drowned at sea, always searching for his beloved, lost young wife. Hush now... (With apologies to the late Dylan Thomas, poet, and playwright of *Under Milk Wood*, the story of a small Welsh village.)

22 The crash test

'It was the best of times, it was the worst of times. It was the age of wisdom, it was the age of foolishness. . . ' (Charles Dickens, commencing *A Tale of Two Cities*).

And so it was in October 1987, after the stock market crash. Some of us cried an ocean while others bobbed like corks on that sea of troubles. Among them, Elders-IXL and Liberal Party chief John Elliott. On Black Tuesday he made a million or so, buying up cheap stock dumped by the lemmings, all the while quaffing Grange Hermitage at a business luncheon in my native Wollongong as steel-workers and miners clamoured at the factory gates.

'YUPPIES ARMAGEDDON—Oh, no, not the Porsche!' a newspaper headline gleefully derided. Panicked, the lemmings scurried off the cliff edge, selling art collections, antique furniture and other status symbols. 'There's going to be the biggest second-hand market in Porsches and Ferraris that you've ever seen,' predicted a *Sydney Morning Herald* financial writer.

By golly, if our future prime minister can do it, why not me? Such were my thoughts, while rattling my piggy bank, which was uncommonly full, for once. Little did I know, as Kurt Vonnegut remarked—or was it John Newell?

Shoulders squared, I strode purposefully down a grotty sidestreet of inner Melbourne town. It looked like the film set of *Taxi Driver*, but I was on the trail of a bargain and not to be intimidated. A Kremer-conversion Porsche in fact, at $55 000 ONO. Such bait makes cautious people lions. Picking my way through the typical detritus of a slum street, I confronted a closed garage door set in a wall of grimed red brick. Above it was the number I sought, barely discernible. From within came the unmistakable, intermittent cacaphony of an automotive workshop. Tired of beating on the giant shutter, I sleuthed into a side alley and found a single door beneath a sign announcing something like 'Fly-by-Night Auto Services'. This had to be it.

'Joe sent me,' I said out of the side of my mouth to a red-overalled man loitering within. 'I've come to look at his Kremer Porsche.'

'Ah, right,' was the non-committal answer.

On the floor of the workshop were numerous Porsches in varying degrees of *déshabillé*, tended by tool-wielding persons in off-white, off-yellow and off-red overalls. Two gleaming Turbo-bodied Porsches were at centre stage, seeming pristine under the dangling neon bar lights. I hoped one was Joe's Kremer conversion. No, his was a 911SC, left-hand drive, with several rear body panels removed—and no wheels. No engine, either, my expert eye detected.

'That's at a performance tuning shop. We only do bodywork and conversions,' red overalls informed me.

'Conversions?'

'Left to right-hand drive, mainly Porsches.'

'What's the story on Joe's car?'

'Got belted up the arse. We're fixing that and making it RHD, when he finds the bread.'

'Could I use your phone to call Joe?'

'No problem.'

'Hello, Joe. I'm looking at your car but there's not much to look at. Where's the engine? In a workshop at Fitzroy? Being tuned... putting out 400 horses... cost the previous owner fifteen grand in Germany... Yes, I know Bob Whyms, the Porsche specialist in Sydney... Why? He has a suitable gearbox... Your car doesn't even have a gearbox? Well look, Joe, I'll have to get back to you...'

His name really was Lothar. At least he said it was. He wore only brief swimming trunks and a gold neck-chain over his still-muscular, sun-tanned body.

Stylishly swirling smoky iced Pernod in his long glass, he gestured with the other hand toward a resplendent motor cruiser moored at the bottom of his Gold Coast key-front. 'I prefer luxury and speed on the waterways, rather than the highways these days. You're in *command* at the wheel of a craft like that. On the road you get no respect, particularly from cops, unless they know who you are...' I nodded respectfully.

'Perhaps we might go for a drive?' I ventured. Lothar had spent the previous half hour telling me about the car he was selling and Porsches in general. He obviously knew nothing about them. The car that had brought me to Surfers Paradise was purportedly a 911 Carrera RS 2.7 litre, *circa* 1975. Mr Porsche stopped making these in mid 1973, some didn't get registered until '74, but calling any RS 2.7 a 1975 model was stretching things a bit—not uncommon in the world of used cars. Never mind, Lothar's phone spiel made the car sound interesting: engine and suspension by English Porsche specialist house Autofarm, body by Gantspeed Engineering of Lincolnshire, phenomenal performance, immaculate, low miles, etc. 'I have all the receipts for the work done,' Lothar assured me. 'It's a real bum-tightener to drive. . . I doubt many drivers could use its potential.'

He had the receipts all right, made out to a previous owner. All Autofarm had done was fit a new clutch and a rally exhaust, plus replace or refurbish the shock absorbers. The bodywork by Gantspeed was no more than an update of the original rear ducktail with a contemporary tray spoiler and a full-body respray. The 'low miles' showed as 143 000. When I remarked this, Lothar said with boyish innocence, 'But since the engine rebuild, it's only done 25 000 miles.'

I didn't pursue the matter because Lothar's previous remarks about motor cars in general and Porsches in particular made it probable he really believed a new clutch and exhaust pipe was an engine rebuild. The car *was* immaculate and the paintwork superb, I'll give him that. When the engine turned over it sounded totally clapped, an impression confirmed when I engaged the clutch. Most of its power seemed to be blowing very noisily out of the rally exhaust, leaving precious little to activate the rear wheels. 'Music to the ears,' intoned Lothar, settling back in the passenger seat, enjoying himself. 'Feel the power!' By this time I knew he wasn't kidding. He really thought he owned a tiger. Or was he the greatest actor since Gielgud? Or did he think I was that stupid? In case the latter, I said mildly 'Have you ever put a stopwatch on this car?' Of course he hadn't. I had mine in my pocket but didn't wish to cause embarrassment.

'Tell you what, Lothar,' I said, jotting some figures on a piece of paper. 'Here are the acceleration times a Carrera RS 2.7 in good condition should do. See if you can get hold of a watch and check your car's performance. If you can get within a couple of seconds of these times, give me a ring and I'll come up and buy your car.' Lothar never rang back. I think I could have made the margin at least five seconds. . .

'The thing that worries me about your car is that the chassis number doesn't match with the engine number,' I said to the owner of the blue 911SC advertised at the bargain price of $63 000 ONO.

'Doesn't match?' echoed the owner.

'No, doesn't match.'

'Should it?'

'If you wish to sell it to me, yes,' I responded.

'Ah, well, all I know is it's a good car. I don't know about technicalities. How should the numbers match?' He sounded quite convincing.

'See this compliance plate,' I said, indicating the flat embossed plate rivetted to the bodywork inside the front boot. 'It says your car was manufactured in 1978, not '79, by the way. It also states the chassis number of your car.' I pointed to the chassis number stamped into the body of the car adjacent to the compliance plate. 'The chassis numbers match, but alas . . .' I walked to the rear of the vehicle, ducking my head under the previously opened engine hatch . . . 'your engine number is not the same as the one shown in your log book.'

'I've only owned the car ten months. I never noticed the numbers didn't match,' the Porsche purveyor said apologetically. 'The reggo is in order and there's no money owing,' he continued.

'I know,' I said, having contacted REVS (the Registrar of Encumbered Vehicles) before viewing the car. 'Do you mind if I use your phone? I'd like to ring a lady called Debbie.'

'No, go ahead,' said the disquieted Porsche owner.

Debbie Day is sort of the keeper of the records at the House of Hamilton in Melbourne. It transpired the car in question had been delivered yellow in colour when new, with a different motor and *with an electric sunroof.* Now it was blue and lacked the sunroof. 'Your car should have an electric sunroof,' I said.

'Yes, I believe they're very good,' said the owner.

'No, I mean it was delivered with one and now it hasn't got one.'

'How could that be?' said the owner, nonplussed.

'I suspect it may have been involved in a tiny accident?' I suggested.

'Oh, yes! Now you mention it I recall the previous owner saying it was stolen for a while and slightly damaged in the rear.'

'Uh, huh . . . and you've finished up with two cars for the price of one,' I mused aloud.

'What do you mean?'

'I think the term is sardined.' I replied. 'It's possible you own the front of one car and the back of another.'

'Oh, *shit!*' exploded the owner, with enough vehemence to half convince me it was news to him.

The major wanted to get out. Only his military training prevented him from saying so. Every time we approached a corner he went parade-stiff, gripping the seat squab firmly. Eventually his instinct for self preservation overcame his macho-reserve and he began making tight-lipped comments like 'I don't think we're supposed to be driving like this around Mosman.' And 'Watch it, man! This next one's a tight one.' And 'That should blow the cobwebs out of her! I don't normally use so many revs.' Finally, 'Slow down! (It came as an order.) We turn right at the next but one.'

Since entering upon my twilight years, I have not been wont to frighten passengers, but when test driving a car you are thinking of buying, it is prudent to give it a teeny bit of stick in the going, turning and stopping departments. Not that I was being reckless. All things in moderation is our family motto. It is just that many Porsche owners don't know how good their cars are, using them mostly as stylish suburban hacks and weekend status symbols. They seldom red-line them, heel-and-toe only when doing the Charleston and abhor the squeal of their usually under-inflated tyres.

The major's 911SC was surprisingly accelerative for this model, which is fitted with the misleadingly named K-Jetronic fuel-injection and therefore not noted for its 0 to 100 km/h performance. (The earlier mechanically fuel-injected models were much faster and less economical.)

'Has the engine been modified?' I enquired. We had just driven the twisty suburban route from Sydney's Taronga Park zoo to the village of Mosman in what I suspect the major regarded as an unacceptably short time.

'Yes,' he said shortly as we got out. 'I'll show you.' We walked to the rear of the car, where he remarked apprehensively 'It smells rather hot.'

'It smells normal,' I reassured him. Under the bonnet were several umpteen-throat Weber carburettors instead of the standard fuel injection system. A full top-end conversion, in fact, of which the major was proud. I was not so impressed, having previous experience of Weber-carburetted Porsches. 'Will it start, now that it's hot?' I asked as we got back in the car.

'Er, it should,' the major said without conviction.

I knew it wouldn't. And it didn't. So we did what you always have to do with this setup and waited quite a few minutes for things to cool down and the vapour locks or whatever to sort themselves out. It was a pretty good car, apart from the Webers, but I was looking for a stock, standard, unmodified 911SC, so the major and I parted company on the note that I would look for another car and he would look for another buyer.

She looked the sort of girl who loiters with intent around Kings Cross or St Kilda. He looked the sort of guy who cruises with intent around the same places, looking for such a girl. A well-matched couple. She knew she was sitting on a fortune and he obviously ran something lucrative but not quite kosher in Sydney's western suburbs. 'I doan like the colour, Dino. You said black,' the girl pouted.

'You hearda resprays?' Dino responded. 'And I can get the seats done any colour or cloth you like, okay?' They were talking about a gunmetal gray 911SC Porsche in the basement carport of a Sydney north-shore home.

'Lissen, who do I talk bikkies to?' Dino asked, addressing me.

'I'm just another looker,' I replied.

'Well, who?' Dino was not one to be fobbed off.

He had arrived only minutes ahead of me, hadn't driven the car yet but was ready to do business. The Porsche's owner was a mysterious absent person, but one of the other two men present was acting for him. I pointed and Dino thankfully transferred his attention. I took the opportunity to inspect what was on offer, a 1979 model 911SC with everything, at $65 000. From the outside it looked good. Inside it was a disaster. The upholstery was split and peeling. So was the body trim. Both tatty seats slid freely back and forth on their runners, refusing to lock firm. The glovebox was permanently open, the sun visors permanently down. And so on. The gear lever lay flat on the transmission tunnel. Miraculously, once you picked it up, it seemed to do the job. The clutch felt incredibly heavy, even for a Porsche. I kept it depressed when I fired the engine, just in case the gear lever had chosen a slot other than neutral.

One of the gentlemen present, clad in shorts and singlet, told me the car belonged to his brother, who also owned a Ferrari and a restaurant, but only a single garage, so obviously one car had to go. Without sighting the Ferrari, I reckoned he had made the right choice to sell the Porsche, which did not inspire confidence. The brother present, recently a used-car salesman, had found the Porsche for his next-of-kin. Now, only six months later, against his expert advice, it was being sold, the better of the two cars. Which didn't say much for the Ferrari. After some hesitation, I accepted the offer of a test drive, largely as a respite from Dino and his girlfriend, now engaged in a noisy altercation.

'Watch the clutch. It has a very short travel,' I was advised. It certainly did. This idiosyncrasy, combined with the immense effort required to hold the pedal floored, made for a rather spectacular exit from the carport. It was a leap, more than anything, down the steep concrete drive to the street far below.

After an alarming progress around several unknown tortuous suburban blocks, I knew how the major had felt. Eventually I got the knack of marrying the Rambo clutch with the limp-wristed gear lever. For long enough to discover the engine was good but the steering and suspension were not. All up, I judged the car needed at least $10 000 spent on it, just to fix the obvious. Which meant it was far from a bargain.

Back at the house, Dino was haranguing the car-owner's brother. 'Whaddaya mean he don't want to hear an offer? It don't cost to hear an offer...' The girl sat disconsolately on a rock wall in the garden, her mauve-stockinged legs and leather mini-skirt somehow inappropriate amid the sedate suburban shrubbery. I made my apologies and left them to it.

Time was passing and all the genuine bargain-priced Porsches eluded me, sold before I picked up the phone. The only cars I saw were disasters as described above. The really good-sounding vehicles were always gone when I rang up, even before 9 a.m. I tried ringing at eight. Same story. Even seven. 'Sorry, it's sold.' I began overnighting in Sydney on Fridays, so I could get my hands on the *Sydney Morning Herald* at dawn on Saturday. (The earliest I could get the *Melbourne Age* was Sunday night.) To no avail. A Sydney advertiser told me he had sold his car to a buyer who had phoned him before midnight on Friday. This at 6 a.m. on Saturday morning! Clearly there were better informed bulls than me out there, picking off the more attractive bears the instant they broke cover.

Provoked, I took certain action which enabled me to know early on Friday night what desirable Porsches were to be advertised on the following Saturday morning in the *Sydney Morning Herald*. A phone call to Melbourne incited longtime friend and *Wheels* founder Jules Feldman to rise early and relay to me interesting information from the Motor Market section of each Saturday's *Age*.

These dubious arrangements enabled me to at least *see* a few of the better vehicles on offer. Getting my hands on one was a different matter. The problem was this: good-sounding cars offered at $5000 or more below the going market price drew a fair gaggle of sunrise lookers, all with cheque books drawn and cocked. For example, a $76 000 market price car is on offer at $68 000. While you are away having your drive, some wretched tyre-kicker offers $70 000. When you learn this, you boldly offer $71 500, because the immaculate, one-owner car is obviously faultless and has only 80 000 kilometres up, barely run in, in Porsche terms. Then another player takes the vehicle for a spin and returns with a cheque already written for $73 000. Which the seller accepts. I played out this scene, with variations, a number of times. What it amounted to was this: as a result of the stock market kerfuffle, rather more Porsches (and other exotics) than usual came on the market, but genuine bargains were few and far between—and once bidding started, lost their financial appeal.

The irony of it was, I had participated in the identical scenario a couple of years earlier as a seller, when I offered my 911 Carrera at $32 000 and got knocked down in the rush—which peaked around $40 000, from memory. Then I was well pleased, but now the boot was on the other foot and kicking hard at my hip pocket.

My sights were set on a pristine example of the 911SC range, vintage 1980-82, market value approaching $80 000, but hopefully down around $70 000 while the stock-market jitters continued. New, these cars had been $45 000 to $50 000 depending on options. If only we had known then!

It came to pass I found myself cruising among the stately homes of St Ives, deep in Sydney's plush north-shore investment belt. Birds chorused their dawn calls in the elms and hedges. The tennis courts were as yet silent, swimming pools still as mirrors, triple garages shuttered tight above long, meandering gravel driveways. A fish out of water, I felt strangely at home, cruising in the massive white Jaguar XJ-S V12 cabriolet featured in an earlier chapter.

The car I sought lived in a sequestered, leafy cul-de-sac reminiscent of an English country lane. It was a 1980 model 911SC, immaculate, pampered by original owner, every option, low kilometres, etc. Asking $75 000, which by this time I knew was the exact going price of such an offering in top condition. Never mind—if the owner was a wounded stock marketeer, perhaps he would be susceptible to an offer.

The car was in unbelievably good condition, giving meaning at last to the over-used adjective pristine. It not only looked new, it seemed never to have been driven, apart from the tell-tale 72 000 kilometres on the clock. 'I take good care of my toys,' Mr St Ives told me smugly. Obviously he did. There was not a mark on the car, inside or out, underneath, in the engine compartment. . . anywhere. The original duco shone with the brilliant lustre of a new showroom vehicle.

Mr St Ives assured me the car had never been parked in the sun, had been always garaged, washed and vacuumed weekly and waxed monthly. I believed him. The car had never been driven in anger ('abused' was his term). In fact, he had never exceeded 4500 rpm, though the redline is close to 7000. I believed that, too. He was that sort of Porsche owner. Needless to say, the logbook showed the car had been impeccably maintained by the official north shore agent, Scuderia Veloce. Driving the car was a dream, like testing a new vehicle. I swear the motor felt stiff! Suspension and steering were tight as the proverbial drum. Every option, of course: air, electric roof, electric mirrors, top-of-the-range radio-cassette player with power aerial, drop-forged wheels, adjustable konis, etc. During our twisty drive down to Bobbin Head in Ku-ring-gai Chase, Mr St Ives remarked mildly 'I've never treated my car like this. The needle has never been in the red before. Are you trying to destroy the vehicle?'

'No, I'm trying to buy it,' I replied truthfully. On the way back to our starting point, when Mr St Ives said 'Next right,' or 'Next left,' I several times turned into private driveways, mistaking them for tree-lined suburban streets. How the other one per cent live. Strangely, there were no rival buyers gathered on the lawn when we returned to base. Christmas was nigh and perhaps they were already on holiday.

Faced with the rare opportunity to buy an absolutely top car at the correct market price, I could not resist a gamble. Putting on my best poker face, I explained I didn't have $75 000 on me right then and the Jaguar was already packed for a week-long wine-buying safari to Rutherglen in Victoria. But I had $72 000 at home, perhaps a little more. Which I would bring along the following weekend, if no one meanwhile turned up with the asking price.

Mr St Ives appeared to accept this with good grace and we parted on the note that he would not sell the car for less than $72 000 before next weekend, when I intended to return and claim it.

Next Saturday, after unloading an astonishing number of bottles from the Jaguar's cavernous boot, I phoned Mr St Ives concerning our arrangement. 'Did you get your $75 000?' I asked in trepidation.

'No, I did not.'

'Anyone offer more than $72 000?' I was holding my breath.

'No, they didn't.'

'Oh, good,' I said smugly, well pleased with my week-long brinkmanship. 'I'll come up with my cheque book.'

There was a longish silence. Then Mr St Ives said 'I'm very sorry, but I sold the car to a Mr Goodman for $70 000.'

'Whatever for?' I moaned.

'I didn't think you were serious.' Mr St Ives's voice was tinged with anguish.

'Did you say Goodman? Not a Mr Dale Goodman, from John Newell's Porsche Centre?' I pursued.

'The same.'

'Back-stabbers' I hissed at John Newell. We were facing each other across his expansive desk, as we have oft done. Arguing about money, as usual. 'You've done this before!' I accused. 'Remember that car in Adelaide I was going to buy and you let slippery Goodman fly down there and buy it out from under me!'

'Calm yourself, Jeffrey, and tell me your problem,' Master Newell responded, unruffled, smiling his usual good-natured smile. I did so, at great length, but failed to convince him of his wrong-doing—or that I had a prior right to the car (which I didn't, but we poker players never give up). He did agree it was a 'magnificent' car. Which was why it was to be offered at around $80 000, after detailing and a few minor refurbishings.

My reaction to this news was unsuitable for verbatim publication. Suffice to say it caused the usually intractable Master Newell to dab several crocodile tears from his cheeks and offer me the car for a mere $76 000. This caused another uproar, but as usual my opponent demonstrated it is difficult to bluff a player with a full hand when you know that he knows you don't have so much as a pair. Dale Goodman arrived, alerted by the commotion, to support his master. I threw down my cards and wrote a cheque. To show there were no hard feelings, I ordered a set of Bridgestone RE71 tyres and a couple of minor modifications which brought the total cost of the vehicle to $79 500.

Postscript: The prophesied crash in second-hand Porsche (and other exotic car) prices never really eventuated. They were mostly leased, you see, so the 'owners' (minders, really) had nothing to sell. Instead, they off-loaded their art collections, antiques, even their real estate. A year later, the Deutschmark weakened against the Oz dollar, causing new and second-hand Porsche prices to drop a few per cent briefly.

By 1989, they were climbing again.

Haggling with John Newell. No prize for guessing the player at the right holds all the cards.

23 Once upon a dream

Due to errors of judgement on the part of a Swedish car maker and the new editor of *Wheels* magazine, in 1988 I attended my first motoring press junket. Enjoyable and instructive though it was, my abiding reactions during the four-day 1200 kilometre 'Adventure' fluctuated between dismay and alarm as my credibility and fear thresholds were constantly exceeded.

You see, the Swedes are an unimaginative lot—countless generations have endured those dark, freezing arctic winters, slowing their creative flow to glacial pace. Traditional hobbies are wood whittling and making Volvo trucks; cars and trucks, actually, though some motor-noters profess to have difficulty telling them apart. Comes the brief northern summer, the Volvo workforce (twenty per cent female) and their countryfolk emerge blinking from winter's darkness and go absolutely mad. Lured by the midnight sun, they migrate north and cavort naked inside steamy makeshift saunas, knocked up from a few saplings and sheets of plastic in the forest, all the while flailing each other with birch twigs. Public relations executives try to legitimise these antics by taking along the latest company products, to be photographed among the Lapps and reindeer. This is something of a problem for the Volvo people, who produce a new model about once each decade. But they go anyway.

Thus it had to happen in Australia. Lacking any new models to introduce, Volvo Australia nevertheless decided to import the traditional practice of going a little bit mad come spring. So off we all went north, with the not very original second motive of using crocodiles, buffalo and 'natives' instead of reindeer and Lapps as photographic props.

Zeus knows how I came to be part of the 'Adventure'. Probably a typing error or someone's idea of a joke, for I knew nothing about the Volvo 700 range (they all look the same to me) and wasn't much interested. Now better informed, I can report they not only look the same, but go the same, with one modest exception. More on this later. And I confess to being more interested than previously, having discovered the hulking, box-like beasts possess a variety of desirable qualities.

But to begin at the beginning, as the Welsh poet once said. Imagine my consternation on being plucked from the bucolic spring torpor of my native Foxground and thrust for an overnight in Sydney's plush Airport Hilton, then into the heady luxury of the executive end of a Darwin bound jetliner full of motoring journalists and photographers who all seemed to know each other. Reeling from this culture shock, I was further alarmed by the revelation that my hosts rejoiced in such nicknames as 'Kakadu,' 'Crocodile', 'Groper', 'Dundee' and the like. Surely I was in the wrong plane, going to an international boy scout jamboree?

In a state of mild shock, I told the hostess I was teetotal when she came around with the drinks, and went to sleep, partly reassured at the last moment by a glimpse of fellow trade veterans Mike Kable and Pedr Davis. Safely back home now in my country refuge, I'm still not sure if I ever regained consciousness, or dreamed the whole episode.

A white cockatoo appeared from stage left and rode a bicycle under the floodlights. Another skated on stage and did various unexpected things, for a cockatoo. Flashbulbs popped and some of the veteran journalists began interviewing the birds' trainer, dressed flamboyant-cowboy style, who had earlier tried to entertain us with some Banjo Paterson, but forgot his lines.

The younger journalists interviewed the trainer's assistant, a comely lass from Queensland. Here memory fails, except to recall there is not much to do when the buffalo steak and red wine runs out after dinner in the town of Batchelor, NT.

We had driven a dozen Volvos 200 kilometres from Darwin through recently created Litchfield Park, a dusty but pretty enough preserve of termite mounds, pandanus, paperbarks and occasional small creeks— sans salt-water crocs (the dangerous species) apparently, because people were swimming in them. About seventy kilometres from the airport, the bitumen had changed to gravel and according to the detailed route notes supplied by Volvo's chief scout, extreme caution was needed to escape dips, sand, crests, creeks, causeways, curves and crocodiles. But it was just an average country road. However, the enormity of our situation became apparent when we stopped at Wangi Falls for lunch and got out of our air-conditioned Volvos. It was 40°C in the real world. The house-block sized pool at the foot of the dry falls was magnificent and full of bobbing, splashing locals and tourists, soon joined by some of our party. Lunch was a typical Northern Territory style stuff-up (no fault of the trusting Volvo scouts)—motel stewed tea and kerosene-tainted rolls instead of the advertised ethnic extravaganza of billy tea and damper. Never mind, Volvo's 'Dundee' pronounced the rolls 'super'.

That night, in the privacy of my motel room, I tried to erase the memory of the evening's entertainment by browsing through the various documents and products supplied by our patron. Perhaps there would be expensive, useful prezzies—I had heard somewhere of the perks associated with this form of exercise.

There was a 'survival kit' in a miniature plastic Esky, containing a jar of vegemite, pencil and paper, matches, band-aids, cotton bud, aspirin, a can of beer, nip of Scotch, plus a small pliable plastic knife like you get at MacDonalds, with some jokesy instructions about using it to fend off 'howling' dingoes, 'slithering' snakes and 'grinning' crocodiles. Boys will be boys. There was also a too-small 'Life, Be In It' T-shirt and a plastic shoulder bag with VOLVO writ large on the side. Patronage suited to our art, I thought, as I drifted off to sleep.

The next bit was a dream, for sure. I was in a large room, seated at a U-shaped table with my fellows and our mentors. Now the democratic camaraderie of last night's dinner table, abetted by the sort of wines served in beer-drinking territory, was lacking. Our chief scouts headed the table, apart from the body of cubs and senior rangers. We were given glossy-sleeved press kits full of reports, statements and claims about Volvo cars that nobody present needed to know, accompanied by some indifferent photos.

Then we heard touchingly sincere speeches from 'Crocodile', 'Groper', 'Dundee', etc., which fairly brought tears to my eyes, so thoroughly was I convinced they believed what they were saying. The most eloquent, articulate speaker told us that 'intelligent, reflective' professional family folk, and the upwardly mobile headed for those ranks, buy Volvos as an expression of their social attitudes which are based on an appreciation of the finer things of life, plus safety, security, longevity, comfort, commonsense, etc. BMW purchasers, we learned, are 'poseurs' and Mercedes fans merely 'buy the star'. My favourite marque was not mentioned, so we Porschephiles remain in ignorance of our sins. Next we saw a lively colour film, rather like an endless musically swinging video clip, which seemed to suggest that Playboy-type bunny girls are the best Volvo drivers, at least in Sweden's snow country.

A middle-aged chap called Brian, at the wheel of an identical vehicle, just couldn't keep up with them. The film was well received, generating much gaiety among the audience, mild hysteria in fact, and I was reminded of a southern prayer meeting. Further exhortations from the pulpit preceded our second, mercifully shorter film. This was a local attempt at the Swedish version.

While struggling to appreciate the significance of all this, I listened to question time, noting a rising tone of hysteria among the congregation as the responses became increasingly soul-searching. Alarmed, I kept an eye on the nearest exit, fearing those guilty among us might be called upon to confess the sin of owning other than Volvo cars. Luckily it never came to this, but for a while we were all under the spell of Volvo's chief evangelist, 'Dundee' I think it was, and for the first time I appreciated what takes the likes of Billy Graham or Ronald Reagan to the top: sincerity.

For a while we sailed the tranquil, croc-free waters of Katherine Gorge, dutifully gawking at soaring, colourful rock walls, rich in local folklore from as long ago as the time when Jedda and Marbuk made their fatal leap in Charles Chauvel's classic film. Our overloaded, roofless flat-bottomed boat got stuck on a rock and for a while it seemed we might fry like sardines in a pan under the merciless Territory sun. Aided by unsolicited advice from our inimitable 'Dundee', the skipper eventually got us off.

Then we were in a bus, not four-wheel drive and seemingly lacking a clutch, driving overland through the trees, with only the stars to guide us. Fortunately the chirpy, colourfully spoken lady who was driving the bus had grown up among the tribespeople of the area and knew every tree and rock and termite mound and its folkloric significance. We were supposed to be going to a corroboree, but our lady-of-the-paperbarks chose to make an unscheduled excursion into the donga, so that we might better appreciate the experience. Speaking in the soft, lilting cadences of the local people, she eloquently recited poetic legends of Katherine's Dreamtime, reducing a busload of mildly raucous journalists to respectful, thoughtful silence. The bark hut banquet that followed was excellent, the corroboree a travesty.

Day three, I think it was, found us heeding the advice on the packet to 'tear along the dotted line'. We were travelling north by the two-lane bitumen toward Pine Creek, three abreast, following a Volvo estate wagon, tailgate aloft, from which young master Warwick Kent, of *Wheels* magazine, was snapping pictures. I had often wondered where and how this sort of thing was done. Now I know. On public roads—dangerously. The occasional oncoming vehicle sent us scattering in all directions, to resume formation on the next straight. Zeus knows what those south-bound motorists thought we were doing.

Master Kent, my travelling companion on the 'Adventure', seemed to thrive on danger. Every time I overtook a road-train, he wound down the passenger window, leaned out into the maelstrom of flying gravel and clicked away through a wide-angle lens. When we occasionally reached an imprudent speed, he would suddenly throw off his seatbelt, climb into the rear of the vehicle and take photos of the speedo. Thus we have it on record that in my hands the Volvo turbo could barely tip 200 km/h during our excursion. It will allegedly go faster. (Dirty fuel may have been the problem, we found out later.)

On roads thick with bulldust, Warwick liked to stand on the other side of blind hill-crests while I drove up and over, usually to find him standing in the centre of the track, blissfully clicking away. I admired his confidence in my driving, but wondered if he would ever become an old photographer. He is certainly a good one, as a riffle through back issues of *Wheels* confirms. Vegetarianism seems not to have impaired his driving (he does it better than me) or potency (he is father of two). Blokes like Warwick Kent cause me to marvel at the younger generation—so talented, so confident, so lucky...

Thoughts that came to me as he drifted us skilfully around blind, tree-lined corners on the corrugated, guttered, rock-strewn Kakadu Highway at well above my fear-threshold. Once or twice I managed to get him to pull up as I glimpsed wild buffalo loitering in the shade of the paperbarks. Then I stalked off on foot for some close-up snapshots of my own, gaining an unwarranted reputation for bravery from some passing fellow scribes, unaware of the ways of buffalo—which are about as dangerous as house cows. But I was brave in the passenger seat.

In a large, translucent pool below Waterfall Creek Falls, a score of tiny tots wearing face-masks and snorkels were swimming in formation, under the watchful eye of a female instructor. A handful of tourists sunbaked on the sandy beach or swam out in the deeper water below the blue-shadowed cliff face. Nearby some young ladies, definitely not potential Volvo buyers, held aloft a colourful banner: NO KAKADU MINE. They told me they were there on behalf of the local Jarwon tribe, who regard the area, under threat of mining by Australia's Big One, as a sacred site. A familiar story, but worth investigating. The ladies were not as neat and clean and well-advised as our entourage, but I felt they deserved better than the jibes that came their way courtesy of Volvo Australia.

Thus far my social standing on Volvo's Dream Safari (the sense of reality persisted) could be described as 'present-but-not-privy'. My fault entirely, due to a temporary lapse into teetotalness, which tends to set one apart from one's fellows, particularly in this trade. Now for the first time I gleaned tidings of what was going on around me, behind other safety-padded steering wheels and at the brief parish pumps along the way.

The cars, by and large, were deemed highly satisfactory in the comfort and appointments departments, but lack-lustre performers, without the grunt of many popular, less expensive family cars. (No one wanted to compare them with BMWs or Mercs.) Only the turbo models had any noticeable get-up-and-go and this was unremarkable by today's standards. There was general grudging admission that Volvos are solidly built for longevity, safety and comfort, rather than derbying, and that the cachet the marque enjoys in some circles, though dubious, nevertheless exists.

None of this stopped some of us from driving the stately machines as rally cars. Which resulted in damaged tyres and suspension components, the removal of a few underparts, including a gearbox casing — plus a few red faces. So far as I know, nothing went wrong with the cars that was not driver avoidable. This says a lot for the dear old things, a dozen of them, subjected to conditions and drivers for which they were not intended.

There was also speculation during our Waterfall Creek Falls luncheon that some of the cars were steadily declining in performance. Doomsayers took this as evidence that Volvos are unsuited to Australia's rough outback. I doubted this, having spent an artic summer in Sweden's far north, driving vast distances on roads as bad as those in Kakadu, where I'm sure Volvo test their vehicles. The true reason for our increasingly sluggish progress was revealed later in the day, after we had belted a further one hundred and thirty rough and dusty kilometres north to Yellow Waters, near the plush Coinda motel complex. By then several cars had expired.

Leaving Big Brother Volvo to do the worrying, our jolly band of scribes and photographers boarded another flat-bottomed riverboat and headed off for a sunset billabong cruise among the wildfowl and crocodiles. Our skipper was a handsome, educated, articulate lady, a suntanned citizen-of-the-world. The two-hour trip was pure magic, a happy combination of uniquely beautiful riverscape, fascinating wildlife, civilised conditions and intelligent commentary. When we stepped ashore, glum-faced Volvo senior scouts told us some of the cars had been fed paint-contaminated fuel from jerry cans. This had slowly blocked filters and fuel lines. Never mind, trained help was on the way and come morning, our full fleet would be mobile again.

The diminished cavalcade pressed on to our overnight camp at Jabiru. The more thoughtful, investigative types among us wondered why the Volvos had been refuelled from jerry cans when pump unleaded was readily available all the way along our route.

At Jabiru, my suspicion that the whole 'Adventure' was a dream was overwhelmingly confirmed. In fear and trepidation, I sent Master Kent ahead into the mouth of the crocodile, following my code of foolhardy first, survivors second. He cheerfully led the way, through hissing, self-opening jaws—into a sequestered wonderland of vast black marble floors, soaring white walls, rampant greenery, curving staircases, chrome, glass, concealed lighting, giant photo murals, stained wood, plush furnishings and smiling, soft-spoken receptionists, their faces blue in the glow of computer screens.

If this doesn't sound much like a reptile's maw, you're right. It was in fact the Four Seasons Motel at Jabiru, built in the shape of an enormous crocodile. A concept that made me flinch (I loathe the Four Seasons' jarringly inappropriate Yulara Motel near Ayers Rock), but in reality it works, largely because the long, low, dark structure blends, more or less, into the landscape and does not look much like a crocodile, except from the air. My last camp at Jabiru was some years ago, so perhaps I over-reacted to the presence of such undreamed-of luxury where once there was only a harsh wilderness, infested with buffaloes, flies and mosquitoes.

Of course, reality overtook us later, as we crawled in darkness on our hands and knees along the flanks of the beast, trying to find our room numbers (embossed on small metal plates below the doorknobs) by matchlight, because all external lights were off and not even the staff knew where to find the switch. In fairness, the place was not officially open and the staff were as new to the premises as us. We had dinner that night in the Escarpment Room as I recall, but of course I was

dreaming—in this country you eat crouched over a campfire, circled by smouldering pats of buffalo dung to drive off mosquitoes. The buffet style meal included crocodile mousse and was followed by the usual NT selection of wines (they didn't know about Perrier water, either).

Then we received the prezzies I had been told about, mine a drinking stein (of course!), amid speeches ranging from dreadful (me), through predictable (Volvo), ribald (Melbourne *Age*) to acute and amusing by Harry Secombe of the *Bulletin* (travelling under a nom-de-plume). While we were thus disporting ourselves, Volvo technicians were tearing 265 kilometres down from Darwin, to work all night removing and cleaning petrol tanks, fuel lines and filters. Why had some of the cars been fed from jerry cans, some of us were eventually brave enough to ask? Well, ahem, the turbos require high-octane unleaded, a beverage not generally available in the far north. So Volvo had brought up some big drums and siphoned this into new jerry cans purchased in Darwin. These were freshly painted, inside and out, apparently with petrol-soluble paint. Mystery solved and now I had the answer to another question that had plagued me.

Arrangements had been made for me to take a turbo for a further ten days into the Kimberleys, after the rest of the troupe returned south, the choice of vehicle being made by *Wheels*. Several times during our safari, rather troubled looking Volvo scouts had suggested perhaps I might be happier in something else, say the 760GLE top-of-the-range luxury model—which, like the bulk of the 700s, runs on standard unleaded. (Thus enlightened, I heeded their advice and was well pleased with the choice, taking the Big One where no Volvo has been before—another story.)

Next morning we floated among the clouds in three Cessnas, over Arnhem Land which contains buffalo swamps, jagged rocky escarpments, the spectacular East Alligator River and the controversial Ranger Uranium Mine. Then we returned to Jabiru, which is basically the unique motel, a service station and small, modern shopping complex, air-conditioned and comfortable, like Volvo cars.

By the time we scudded back up the bitumen to Darwin on day four, I had driven the full Volvo 700 range and managed to segregate the six vehicles into three groups: ordinary Volvos, faster Volvos and luxury Volvos. No mean feat, considering they still all looked the same, apart from the estate versions. All seem well made, comfortable and durable, with better-than-average appointments, including leather upholstery and (in some) air-conditioned gloveboxes, a feature I had thought exclusive to Porsche 928s. They handled predictably and well, considering their bulk, on bitumen. Volvo make no claim to being sporty. The 760GLE luxury Big One, with independent rear suspension, was sheer undemanding joy and idiot-proof. (This particular idiot speaking from the hindsight of my later Kimberley excursion.)

So, the verdict on my first motor vehicle PR junket? Well, if it really happened and wasn't just a dream, I can only echo the bride's comments, which were to the effect that it wasn't so bad after all and I might do it again, given the right mount. Volvo cars? They're excellent, for their intended market. If I had one, it would have to be the 760GLE, complete with one of those snow bunnies as co-driver.

24 Kings in grass castles

He lay on the hard, burnt earth under the paperbarks. Across the plain of Mitchell grass stubble he could see pandanus palms and ghost gums, indicating the line of the river where the bodies had been found. A woman and a man, floating and bloody from gunshot wounds. He wondered about their killer and felt his heart beating against the black, fire-baked earth.

Then he was up and running, close on the heels of the man with the .308, watching for him to kill again. Further back the Dutch girl was running also, trying to keep up. The rifleman skidded to a halt, sending up dust as he knelt and got off two quick shots. Then they were all running again, the girl's blonde hair streaming in the harsh, point-blank Territory sun. The shattered, breathless silence returned. They made no sound crossing the bare claypan. Two brolgas that had wheeled away overhead resumed their course to the river. The gunman propped suddenly, leaned against a melaleuca to steady his aim and loosed another shot. The victim fell in the sun dappled shade under the trees, then began threshing so that light-shafts formed in the rising dust fog.

Fiction in this book of hard (and sometimes funny) facts? Never. So what sort of mess had I gotten myself into this time? Well, I was the man in the middle of this Hemingwayesque tableau. The girl was photographer Jacque Lampe. The marksman we trailed was Cameron Sinnamon, grazier, tour guide and donkey exterminator. Cameron was shooting the animals, I was shooting Cameron (with my camera) and Jacque was shooting me (with her camera) shooting Cameron. Got it?

The episode was not as horrific as first impressions suggest, though shocking enough by southern standards. There *had* been a spate of murders nearby (in 1987), Cameron finding two of five bodies, victims

219

of a crazy, Rambo-style German tourist with an arsenal of weapons. The scene described is common throughout the Kimberleys, where some 20 000 feral donkeys have been shot in recent years. Unfortunately, this seems the only practical (but bloody) way of reducing the number of donkeys that are helping transform the already degraded landscape into a desert.

Of course it can be argued that the even bigger population of beef cattle causes more devastation than the donkeys, but that's another story.

How came I to these murderous parts? I was convalescing from my first motoring press junket, courtesy of Volvo Australia, to Kakadu National Park in the Northern Territory. At the end of that four-day circus, the other journalists and photographers all flew south leaving me in Darwin with a 760GLE Volvo sedan, the marque's ultimate offering. The plan was for me to navigate this flagship limousine, the epitome of elegant motoring, through the land of legend, the so-called 'wild, untamed' Kimberley region. Via the famous route-of-no-return, the Gibb River Road, linking the ports of Wyndham and Derby. Until 1988, this back road had been a dicey adventure, even in four-wheel drive. But there were rumours the Gibb was now trafficable to conventional vehicles, at least during the dry season. The northwest is always full of rumours.

Volvo's Darwin outpost wanted the 760GLE overnight, in order to repair the ravages of the Kakadu junket and prepare the vehicle for its Kimberley ordeal. How does one fill in 24 hours in this fair city? 'Drinking!' chorused the staff of the wild north's prestige car centre. In a borrowed 740GL, I set out to find alternatives to their well-meant suggestion. There were few, on or off the sun-blasted streets, thronged in late September with courting back-packers and aimless tourists. But that night I dined in the suburb of Parap, where the (upstairs) Happy Garden Chinese Restaurant provided one of the best meals of my life. Darwin reprieved!

Next morning, my Volvo advisers assured me the still unwashed 760GLE was ready for its 3500-kilometre voyage to the Kimberleys. There was an extra spare wheel in the boot and the tank was half full. Why only half full? Well, we don't have a bowser here, mate, so we used the left-over fuel from the Kakadu trip. You mean the high-octane unleaded from the paint-contaminated jerrycans that stopped half the cars with blocked filters and fuel lines? Yairs, mate, but we filtered it; you'll be right.

It could only happen in the NT I brooded as I drove the stately limousine into the service station opposite, topped the tank with standard unleaded and put the grubby vehicle through the automatic car wash.

I also filled my own spare jerrycan, brought up from Sydney with my camping gear in the boot of one of the Kakadu junket Volvos.

First stop was the airport, to pick up Jacque, just arrived and bedecked with cameras for every occasion. It was a scorcher of a day, nearing 40°C on the tarmac, but we continued cool as we sped south-east down the blacktop toward Jabiru in the supremely well air-conditioned Volvo. For about one hour. Then you know what happened, don't you? Yes—120 kilometres from Darwin, our magnificent 760GLE quietly expired, its filters and fuel lines blocked with paint contaminated petrol. Within sight of the Bark Hut Inn and caravan park, fortunately. To this establishment we trudged half a kilometre under the blistering sun.

The Bark Hut beer garden, site of the only public phone, is not my idea of a place to spend Saturday afternoon. The locals favour it as a place to demonstrate their drinking prowess, lung power, muscles, tatoos and boobs—and to make long, chatty phone-calls to mates down the track. *Eventually*, I made contact with Darwin–Volvo.

At sundown, a team of the firm's best available mechanics arrived and began dismantling the 760GLE, removing its tank, fuel lines and filters. For the second time within days. One was their man-in-charge-of-fuel-filtering—poetic justice. Good workers, slow learners, but consistent. . .came darkness and they didn't have a trouble light! I loaned them my torch. Around 11 p.m., I persuaded the Bark Hut's proprietor to switch on his pump, filled the Volvo with clean, pure unleaded and we were on our way. Just after midnight and a further 135 kilometres down the track, we gratefully allowed the giant Four Seasons crocodile at Jabiru to swallow us.

Next day we really put the 'swift Swede' to the test, heading first into Arnhem Land toward Oenpelli, then back and side-tracking to every sign-posted tourist attraction along the Kakadu Highway south to Pine Creek. Most of our journeying was over corrugated, pot-holed gravel and earth roads, or guttered, rocky side tracks with patches of bulldust concealing all manner of hazards. Nothing bothered the sumptuous, unflappable 760GLE.

It transported us in air-conditioned luxury to some outlandish back-waters (to the surprise of assorted macho four-wheel drive expeditioners), soothing us the while with soft music from six concealed hi-fi speakers. I think the only major Kakadu track we passed up was to Jim Jim Falls, heavily sign-posted 'four-wheel drive only'. At Pine Creek, where once 10 000 Chinese miners toiled on the diggings in search of gold, we turned south down the sealed Stuart Highway. Our stately flagship liked the wide bitumen and sped effortlessly through the night at speeds that would have had us jailed in the southern states (no highway speed restrictions in the NT).

At Katherine, we managed to talk our way into the Paraway Motel's dining room, somewhat later than the strict 'last orders' curfew hour of 9 p.m. Over our well-done 'rare' steaks, I figured we had notched just short of 600 kilometres for the day. Effortlessly, a tribute to the big car. Plus several hundred Kodachromes between us—Jacque being at least as shutter-happy as I, on this her first photo assignment in the NT.

The morning sun on our backs, we cruised the endless bitumen, not much wider than the Volvo, to the edge of the known world. Then, like Ancient Mariners, dipped below the furthest horizon and landed in strange country, such as that once marked on mediaeval maps with the warning: 'Here be Giants'! Inside our time capsule, all was cool luxury and the smell of leather, with soft music playing over the relaxing hum of the smooth vee-six. Familiar reality. Outside, in the dancing heat, we saw an increasingly surreal landscape of raw hills and tortured gullies dotted with grotesque, drunken boabs. Only the occasional stops for fuel, snacks and photography jolted us back to reality. Which was different enough, with more dark faces now than light; unfamiliar, lilting accents, every remark ending with 'Eh?', and the tempo of life so slow that time seemed to have stopped... lanky, high-booted, dusty figures under broad hats, frozen in silent tableaux on store verandahs and inside pub bar rooms.

By mid afternoon we had travelled half a thousand kilometres and now the track was rough and dusty, marked on the maps as 'four-wheel drive recommended'. Smoke fogged the sky in every direction. Mostly it billowed, cloudlike, but there were some dark, ominous spirals above the glow of active fires. The scorched earth was black with burnt Mitchell grass and charred logs, the countless termite mounds stark monuments in a vast, smoke-stained graveyard. Miraculously, along some of the river lines, pandanus, melaleucas, grevilleas and other vegetation had survived as welcome ribbons of green, hiding the clear, slow-moving water and sandy beaches, where red-winged parrots flew.

We crossed the King and Pentecost, almost dry now, but often impassable during the Wet. Close by was the Forrest, where in 1926 the waters darkened with the blood of scores of Aboriginal men, women and children, massacred by posses of white settlers and police. Such atrocities were commonplace during the so-called 'pacification' of the Kimberleys. After that holocaust, the 'kings in grass castles' took over the land, replacing the original inhabitants with cattle, sheep and donkeys.

At a lonely out-station, a stockman offered us simple hospitality for the night, in a corrugated-iron shed. Over dinner by hurricane lamp, he told us: 'The history of this place is the whites took it over and shot half the blacks—the mistake they made was they didn't shoot the other half.' Unlike many of the locals we met later, he was born in the area and not averse to recounting some of the chilling oral history of 'the good old days' in the Kimberleys. Horrible chapters that escaped the flawed memories of the authors of most published memoirs of the area. The Aboriginal survivors have not forgotten and this is why fires ravage the landscape every year during the dry season. Once they were lit to drive out game. Today the scorched-earth policy is aimed at driving out the whites—by starving their cattle of feed and sending them broke.

On a happier note, I can report the Kimberley region still has much to offer the adventurous visiting motorist, despite the fires. Don't do as I do, though. Do as I say. Although we completed the rough and dusty odyssey without mishap in the Volvo 760GLE (not so much as a flat tyre), I would not particularly *recommend* conventional vehicles for this country. Certainly not if you wish to explore the many side tracks available.

We stuck to the main Gibb River Road linking Wyndham and Derby, plus the Kalumburu Road north as far as Drysdale River homestead. Both these roads are now trafficable during the dry season in conventional vehicles—but the way is extremely rough in places, facilities are few and distances are considerable. Low clearance vehicles are at a disadvantage (the Volvo just got through in places) and of course your car must be strong and in tip-top mechanical order, particularly suspension and *tyres*. Retreads won't survive the corrugations, gutters, jump-ups, stone gravel and sharp rocks.

Along the eastern section of the Gibb River Road, conditions are rough and the most scenic attractions are located on private grazing leases. By and large, free camping beside the track is just not on (no fires allowed), so it's best to head for the organised centres. These are Jack's Waterhole on Durack River station (the best) and at Home Valley station, on the Pentecost, nearer Wyndham. Both places are operated by the Sinnamon family: Ian, Sue and Cameron, late of Goondiwindi on the NSW–Queensland border. They lease almost 2 million hectares of cattle country astride and between the two rivers, once the domain of the pioneering Durack, Costello and Emmanuel families. There are basic but excellent facilities at both places, including showers, flushing toilets and barbecue facilities. Or you can sample NT-style homestead accommodation, which includes all meals and twin-share rooms in the corrugated-iron, cement-floored station complex. (Termites can eat a wooden building overnight, locals claim). Cooling is by Casablanca ceiling fans and frequent showers or dips in the nearby billabongs—the most picturesque at Jack's Hole, which has the added advantage of no crocodiles! The Sinnamons run safari tours from both centres, to beauty spots and other places of interest not accessible to the independent traveller. These vary from one to several days, and are organised to suit guests' requirements and finances. Added attractions at no extra cost (according to season) include attending cattle mustering operations, wildlife watching, canoeing and fishing expeditions, fire fighting, de-bogging, and observing donkey shoots. Dinner by candlelight is standard at Home Valley homestead, where the Sinnamons keep an interesting cellar of wines, liquors and beers.

The Kalumburu Road north to the coast (275 kilometres) is rougher than the Gibb River Road east of the junction to the Great Northern Highway (245 kilometres). I'm sure the Volvo would have made it beyond Drysdale homestead to Kalumburu, driven cautiously. But our time was limited. The Kalumburu community-run coastal camping area is picturesque enough, with coconut trees and secluded estuaries towards Mission Bay. But the real value of Kalumburu Road derives from the various major detours to such places as the Mitchell Plateau (atop as yet untapped bauxite reserves), where something more suitable than a Volvo 760GLE is needed. Say a Range Rover if you can afford it, or a Nissan Pathfinder if you can't. From the junction with the Kalumburu Road, we found the Gibb River Road south-west toward Derby in comparatively excellent condition. It has been thus for at least twenty years to my knowledge, when it was first graded as a 'beef road', providing local cattle properties with access to the port of Derby.

Thirty or so kilometres south of the junction, we detoured another thirty kilometres to Mount Elizabeth homestead on the Hann River, which has a store, fuel, camping facilities and basic accommodation. This is the recommended place to refuel and re-stock when travelling the Gibb River Road between Derby and Wyndham. But don't expect anything more than basic supplies—definitely no boutique lines.

Further down the main road some 40 kilometres, Mt Barnett station, run by the Kupingarri community, also advertises fuel and basic food lines. Again, don't expect too much. There is good camping here at nearby Manning Gorge, where the river provides safe swimming and fishing. A guided safari tour is sometimes available, we were told. (Perhaps to view the mysterious Wondjina cave paintings along the Prince Regent River, those strange, robed and turbanned figures, supposed by some to have been inspired by visits of Egyptian or Persian mariners back in the mists of time—or travellers from outer space!) Three other nearby gorges are advertised as tourist attractions, but not for Volvo 760GLE drivers, if the track I investigated is a typical example.

By contrast, there is good access to Windjana Gorge National Park. The place is a scenic knockout, complete with basking freshwater crocodiles on the sandbars—a surreal limestone landscape of soaring red bluffs, grotesque boab trees clinging to high cliff faces. Basic but good camping facilities, supervised by rangers. We stayed, with no regrets, so take it as recommended.

Next morning we paused briefly at Tunnel Creek, a few kilometres along the track toward Fitzroy Crossing, and spared a though for Sandamara (or Jundumura), the Aboriginal 'outlaw' who made his last stand here. The 750-metre tunnel through the Napier Range was Sandamara's hide-out. Today, tourists splash through it by torchlight almost every day of 'the season' (April to November).

Smelling blacktop to the west, the Volvo took barely half an hour to transport us to the Great Northern Highway, which was to lead us back to Kununurra and eventually Darwin.

We refuelled at Fitzroy Crossing, now with a roadhouse but hardly your destination-resort (the old rip-roaring pub and settlement are off the highway, about a rifle shot away). And hurried on to nearby Geike Gorge National Park, the most accessible and possibly the most impressive tourist attraction in the Kimberleys. The water helps, of course, particulary on a hot September day. The gorge really is magnificent, an eroded wonderland of white, wine-red and pink limestone cliffs, broad, deep waterholes and seasonal sandy beaches. (A few years back, the excellent camping area was briefly seven metres under water!) Safe swimming, the rangers told us, despite plenty of freshwater crocs. Also prolific vegetation and birdlife, all best seen during the regular two-hour 16-kilometre boat tours. But Jacque was acutely disappointed, running out of film mid-voyage.

Near Geike Gorge is Fossil Downs station, founded by the pioneering MacDonalds, whose family crest featuring the 'bloody hand of the MacDonalds' graced the homestead entrance for more than a century. An appropriate reminder of some early 'kings in grass castles', I mused as the big Volvo sped up the bitumen into the tropical night. Out in the darkness were the remnants of empires established by the Duracks, Costellos, Emmanuels, Kilfoyles and other beef barons.

Today many of them are eroded wastelands. The descendants of the cattle aristocracy have departed, leaving only a handful of dust and a decimated, bitter local community who can still remember 'the good old days'.

25 In the steps of Don Quixote

It was the winter of my discontent. Zeus knows why. There was a fully-paid-for, mint-condition guards red Porsche 911SC in the hayshed. The view across the Great Table, of lush, sub-tropical Foxground valley and the Tasman Sea above Seven Mile Beach was magnificent as ever. Tame kangaroos grazed the lawns under a picture-book sky. The printing presses somewhere in south-east Asia were churning out my umpteenth book. Various magazine editors had lately sent me cheques. My bank manager was in user-friendly mode. I had clothes to wear, food in my belly. All was quiet, relatively, on the domestic front. But something was missing: a worthy challenge.

For one stumbling through the twilight years, many traditional forms of male challenge are best left alone. After deliberating a few moments, I pounced on my usual solution to ennui. With a fresh steed, like a knight of yore, I would sally forth in search of new adventures and encounters. It would have to be a thoroughbred worthy of the task—perhaps from a new stable? Editors and fellow scribes had long urged me to consider blood lines other than those from Zuffenhausen.

A Ferrari? No! They were still astronomically expensive to stable, flighty and inclined to go lame, incurring catastrophic veterinary charges. Impractical, too, if you wished to carry more than a cut lunch and hip flask. A Lamborghini? Unbelievable cost aside, who wanted a mount from what is now (since the Chrysler takeover) a plebeian mass-production stable?

A Jaguar XJ-SC V12, complete with leather briefcase toolkit? Thanks, but no thanks, to borrow singer Koko Taylor's lines. As you recall, I'd hacked one of those, for *Wheels* magazine, through Victoria's winelands and found it more of a steeple-chaser than the sort of lively stock pony I prefer. It was slow to respond to the spur, hard in the mouth—and its cabriolet roof, inadequately secured by toy clips, blew back resoundingly at near two hundred kilometres per hour (which will be news to JRA, the importers—*Wheels* never ran my story).

Maybe a BMW or Mercedes? Fine hacks, no doubt. But though confessing to my years, I was not ready to adopt senior citizen status. Something from Japan, such as the Mazda RX7 Turbo? Hmm. A flightier, livelier, more willing pony would be hard to find. I had enjoyed that week-long trail ride with one to Eden on NSW's far south coast. But instinctively I felt it was not the right image for me. There is something mildly unseemly about a grey-bearded RX7 conductor.

An American mount? Swallowing my prejudices, I tried to give the idea serious consideration. *Car & Driver* magazine had lately done a comparison test of a Porsche 911 Carrera and a Chevrolet Corvette Z51, awarding the blue ribbon to the home product—on performance. But they frankly admitted the Porsche was a clear winner in build quality, which is where it counts for us endurance riders.

So I was back to square one, where I had been stuck some twenty-five years. All things considered, if you have to purchase and maintain a mount out of your own pocket and wish to sell it some day, the cheque has to go to the Porsche stable. But for which mount?

Since 1963, when the 911 was first introduced, there was only one Porsche to buy for some dozen or more years. But with the introduction of the 924 and 928 models and then the 944 range, all with front-mounted, water-cooled motors, the problem of choosing the correct mount arose. Reading the most revered of the world's motoring magazines wasn't much help, because inevitably their reviews were based on brief test runs, usually in the hands of conductors who openly confessed their dislike of oversteering cars (911s). So for a time at least, each of the new breed front-engined Porsches was hailed as the ultimate creation from Stuttgart—the 911 was dead.

My penchant for reading between the lines was fine-honed during those evocative years when the 928 grew into the 928S4, the 924 fell from grace and the 944 sired various offspring, culminating in the 944 Turbo SE. When all the purple prose and lyricism was boiled down, certain hard facts emerged: the new cars did not out-perform the top 911s—they were just easier to drive, had more creature comforts and their appearance was more in keeping with current trends. (And they had yet to stand the test of time.)

I pondered these claims as winter turned to spring in 1988 and came always to the same question. If the new style Porsches were so good, why were there model changes almost every year, just like popular mass-produced cars, whereas the 911 had endured for twenty-five years with scarcely any outward change in appearance? To be fair, there had been minor alterations: acceleration and handling were *down*, in spite of power increases to cope with the additional weight of air-conditioners, power windows and roofs, luxury packs, etc. Oh for the good old days, when lightweight Porsches were designed to accelerate and go round corners faster than any other road car, with little thought for comfort and noise levels. . .

About this time I chanced on a recent issue of English *Autocar* magazine in which they reviewed a new limited-edition 911 Porsche called the Club Sport. This was in truth not so much a new model as a stripped, lightweight version of the current Carrera, with a few engine and suspension modifications to improve acceleration and handling. Just the sort of car I was pining for!—weighing in about the same as 'Little Red', the 1975 model I had raced so pleasurably—but with an additional thirty horsepower!

At first Sydney's leading Porsche purveyors, the House of Newell, spurned my efforts to order a 911 Club Sport. Both Master John and his servant Dale Goodman were derisive. 'We call it the Third World Porsche,' they chorused. 'No air, no sunroof, no power windows, no rear seats, no sound-proofing, no rear wiper, not even a passenger sun visor.'

'I want one,' I said.

'They're only making a few. Production finishes early in 1989. You can't have central locking, or leather trim.'

'I believe it goes near as well as the legendary 1973 Carrera RS,' I suggested.

'It goes like hell,' Dale admitted.

'But the noise,' interrupted Master John. 'Only a lunatic would want one. . .' He eyed me speculatively, then nudged his servant.

'I'll put you down for a Club Sport,' Dale said smoothly, flicking open his order book.

Committed to the purchase of a new car, I had to divest myself of the 1980 model 911SC garaged in my hayshed. As mentioned earlier, I purchased this in the aftermath of the 1987 stock market crash, when the price of used supercars was supposed to tumble, but it had cost me dear on what had turned out to be a sellers' market after all. The ink was barely dry on my order for the Club Sport when the Australian dollar commenced to strengthen against the Deutschmark, threatening to depreciate the value of second-hand 911SC Porsches like mine.

Christmas was nigh and luckily a well-heeled litigation lawyer was urgently seeking a last-minute gift as a holiday runabout for his wife. After three days of financial brinkmanship, I was glad to let him have the car for a smidgin less than I had paid for it a year earlier. It was my first experience in twenty-seven years of Porsche ownership of losing money on a car turn-over.

But what Zeus takes away with one hand he sometimes gives back with the other. The Deutschmark continued to cheapen against our dollar, which a year earlier had been worth scarcely DM 1.2. Now it was 1.4, a few weeks later 1.5 and climbing.

When it approached 1.6, I rang the House of Newell and said I wished to collect my Club Sport at the factory in Stuttgart. (In just a few months, the German price of the car had dropped by almost $20 000—but not in Australia!) Then I converted the lawyer's bank cheque to Deutschmarks, paid for the Club Sport in advance at the factory—and found myself with enough left over for three months in Europe including return airfare!

Of course, when the car finally arrived on Australian shores, I would face import duty and sales tax amounting to eighty-seven per cent of the German taxfree price, but with a new book just published and another due in late 1989, I reckoned I could let tomorrow take care of itself.

All this wheeling and dealing saw me out of my winter of discontent and cleared the way for my proposed Odyssey in search of adventure. Europe was hardly new to me, but I was determined to make the Club Sport caper a memorable experience, something worth writing home about—personally as well as professionally. But old habits die hard.

As usual, I rang my friend Hermann the German at his hideaway in the Taunus mountains not far from Frankfurt airport, who suggested, as usual, that I go to Greece with him. Hermann makes a living as host and guide of his own walking tours of the Greek islands. These are popular with Germans, who are inveterate walkers. Hermann has the idea that if I go on one of his tours and write about the experience, he will be inundated with Australian customers. Useless to explain that we are not walkers in the German sense and would not take kindly to his daily itinerary of 'forty kilometres or so'. Having walked with Hermann in the Taunus forests, I know few Australians could stand the pace—particularly those who could afford to pay for the tour.

I explained to Hermann that his idea of me going to Greece was not very original. He countered by saying that no doubt I would fetch up, as usual, in Spain's northern province of Catalunya, roaming the Pyrenees to Andorra and the Basque Lands.

'If you must go again to Spain, you should go further south, to the real Spain,' he announced. 'Andalucia, the land of bull-fighting and flamenco, or perhaps La Mancha, where Don Quixote fought the windmills on his old nag, Rosinante...'

In fact I had spent some time in Andalucia, where flamenco, the music and dance of *los gitanos* (the gypsies), is not all that common, once running with the bulls at Easter through the streets of Paterna de Rivera.

La Mancha was new territory for me and Hermann's reference to Don Quixote struck a chord. Had not author Graham Greene written a modern version of Miguel de Cervantes' classic, in which the hero priest's decrepit car substituted for Quixote's sway-backed Rosinante?

Why not a modern, trim and toey Rosinante in the form of a 911 Club Sport? I could readily double for Don Quixote, the original 'knight of the rueful countenance'. But who to play my faithful retainer, Sancho Panza? When news reached him that I had ordered a new Club Sport Porsche, number three son Vandal unhesitatingly volunteered to fill the gap in my cast. Provided he could do the driving. This was fine by me. Van could stay only a month and I had already decided to stay for three, so there would be plenty of time for me to get behind the wheel after he flew home to Foxground.

Plans were made to fly to Frankfurt late in February 1989, pick up the car at the Porsche factory in Zuffenhausen, then proceed directly south to Spain. There we would make for La Mancha, the 'parched plain' so named by the Moors when they overran the Iberian peninsula a thousand years ago—and scene of the mythical adventures of Cervantes' fictional knight.

Don Quixote, the aged grandee, spurred by a desire I could well understand, had determined to revive the age of chivalry, in a gallant last attempt to fan the embers of his waning fire. Alas, he was ill-equipped for the task, being somewhat decrepit, poor of eyesight and mounted on a sway-backed old nag more suited to a knacker's yard than the jousting lists. Inspired also by his romantic obsession for the beautiful Dulcinea, a somewhat oafish farmgirl in reality, the knight made his own Crusade across La Mancha, seeking to confront the forces of darkness and to protect the honour of his chosen maiden.

Unfortunately (or fortunately), he encountered no real enemies or adversaries and spent most of his time tilting fruitlessly at the windmills of La Mancha, which to his rheumy eyes appeared as rival knights. His adventures proved so popular with generations of readers (Cervantes published the story in 1605), fiction became accepted as fact in many quarters. Today the towns where his alleged encounters took place are prominent on the tourist maps of Spain. Colourful brochures imply the knight and other fictional characters really existed.

What drew me to the notion of retracing Don Quixote's odyssey I'm not sure, though I suppose some parallels were there—the ageing adventurer, the impractical romantic...even the fair young princess, by a stretch of the imagination. But in reality I think it was another of those cases best explained by the old standby: *it seemed like a good idea at the time.*

So Van and I set out for La Mancha no better equipped for our task than the original characters, without a firm plan and little knowledge of what we were getting ourselves into.

Our intention was to go directly by train from Frankfurt to Stuttgart and pick up the Club Sport next day. But Hermann was waiting at the airport and got us involved in going first to Wiesbaden to see his son Roger, an aspiring photojournalist, then to his hideaway in the Taunus mountains to observe the deer in the surrounding forest. Hermann is a politically active conservationist.

Next he drove us to a village close to Stuttgart, where we spent the night being entertained by a wacky chemist friend well known locally as an art collector and practical joker (he had lately written a series of letters to Helmut Kohl, West Germany's head of state, recounting their totally fictitious adventures together on one of Hermann's walking tours in Greece). Somehow the letters got published, causing Helmut Kohl acute political embarrassment because of his apparent association with Hermann and the Green Party. The president was aghast at being linked with the radical conservation lobby and issued official denials.

Next morning we presented ourselves, somewhat the worse for wear, at the Porsche factory in Zuffenhausen, an implausible trio, Van in track pants, joggers and BERRY RURAL CO-OP T-shirt, Hermann sartorially immaculate but somehow raffish in a green leather jacket, myself in ankle-length Drizabone coat and 'Down Under' model Akubra hat. The svelte female receptionist shuddered visibly as we approached.

'These are important press people from Australia,' Hermann announced. 'They come to buy a Porsche and make photographs of the factory . . .'

'You cannot take photographs of the factory,' retorted the receptionist sharply. 'And foreigners cannot just come here and buy a Porsche,' she added.

'Wrong!' cried Hermann. 'They *are* buying a Porsche!'

'No, no! You cannot just come here from Australia and buy a Porsche,' the receptionist repeated. Things were getting out of hand, as they usually do when Hermann makes the pace.

'We have made arrangements already and paid for the car,' I interrupted.

'*You* have paid for the car?' The svelte lady accented the first word, emphasising her disbelief.

'Yes,' I responded, adopting as humble a stance as the Drizabone and Akubra would permit. 'And I have arranged permission for the photography through your public relations person, Fraulein Ina Schlegl. The pictures are for Australian *Wheels* magazine and *Car* magazine in England.'

'Ein Moment, bitte,' the lady countered, taking refuge in her telephone. Apparently she contacted Porsche's public relations department, because she announced: 'Ina Schlegl is on holidays and no one knows anything about photography for those magazines.' Her tone implied suspicion that *Wheels* and *Car* might be pornographic publications. 'What is your name, please?' I told her and she consulted her diary. '*You* are Herr Carter?' Again the note of disbelief.

'Yes.'

'You have the official order for the car and your passport, please?' It was a demand, rather than a question.

'Yes.' I handed over the documents. 'And I have also the compliance plate for the car. Your mechanics must now fix it to the vehicle.'

'*You* have the compliance plate?' This time her disbelief was undisguised. 'That is most irregular.'

She was right, but I spoke true. My Club Sport had come off the assembly line on the Thursday before the Monday I was scheduled to collect it. Compliance plates, stamped with the engine and chassis numbers of the car, are manufactured in Australia. Having received this information only on Thursday, the Australian Porsche distributor had no time to get the plate made and to Zuffenhausen before I arrived there. In desperation, they delivered it to me as I boarded the plane at Mascot, to deliver to the factory for installation. *Most* irregular, as the lady observed.

'This is all very unusual,' she repeated, comparing my passport photo with reality several times. She made another brief phone call. 'The car is not yet ready.'

I began to feel that, like Don Quixote, I was tilting at windmills and getting nowhere. 'The paperwork is in order?' I asked. I know enough about Germans to know that nothing can get done until the documentation has been dealt with.

'Yes, everything is in order.'

'Then perhaps we could take some photographs?'

'You cannot take photographs in the factory.'

'You have already explained that and I have already explained I don't wish to take photographs in the factory. Only of the car being delivered to me. Fraulein Schlegl told me this would be no problem.'

The receptionist hesitated a moment, then reached her decision. 'It is not a problem. You can take the photos.'

'*Ole!*' I exclaimed involuntarily.

'*Bitte?*'

'*Vielen dank,*' I responded in the correct language. 'I go now to get my cameras.'

'But the car is not ready until after lunch,' the receptionist responded. 'You must first have lunch in our company restaurant.' She spoke as if to a child, not condescendingly, but with understanding.

'*Sehr gut,*' I replied. 'But first I will take some photos here.' I indicated the plush company foyer. 'Including one of yourself, as the representative of Porsche...'

'Oh, no, you do not want such a photo,' the svelte lady fluttered, involuntarily patting her immaculate coiffure. But when I returned with my cameras, she offered no further resistance as Van and I snapped irreverent compositions under the baleful gaze of assorted portraits and busts of the company founder, Dr Ferdinand Porsche.

The lunch was excellent and so was the Club Sport when we were finally ushered into its presence. Shining metallic silver, which showed its lines to perfection, black trim and no frills, it was a fit mount for a modern day Don Quixote. Hardly a sway-backed nag like the original Rosinante, but at least its master was close to the marque, being of unquestionably rueful countenance, impractical, romantic... and getting a mite long in the tooth.

After a brief familiarisation lecture from another company representative and a second photography session, Van and I said farewell to Hermann and Zuffenhausen and gave our new mount its head toward Spain.

Apart from suffering a broken headlight lens on the autobahn, all went well as far as the Spanish border, where we found ourselves jousting with the customs officials and the Guardia Civil. The problem: no visas. On my previous half dozen visits ranging over fifteen years, a visa was always necessary, but this time our travel agent assured us things had changed. Well, they hadn't, the border guards told us. After half an hour of bickering and a similar time waiting, we were reluctantly issued with thirty-day visas.

We then proceeded exactly three metres and fell into the hands of the Guardia Civil, who had observed proceedings and decided we were prime suspects for something or other. Probably just another example of the Spanish giving you a lot of trouble if you make even a small problem for them. We were ordered brusquely into the parking area, where the car was searched, its papers checked and our passports carefully examined *to make sure our visas were in order*!

Eventually we made off at full gallop into Spain. Like the original Don Quixote and Sancho Panza, we were far from satisfied with our encounter, which had been neither a victory nor defeat—a typical Cervantes-style contretemps. Once properly into Catalunya, we headed for the village of Palau Saverdera, where I had once lived for two years. There we were the recipients of many *abrazos* (hugs), kisses and salutations from old friends. We dined in style with the family of Senor Ramon Nogue, *el maestro*, the village schoolmaster, feasting on such local delicacies as pigs' muzzles and ears (for starters), followed by rabbit with snails and topped off with the popular local dessert, *creme catalan*. By way of refreshment, we drank the local wine, *ganatche*, from the traditional glass *poron*, which squirts out a thin stream of liquid when held aloft and tilted.

We slept at the Casa Nogue and in the morning were shown, in the open courtyard cellar beneath the kitchen, a pig destined to be killed the following week, plus other items of interest to us bush folk (Van is manager of the Berry Rural Co-Op produce store). The Club Sport was securely stabled in an ancient barn with huge wooden stockade-style doors, its cobbled floor littered with the moulding detritus of centuries, museum status agricultural implements ranged all around in the deep shadows.

Sleepy Palau Saverdera is not typical of modern Catalunya and as we later sped south it was obvious the province has prospered since it achieved limited self-government a decade ago, following the death of dictator Franco. Like Kansas City in the song, everything now is up to date in Catalunya, whose capital, Barcelona, hosts the next Olympic Games in 1992. The last stronghold of the Republican forces during the dreadful Civil War, Catalunya was literally held to ransom by Madrid, Franco's capital, for some forty years.

Now it is flourishing, the roads are good, buildings are going up, living standards are the best in Spain and the language, banned under Franco, is in common use again. Incorporated into a newly united Spain in the fifteenth century and struggling for independence ever since, Catalunya is out of its Dark Age and now belongs to the twentieth century.

Not so La Mancha, the land of Don Quixote, which remains almost medieval by contrast. The name derives from the Moorish description of the country: *manxa* meaning parched land. The plateau is scenically exciting, with vast plains of cereal crops and vineyards set against stark mountain ranges, but the overall impression is of poverty and backwardness. The province may be Spain's largest wine area, producing also huge cereal and olive crops, but apparently the profits don't stay in La Mancha.

There seems to have been a lack of progress in social areas, too: rampant poverty in cities and towns and everywhere the oppressive presence of the Guardia Civil, still patrolling in pairs, well-armed, as if in occupied territory, with quarters in all but the smallest villages, their imperative motto emblazoned above the barrack entrances: '*Todo por la Patria*'.

In the towns featured in Cervantes' epic, little has changed. Today there is a suburban and industrial sprawl around some of the immortal place names, but at their centres, the Knight of the Rueful Countenance would feel right at home.

El Toboso, where he encountered the peerless Dulcinea, may not have changed at all, except for some bitumen on the narrow, winding streets. Alas, at Mota del Cuervo, another village probably little different since the knight visited, the windmills he challenged are mostly in ruins, only one partly restored at the time of our visit (March, 1989).

At Consuegra, where Van and I overnighted in the excellent Hostal de las Provincias, the ridge above the town on which the mills and a twelfth-century castle stand remains timeless. The heart of the ancient town would be recognisable to Don Quixote, but not the suburban and light industrial sprawl which now mars the approach to this best of all Manchegan mill towns.

The same could be said of Campo de Criptano, where the rolling landscape surrounding the mills continues unchanged, except for a rubbish dump! No matter, the half dozen or so mills are well preserved and photogenic, once you find your way to them through the labyrinthine town below. Small herds of sheep and goats graze the nearby ridges (and rubbish dump) and it's not hard to imagine the myopic knight charging across the open ground, responding to the perceived challenge of the mills, which he mistook for rival knights.

The wind-powered mills, always set on high ridges, were used throughout La Mancha to grind cereal crops harvested on the vast plains below. The typical long pole angling down from their conical revolving roofs was used to position the mill blades into the wind, pushed by a team of men and than lashed into position.

Gypsy youths hang about what is now a public park surrounding the mills of Campo de Criptano, playing flamenco music on cheap portable cassette recorders. Benign oldsters, uncertain on their pins, their minds in the past, potter about, engaging tourists in conversation, seeking only company.

The scene, as in much of La Mancha, is bound up with wistful memories of a more glorious past, when there were exciting, more important things to do than tending sheep and goats grazing among the town's rubbish.

The mood of the Manchegans was contagious. After a few days, both Van and I became introspective, almost melancholic, dreaming of other places, other times. Unlike Don Quixote, we realised an era had passed, become lost in the mists of time and would not come again. As the knight had failed to recognise, you cannot go back to yesteryear, no matter how seductive the prospect, how fond or sweet the memory.

To cheer ourselves up, we indulged in some frivolous photography, involving the epic landscape of La Mancha—plus myself as Don Quixote, replete in Drizabone coat and Akubra hat, tilting at the mills with camera tripod substituting as a lance. The Club Sport stood in as my unlikely Rosinante, while Van played out the part of the eminently sensible Sancho Panza.

Over many a glass of local wine, we agreed that the best offerings from La Mancha today include their justly famous Manchego cheeses (the best made from ewes' milk), wine, scenery and ceramic wares. Trying to capitalise on the legend of Don Quixote doesn't work very well, for literary buffs or snapshotting tourists. The Rueful Knight's exploits are best relived through the pages of Cervantes' immortal novel.

Eventually Van and I headed for Granada, where five hundred years before us, the Moorish king Boabdil had sighed for the loss of his city to the re-conquering Spanish as he looked back for the last time from a high point on his retreat to the coast. (This landmark, on the Motril road, is now known as *Suspiro del Moro*, the Sigh of the Moor.)

Glancing back at La Mancha, I could not supress a nostalgic sigh at leaving the land of Don Quixote, the romantic buffer who never learned that you can't go back to what was. Half his luck.

Epilogue

When I took up club car-racing at age fifty-five, it was pointed out this might have been better attempted at, say, twenty-five, the age of most of my competitors. My thought was: I had always wanted to try the sport and somehow missed out, so it was now or never. Better to try and fail, than never to try at all . . . That I succeeded modestly well stroked my pride and gave me great pleasure.

Pride goeth before a fall, to quote another old saw. Concurrent with car racing, I tried other changes in lifestyle, again amidst comments that my timing was out by perhaps three decades. Better to make the attempt, I thought, than shuffle into the twilight zone, forever brooding on what might have been. Now I know.

On balance, I think it was the right decision, although the price, like that of a good car, was high. Emotionally I reaped the whirlwind, but the experience was a creative bonanza. I certainly have a lot to write about. As fiction, to make it believable. So once again I have come full circle, returning to my original craft of short story writing. Like Don Quixote, the subject of my final chapter, I shall soldier on, tilting at all manner of worthy targets and adversaries—from the safety of the fiction lists.

Jeff Carter
Glenrock Farm
Foxground
April 1989